THE
VIABLE
POLITY

THE
VIABLE
POLITY

Edward W. Lehman

TEMPLE UNIVERSITY PRESS
Philadelphia

Temple University Press, Philadelphia 19122
Copyright © 1992 by Temple University. All rights reserved
Published 1992
Printed in the United States of America

The paper used in this publication meets the minimum requirements of American
National Standard for Information Sciences—Permanence of Paper for Printed
Library Materials, ANSI Z39.48-1984 ⊚

Library of Congress Cataloging-in-Publication Data

Lehman, Edward W.
    The viable polity / Edward W. Lehman.
        p.   cm.
    Includes bibliographical references and index.
    ISBN 0-87722-994-5
    1. Political stability.   2. Legitimacy of governments.   I. Title.
JC330.2.L45   1993   92-9854
320′.01′1—dc20   CIP

The figure that appears in Chapter 1 is from Jeffrey C. Alexander's four-volume
Theoretical Logic in Sociology, Vol. 1, *Positivism, Presuppositions, and Current
Controversies*, p. 3. Copyright © 1982–1984 Regents of the University of California.
Used here by permission.

For my mother, Kate Lehman,
with love and appreciation

Contents

Preface

The political events of the last four or five years are outrunning even journalists' copy. This is particularly the case for the print media, where the written page is so quickly relegated to the realm of history that it often ceases to be "current events" even before it is read. The same problem plagues political sociologists. Analyses of the Soviet Union, command economies, the bipolar world, and the Iron Curtain now seem almost as remote as studies of the Franco-Prussian War.

With the political landscape changing so rapidly around us, the description and explanation of political processes becomes an all the more demanding operation. How do we make sense of this rapidly shifting terrain, recognizing, as we do, that facts do not speak for themselves? This book focuses on this question. While appreciating that social science is driven by the twin pistons of empirical research and theory, I take one step back from these two standard ingredients of science in order to consider the fundamental assumptions on which they are based. In Kuhnian terms, I am engaged mainly in paradigm building rather than in generating falsifiable propositions or in their empirical testing.

This enterprise, I argue, is necessary for all social science. It is especially critical for political sociologists today. Our speedily changing subject matter pushes us to an examination of first principles more acutely than in other parts of our discipline. Moreover, long-standing ways of thinking that used to provide many of us with basic assumptions (neo-Marxism and structural-functionalism are the most prominent manifestations, but hardly the only ones) have lost much of their credibility. This has unfortunately led some to disparage all search for acceptable first principles as "grand theory" and hence not worthy of serious attention. We cannot give in to this reemergent positivism, for to do so not only diminishes theorizing but also limits the scope of empirical findings and our ability for understanding the world as well as for changing it.

This book's special focus is on the first principles that enhance our competence to analyze political failure and success—that is, to move beyond the rhetoric of "crisis" and "stability." One way of thinking is a notable stumbling block in this regard; I call it the "legitimation-crisis paradigm." This approach, which I argue is not restricted to neo-Marxist or radical analysts, is theoretically and empirically constricting. My aim is to contribute to the construction of an alternative paradigm that helps make better sense of the political world around us. Thus my focus is primarily on the criteria for shaping new arguments and hypotheses as well as for assessing the relevance of potential evidence and only secondarily on helping to build the hypotheses that purport to directly account for political success and failure.

Yet the issues this book explores are not merely "technical" or conceptual. In addition, political sociology should be applied to the dilemmas of modern politics—but without lapsing into pure ideology or rabble-rousing. Any alternative paradigm must also ultimately be judged by how well it has contributed to this effort.

Without Ethna Lehman's suggestions, encouragement, and affection, this book would never have been finished. I hope that I have more than occasionally met her excruciatingly high standards. I also would like to acknowledge the comments and useful suggestions of Robert R. Alford, Edwin Amenta, Bernard Barber, Steven Brint, Kevin Dougherty, Amitai Etzioni, Eliot Freidson, Jeffrey Goodwin, Wolf V. Heydebrand, James M. Jasper, Lawrence Mead, Marvin Olsen, Edwin Schur, Hillary Silver, Beth Stevens, and Dennis H. Wrong. Caitilin Rabbitt has been an exceptionally able and dedicated research assistant whose excellent substantive and editorial help I greatly appreciate. My fellow members of the Workshop on Politics, Power, and Protest in New York University's Sociology Department provided me with indispensable suggestions for the Introduction. I want to acknowledge the comments and advice of Ed Amenta, Jeff

Goodwin, Jim Jasper, and Caitilin Rabbitt along with that of other Workshop members, especially Amparo Hoffman-Pinilla, Howard Lune, Franceca Polletta, Jane Poulsen, Harold Wenglinsky, and Yvonne Zylan.

Chapter 1 is a revised and expanded version of a paper that first appeared in the *American Sociological Review* (1988). Chapter 3 incorporates elements from an article I published in the *Journal of Political and Military Sociology* (1985), while a preliminary version of Chapter 4 first appeared in *Research in Political Sociology* (1987); both chapters represent a considerable expansion of my views.

■ Introduction
Paradigm Lost

The appropriate powers of the state in Western societies have become a crucial source of political conflict and a topic for theoretical debate. The scope of democratic participation, the capacities of public bureaucracies, the inefficiencies of a regulated capitalist economy, state responses to fiscal crises and structural unemployment have become hotly contested public issues. These political conflicts resonate in the seemingly more dispassionate world of academic discourse. As a result, the state has once again become a central topic for research and theoretical assessment.
—*Robert R. Alford and Roger Friedland,*
Powers of Theory

Capitalist democracies may have outlasted their principal competitor but they still face serious challenges. The dilemmas of the modern democratic polity are numerous and wide-ranging and cannot be reduced to any simple, easy formula. Moreover, political sociologists must consider the complaints that average citizens have made over the past quarter-century and try to make some more inclusive sense of these diagnoses. Diverse voices among the American general public have raised a plethora of apparently contradictory concerns: (1) today's democratic regimes are too strong *or* too weak; (2) these systems either fool most of the people most of the time *or* are confronted by massive erosions of support; (3) they are captives to the demands of a powerful few "special interests" *or* are stymied by an excessive dispersion of power; and (4) they are challenged by the incessant demands of citizens who lack trust in their leaders *or* face citizens who are quietly sinking into apathy.

Each of these eight popular diagnoses will ignite a spark of recognition in political sociologists. While we also realize that the four sets of lamentations by citizens are on different levels of analysis and that glaring inconsistencies abide within and among them, closer scholarly inspection reveals that people's concerns provide a less haphazard picture of contemporary politics than first meets the eye. Unfortunately, most recent social science analyses of political success and failure have been seriously flawed because, explicitly or implicitly, they have built their inquiries around a misguided "legitimation-crisis paradigm." This book attempts to move beyond this constricting approach to reveal the deeper symmetries among these seemingly discordant diagnoses in the popular sphere. It shows how greater theoretical precision magnifies our ability to plumb the basic issues related to political success and failure in our times. My main spotlight is on the United States, although much of what is said applies as well to other contemporary systems, particularly other advanced capitalist democracies.

The notion of the legitimation crisis of the modern state, which in varying degrees informs the work of many analysts across the political spectrum, is a special target of this book. The simplistic, often implicit, formula that is at the core of all the variants of this approach cannot satisfactorily address our current political conundrums. In fact, this way of thinking is even incapable of getting us started in understanding our original four pairs of oft-repeated and seemingly contradictory popular lamentations. Let us look first at the general elements common to the legitimation-crisis approach. We are then in a better position to ponder how this paradigm fails to do justice to the issues embedded in the diagnoses cited above and, hence, to begin to see why this way of thinking has borne such meager theoretical and empirical fruit.

The Legitimation-Crisis Paradigm

Both social and natural scientists draw on overarching sets of assumptions, often referred to as "paradigms," to help define their subject matters (Kuhn 1970).[1] Paradigms contain not only testable theories and empirical research as these have traditionally been conceived (see, e.g., Merton 1968, pp. 139–71); they also encompass varying philosophical, ideological, and even aesthetic assumptions that point to appropriate scientific "puzzles" and how to solve them. When a paradigm—such as the legitimation-crisis perspective—fails to be sufficiently theoretically comprehensive and consequently limits the scope of empirical findings, our prospects for understanding the world better, let alone changing it, suffer.

Students who scour the political sociology literature will be at a loss to find references to an explicit legitimation-crisis paradigm; no summary work that I know of singles out such a distinctive school. In contrast, many analysts are comfortable with Alford and Friedland's (1985) division of major approaches into the class, pluralist, and managerialist perspectives, with their respective emphases on the rise of capitalism as a decisive form of social production, the establishment of democratic institutions as vehicles for political participation, and the emergence of bureaucratic states as centers of binding decisions. Others, of course, find such a list too truncated. My colleague Jeffrey Goodwin, for example, believes that the dominant perspectives in contemporary political sociology are more adequately rendered as pluralist, elitist, neo-Marxist, state-centered, political conflict, and rational choice.[2]

Neither of these two lists breathes a word about a legitimation-crisis paradigm. While the notion of such a crisis is essential to the neo-Marxist perspective, the pivotal formulation at the center of this paradigm cuts across the dominant perspectives in political sociology as they have more conventionally been conceived. The legitimation-crisis paradigm is not one visible theoretical camp with unambiguous adherents. Rather, it is a perspective that informs a broad array of political analysts influenced as well by other, more visible paradigms, even though many of them would not in any way identify themselves as adherents of the way of thinking about the political world that I am examining.[3]

The rise of the legitimation-crisis approach can be traced back to the mid-1970s. The most vocal advocates of such a crisis at that time were neo-Marxists, although distinctive neo-Marxist and non-Marxist versions existed. Virtually all those who have worked within its essential framework since then share a common lineage. Ultimately, like most sociological students of legitimacy, they are rooted in Max Weber's work on the role of moral support in the state's right to command and the subject's obligation to obey (Weber [1924] 1968, especially pp. 212–99, 941–1372).[4] However, Joseph Schumpeter ([1950] 1975) is this broad perspective's more contemporary and most specific proponent. The fate of modern democratic regimes, in his view, hinges on their ability to trade off the delivery of state services for political support.

The legitimation-crisis paradigm's unfortunate penchant for simplistic binary frameworks is undoubtedly anchored in Schumpeter's formulation. In Schumpeter's binary model, crisis results from the state's failure to match its capacity to respond with the level of citizens' demands. Political support is withdrawn because governing elites have either made too many promises or are unable to deliver on specific claims that citizens have pressed. Only two solutions to the resulting crisis are possible: increasing state capacities or decreasing citizens' demands. Neither, however, can stave off crisis permanently. Enhanced state capacity, Schumpeter believed, entails bureaucratization, which, while needed to implement the popular will, is ultimately inimical to democratic institutions. (For a more recent analysis of the potential conflicts between bureaucracy and democracy, see Etzioni-Halevy 1985.) Moreover, in his mind, any augmentation of the state's ability to deliver services only escalates citizens' demands and so again throws the system toward crisis. On the other hand, although a reduction in demands (and consequently in state capacities) was Schumpeter's preferred solution, he recognized that this option is incongruent with democratic politics. Schumpeter regarded electoral competition, in which a party's promises are exchanged for votes, as the essence of a democratic polity. Democratic politics, in other words, is premised on the periodic fostering of new demands, at least some of which newly elected leaders are expected to meet.

Lipset ([1960] 1981, 1963b) is the primary source of most recent legitimation-crisis formulations. Although he has never consciously associated himself with the approach, his earlier work has promoted this line of thinking in two ways. First, he was very much concerned with prospects for "democratic political stability" (in light of the rise of totalitarianism abroad and right-wing extremism at home) and ultimately defined this pivotal concept within the binary framework of effective state capacities *and* legitimacy. Second, his empirical analyses of democratic political stability centered on how state effectiveness—notably in the realm of economic growth—can substitute for legitimacy in the short run and generate it in the long run. In this instance, Lipset made state effectiveness his independent variable and legitimacy his dependent variable. Lipset's contributions in each of these two areas are sufficiently important that I scrutinize them more closely in subsequent chapters.[5]

Lipset adhered to Schumpeter's rigid binary framework throughout his earlier writings, only in later works (see particularly Lipset and Schneider 1983) breaking out of this mold. This split with the binary style permitted him to move beyond the questions of effective state capacities and legitimacy and to recognize that, in fact, diffuse support for the system (legitimacy) may go hand in hand with lowered confidence in those who are running it.[6] Unfortunately, the underconceptualized legacy from Schumpeter and the early Lipset survives. As Weil (1989, p. 683) notes: "The image of political support as a balance between citizen demands and state capacity was generally accepted by crisis theorists on both the left and the right."

Neo-Marxists have unquestionably been the most numerous and outspoken advocates of the inevitability of a crisis of political legitimacy in capitalist democracies (see particularly O'Connor 1973; Offe 1974, 1984; Habermas 1975; Wolfe 1977). At the heart of their argument is a binary view similar to the ones we have already seen: Their anticipated crisis stems from the state's growing inability simultaneously to deliver economic growth via capital accumulation and legitimacy via the provision of social services. Crises are inescapable, they predict, because capitalist states must give priority to the capital-accumulation needs of the private economy.[7]

The correspondence between neo-Marxist and non-Marxist applications of this way of thinking is striking, although not all non-Marxists adhere to it explicitly and they are less likely to predict a legitimation crisis unequivocally. Non-Marxists are more likely to predict such outcomes when the analyst's ideological sympathies are left-liberal (e.g., Poggi 1978, pp. 132–34; Thurow 1980). The emphases of writers who are further to the right are a bit more distinctive. Despite differences among them, their analyses recall Schumpeter's own assessments insofar as the lowering of demands is the preferred remedy for the tension between strained state capacities and citizen support (see, e.g., Bell 1973; Crozier, Huntington, and Watanuki 1975; Rose and Peters 1979). Analysts who have been linked to the neoconservative movement of the 1970s provide perhaps the most unusual analysis of legitimation crisis. Next to neo-Marxists, neoconservatives most explicitly invoke the rhetoric of legitimation crisis. Yet they tend to associate this crisis with deeper "moral" or "spiritual" problems in the encompassing general culture of advanced capitalist democracies (especially Bell 1970, 1976).

Predictions of an impending legitimation crisis peaked in the late 1970s, and the substantive focus of most political sociologists has since shifted elsewhere. In light of this fact, one is justified in asking: Why should we focus our theoretical arsenal on a relatively diffuse paradigm that may have seen better days? The answer is: While substantive concern with legitimation crises has ebbed, this way of thinking has become so deeply ingrained in how social scientists analyze political success and failure that it survives the inadequacy of its forecasts. The tendency to frame political viability in the simplistic binary formula of state effectiveness and legitimacy persists among people who would be stunned if they were called adherents of the legitimation-crisis paradigm. In other words, the precursors and conscious advocates of this approach have dug such deep intellectual ruts that many of us continue to fall into them unreflectively. Indeed, the fact that the legitimation-crisis paradigm today flourishes mainly in implicit forms makes overcoming its difficulties a more intractable problem than it was in the 1970s.

Let me cite a few examples to illustrate how widespread reliance on the binary formula of effectiveness and legitimacy remains. Clearly, it remains entrenched in neo-Marxism, particularly in Critical Theory (for divergent overviews, see Carnoy 1984; van den Berg 1988). Neo-Marxist renditions of the paradigm are especially prevalent in contemporary treatments of the dilemmas of Third World polities. Diane E. Davis's (1991) study of the constraints that foster "urban fiscal and political crisis" in the cities of developing countries using Mexico City as her strategic research site is typical here. She focuses her analysis entirely around two poles: the constrained policy options available to political authorities and their prospects for legitimizing their rule among the populace.

But neo-Marxists are not alone. For example, Mishra's analysis of the problems of the modern welfare state begins with the assumption that "the broad consensus concerning the mixed economy and the welfare state so characteristic of western societies since the second world war has weakened a good deal in recent years. The welfare state is faced with a crisis of legitimacy" (Mishra 1984, p. 25). Even analysts who reject the likelihood of an imminent crisis tend to fall back on the binary formula. Hirschman (1982), for example, after reviewing several "crisis of the welfare state" theories, rejects them merely because the conflicts between ineffectiveness and legitimacy are "quite possibly temporary growing pains. These pains may well cause considerable trouble when first encountered, but can eventually be brought under control as a result of various learning experiences and mutual adjustments" (Hirschman 1982, p. 43).

The binary formulation even extends to the study of political parties. Angelo Panebianco (1988), an Italian political analyst steeped in mainstream American social science, applies this logic to the analysis of European parties and the role of party leaders. Party leadership, he argues, is limited by *"legitimacy:* the leadership's legitimacy is a function of its control over the distribution of 'public goods' (collective incentives) and/or 'private goods' (selective incentives). When the flow of benefits is interrupted, the [party] organization is in serious trouble" (Panebianco 1988, p. 40).

Experts analyzing the events in Eastern Europe over the past five years have also been unreflectively slipping into the binary mold. For example, as he scanned the crumbling Communist regimes in the late 1980s, Chirot (1987) observed:

> In Eastern Europe, perhaps more than in any other part of the industrialized world, there exists a crisis of legitimacy that may well produce a political upheaval of major international proportions. . . . Socialist economies have not worked well . . . economic problems have created a sense of urgency and a search for solutions. . . . Crises of legitimacy now also face these systems because Eastern Europeans compare themselves to their Western European counterparts not the Third World. (Pp. 1–3)

A recent book by Gianfranco Poggi (1990) on the state summarizes succinctly how contemporary non-Marxist analysts move along the formal ruts set by the explicit advocates of legitimation crisis.

After noting that most modern states rest on democratic legitimations, he goes on to argue that

> the state claims to see its own existence as justified by the services it renders its people, and the people's compliance with the political demands placed upon it as constituting both a dutiful acknowledgement of the services rendered it, and a necessary condition of further services being rendered. (P. 28)

In short, the common core of the legitimation-crisis paradigm is formal rather than substantive. That is, those who explicitly or implicitly adhere to this way of thinking are not united by a prediction of an inevitable crisis in popular support; rather, they share the formula that the success or failure of capitalist democracies (and perhaps all modern regimes) is simply a matter of ascertaining the degree of legitimation crisis within states that are doomed to be less than totally effective in satisfying citizens' demands. While neither state effectiveness nor legitimacy has been given adequate theoretical definition, a still more serious problem confronts us. The failure to render "legitimacy" in a theoretically satisfactory manner has resulted in its being "lumped," "confused," or "conflated" with other kinds of political trust or support. The conflating of diffuse support for the system (legitimacy) and trust in a specific set of officeholders (confidence) is an especially egregious liability. As we see later, potential crises of legitimacy have thus been conflated with breakdowns in welfare-state programs, the modern state's extravagant emphasis on and failure to sustain economic growth, and the purported rise of hedonistic themes in America's overall value system. While all these issues are potentially crucial, they cannot receive a fair hearing so long as they remain analytically entangled with the concept of political legitimacy.

The legitimation-crisis paradigm tends to lump legitimacy together with concepts that warrant separate, nonoverlapping definitions because of a characteristically binary logic that is both simplistic and underconceptualized. This book argues that a satisfactory paradigm must recognize both the multiple facets of political life and the relations among them as well as show what "multidimensionality" entails both theoretically and empirically. A new paradigm for political sociology, as I comment below, requires additional distinctions and clarifications, including such key differences as political power versus other kinds of power, the state versus the political system, and state effectiveness and legitimacy versus political viability.

An acid test of a paradigm's multidimensionality is its empirical openness. That is, does it close off the range of decisive research questions, possible answers, and sources of data, or does it enrich the research process? I believe the legitimation-crisis paradigm unnecessarily limits the empirical scope of political sociology; and I propose to develop a new paradigm and to show how it is more empirically open. Let us begin by examining the liabilities of the legitimation-crisis perspective through an analysis of why it cannot even address adequately the four popular pairs of diagnoses with which this book began.

Eight Popular Diagnoses

Any empirically open paradigm in political sociology must achieve a fuller scholarly appreciation of the failures that "average citizens" impute to modern democratic politics. The eight diagnoses cited in the opening paragraph are fairly representative of the range of complaints one hears directly from the general public and through the mass media. How well does the legitimation-crisis paradigm perform in providing theoretical integration to seemingly contradictory laments over (1) state strength, (2) levels of support for the system, (3) dispersion of power, and (4) citizens' political participation?

My assessment is that this paradigm's performance is unsatisfactory because it rivets our attention on the first two pairs of diagnoses while relegating the others to second-class citizenship. That is, its binary framework locks together inquiries about whether the state is too strong or too weak *and* whether the general public has been seduced or is rapidly losing faith in the system. (The core hypothesis that ineffective state capacities lead inexorably to legitimation crises is prototypical here.) Moreover, the paradigm's adherents are inclined to treat the other two pairs of diagnoses—namely, questions about whether the state is dominated by a tiny elite or stymied by the dispersion of power *and* whether distrustful citizens are pressuring authorities too much or are too apathetic—as if they are merely special instances of the first two.

The first pair of complaints focusing on whether today's states are too strong or too weak invokes two of the most popularly debated issues of our time. Indeed, although these concerns are central to the legitimation-crisis paradigm, they are so widely shared that we can in no way treat them as features unique to this way of thinking (unless they are unequivocally tied to loss of diffuse support for the system). Alarm about the dangers of strong regimes is by far the more extensively voiced fear in the first pair; even into the post-Reagan era, challengers and incumbents alike continue to flail "big government" and urge new "limits" on state capacities. To be sure, there is disagreement about the source of this ineffectiveness. While the enemies of "big government" cover virtually the entire political spectrum, they generally have different targets in mind. In the United States, for example, the right seems most concerned with affirmative action programs and social service or regulatory agencies that allegedly restrict market forces; the left, on the other hand, denounces the intrusive power of the military-industrial complex or the Central Intelligence Agency and, more recently, a conservative Supreme Court controlled by Reagan and Bush appointees.

Yet worry about weak state capacities does not always contradict alarms over "big government." In particular, when these two diagnoses are expressed as fears that the state either meddles too much or accomplishes too little, they may even be mutually supporting. In this case, government "bureaucracy" is usually roundly denounced, with "bureaucracy" connoting both the notions of large-scale formal structures and bumbling red tape. Legitimation-crisis theorists have been especially adept in recognizing that today's states can be both intrusive and ineffective. (See, e.g., Habermas [1984] on how economic and political structures are allegedly "colonizing" the public sphere—or what he calls the "reproduction of the lifeworld"—while at the same time failing to come to grips with their own internal contradictions.) But these theorists' reliance on the binary formula of state-effectiveness-and-legitimacy prevents them from exploiting the implications of this insight.

The alternatives present in this first pair of laments are complementary in additional ways. Analysts who plow this field—including legitimation-crisis paradigm adherents—share a view of the state as a deliberately constructed "delivery system" whose performances have not always been satisfactory. Regardless of which pole they emphasize (or if they try to combine the two), these observers recognize that problems arise because states have more than one goal. In general, analysts who make this point agree that we are witnessing the simultaneous complaints that the government interferes too much (in areas of interest to others) and achieves too little (in realms that matter to me).

There are also concrete disagreements, however. Criticisms of government meddling are often cast as the state having too many irons in the fire; the state needs to prune its agenda, it is asserted. Those who worry that too little is accomplished, on the other hand, are more likely to accept the inevitability of a diverse agenda. Their despair is over the state's inability to achieve potentially conflicting goals. As we see in Chapter 2, legitimation-crisis theorists have been especially prone to apply their binary conceptualizing here and to couch this dilemma in terms of economic growth versus social entitlements; but the underlying issue is more complex than this simple-minded formula implies. While those who blame government "meddlers" tend to be politically conservative, there is more ideological variation among those who lament the state's ineptitude in dealing with more than one goal. Among legitimation-crisis analysts who focus on economic growth versus entitlements they range from neo-Marxists to conservatives.

Although adherents of the legitimation-crisis paradigm are single-minded in their emphasis on the first and second pairs of diagnoses, those who explicitly anticipate a "crisis of legitimacy" give far greater weight to the second pair, with its focus on whether the citizenry remains duped or is losing faith in the system. Indeed, for most of these analysts, a crisis of legitimacy boils down to only one pole of the second pair: the loss of political faith or trust. We have reviewed how this particular formulation has been used by observers of all political persuasions, although it is most commonly associated with contemporary followers of Karl Marx (even though their pivotal imageries owe more to Max Weber). These analyses focus on the purported contradictions in advanced capitalist democracies. The crisis of political legitimacy is but the latest in a series of anticipated final upheavals of that system and has always been tied with the inevitable failure of state capacities under capitalism. As I have indicated, a major aim of this book is to put forward an alternative approach that is more theoretically comprehensive and empirically open than this formulation.

Yet the label of legitimation crisis is also appropriately applied to the diagnosis that modern regimes manage to fool most of the people most of the time, insofar as it retains the paradigm's characteristic binary formulation. Neo-Marxist approaches provide perhaps the clearest justification for this extension. In particular, Marcuse (1964) presented a dramatic inversion of the explicit legitimation-crisis approach when he argued that the "repressive tolerance" of capitalist democracies narcotizes most of the population. Only those at the very periphery of society (e.g., blacks, the lumpenproletariat) escape the governing elite's seduction via manipulation of mass consumption patterns and the mass media. In this substantive respect he might be called an "anticrisis" theorist. On the other hand, he remained within this school of thought, since he never swerved from the binary formula of state capacity and legitimacy. For Marcuse, the near-pervasive legitimacy of capitalist democracy is inauthentic and a distortion of people's real biological, psychological, and social needs.

More recently, a similar message has been promoted among observers who were labeled as neoconservative during the late 1970s and who overtly invoke the possibility of a "crisis of legitimacy." They too decry the stultifying consensus of advanced capitalist democracies as well as its corrosive effects on citizens' willingness to contribute to the well-being of the economy and state. This branch of the legitimation-crisis paradigm is not concerned about "repressive tolerance," nor are its complaints always specifically political. Rather, those in this tradition worry about the decline of the work ethic and the rise of hedonism, an "ethic of self-fulfillment," and even a "voluptuary system" (see, e.g., Bell 1976; Yankelovich 1981). Both Marcuse's and the neoconservative variants of legitimation-crisis analysis focus our attention on the alleged costs of consensus and on the larger culture's destructive impact on political support.

While such theories and the more mainstream legitimation-crisis diagnoses anticipate kinds of predicaments that differ in part, they share the perspective that a moral malaise in modern life has arisen largely from deep-seated contradictions between contemporary capitalism and democracy, with the former reflected in weakened state capacities and the latter in eroding legitimacy. Thus those who see the masses as compliant dupes and those who say we face widespread decay in public trust are less antithetical than they appear. Moreover, diagnoses of overt legitimation crisis coupled with ones of a more general moral decline, as we have observed, are no longer the exclusive concern of the political left. Yet both remain trapped within the paradigm's binary framework.

The legitimation-crisis paradigm has an even more difficult time dealing with the third and fourth pairs of concerns. Those who work under its aegis try to cram these into their binary formula: treating the question of whether the state must respond to the demands of a tiny elite or is whiplashed by the whims of dispersed centers of power as if it were simply an aspect of the problem of whether states are too strong or too weak; and conflating the question of whether authorities face distrustful citizens who make enormous demands or confront largely apathetic masses with the question of whether citizens have lost faith in the system or remain hoodwinked.

Legitimation-crisis theorists of all political stripes are inclined to collapse the issue of elite domination versus the dispersion of power into the issue of state capacities. They agree that states are relatively ineffective and are prone to give special weight in their analyses to the problems of managing demands; but they disagree on how they frame this dilemma. Moderates and conservatives in this tradition concur with Janowitz (1978, p. 546)—a self-proclaimed opponent of legitimation-crisis analyses who was nevertheless susceptible to such binary formulations—that faltering regimes reflect "new forms of dispersion of political power which leads to the inability to create meaningful majorities which can effectively govern." They have used terms such as "veto groups" (Riesman et al. 1951, pp. 244–54, 266; Kornhauser 1961, pp. 252–67, and [1953] 1966, pp. 210–18) and "stalemate" (Bell 1973) to capture the same experience.[8] Neo-Marxists within the legitimation-crisis paradigm, on the other hand, have exactly the opposite image: The inevitable ineffectiveness of the liberal democratic state is rooted in its unavoidable dependence on the capitalist class and its agents as well as on the need to satisfy their requests.

The third pair of diagnoses is shrouded among all camps within the paradigm by this tendency to conflate the sources of compelling political demands with the state's capacity to respond. When the problem of state capacity is reduced to the question of the management of citizens' demands, the third pair becomes merely a contemporary manifestation of the timeworn power-elite versus pluralist debate (for an overview, see Prewitt and Stone 1973), whose either/ or style has increasingly been rejected by social scientists.

A variety of contemporary approaches alerts us to the risks of confounding the issue of state capacities with positions on the power-elite debate. Perhaps most pivotally, so-called state-centered researchers now regularly remind us that state capacity entails much more than the adjudication of demands. States, they have found, may sometimes be autonomous actors pursuing their own agendas and not just responding automatically to powerful elites or dispersed centers of power (see, e.g., Skocpol 1985a). The organization of influence in capitalist democracies also seems to be far more complicated than was conceptualized by either elitists or pluralists. Analysts who focus on social structure, for instance, have made us more conscious of the fact that larger economic and social units and supraunits ("structures") often account for more of what is finally decided than do partisans within them, whether such partisans are seen as an array of contesting coalitions or as tiny elites. Dominant-coalition theorists, on the other hand, recognize that those with inordinate clout may be neither a minute, willful, and homogeneous elite (as envisioned by power elitists) nor mutable coalitions that may shift from issue to issue (as originally propounded by the pluralists); instead they stress the importance of relatively enduring coalitions (especially on the local level) of constituencies with heterogeneous attributes (including class traits). They nevertheless admit that the rise of such coalitions does not mean that previously unrepresented constituencies now have an advocate; the less privileged still have trouble articulating their demands. (For an interpretation of dominant-coalition theory as a synthesis of other approaches, see Mollenkopf 1989.) Moreover, the rise of new advocacy groups does not seem to generate countervailing political forces who can check

their excessive claims as envisaged in pluralist theory (see, e.g., Mc-
Connell 1966; Moore 1972, pp. 139–47).

Other observers worry that today's political partisans, however
permanently organized they may be, are increasingly narrowly focused special interest groups incapable of negotiating the compromises upon which democratic politics thrives. Such advocacy groups
have grown in relative and absolute size in the past two decades.
Washington, it has been said, has never been so swamped by single-
interest pressure groups (see, e.g., Etzioni 1984, pp. 169–218). Further, analysts outside the power-elite and Marxist traditions have
come to recognize that business's special responsibility for economic
growth in capitalist democracies gives these potent economic interests enormous clout. For example, Lindblom, an anchor of the pluralist school, concludes in *Politics and Markets* (1977) that the business elite inevitably dominates economic policy in capitalist society.
His final sentences are striking: "The large private corporation fits
oddly into democratic theory and vision. Indeed, it does not fit"
(p. 356).

Thus, those of us concerned with understanding nonstate influences on policymaking would do well to avoid the legitimation-crisis
paradigm's conflation of this issue with queries over state capacities
and, hence, to abandon the shibboleths surrounding the moldering
power-elite versus pluralist debate. Concerns about the unequal dispersion of such influence and the costs of too much dispersion are
not as incompatible as they might have seemed a decade ago. Why
is this now possible?

As the foregoing discussion indicates, there is growing agree-
ment on five points: The structures of political influence are far more
intricate than envisioned by either elitists or pluralists (or neo-Marxist legitimation-crisis theorists); the number of interest groups making claims on the state has grown in the past generation; these
newer advocates are more likely to be narrow single-interest rather
than broad multi-interest groups; powerful economic interests continue to have inordinate influence while many constituencies go un-
der- or unrepresented; and yet the state has powers and interests of
its own, not wholly subordinate to these economic interests. This
revised image of political influence in capitalist democracies has implications for our final pair of diagnoses inquiring whether these

polities are marked by too much apathy or too many demands. The linkage is made explicit by contemporary moderate and conservative followers of Schumpeter, who regard the proliferation of new interest groups and demands as a critical source of the "stalemating" and "overloading" of the political process (Bell 1973; Crozier, Huntington, and Watanuki 1975; Rose and Peters 1979).[9]

While legitimation-crisis theorists confuse the third pair of diagnoses with queries about ineffective state capacities, they tend to subsume discussion of whether distrustful citizens are pressing authorities too much or remain apathetic under the rubric of "crisis of legitimacy." Most who practice under this paradigm have obdurately resisted separating questions about diffuse support for the system from trust in specific incumbents. Indeed, they often see both poles of this question as occurring simultaneously. Wolfe (1977, pp. 295–305), for example, regards the "schizophrenic citizen" as symptomatic of the legitimation crisis of the "late capitalist state." "One side of his personality," he says, "is victimized by the depoliticization process, leaving him withdrawn, apathetic, and sullen. The other side is filled with rage and can express itself at any moment through a political urge, ranging from a sudden burst of intense conversation to collective violence" (Wolfe 1977, p. 296).

Concerns about citizen participation have also alarmed other analysts who, while not relying on this paradigm, are inclined to emphasize one pole or the other. Liberal and left-wing commentators have typically been at the forefront of those who worry about citizen apathy or alienation as they stress inefficient political mobilization, the erosion of the democratic party system, and the debasement of electoral politics. Today some of these thinkers deplore what they see as a turning away from public interest toward a newly justified privatism (see, e.g., Bellah et al. 1985; Hirschman 1982); others focus their criticism mainly on the apparent decline in citizen electoral participation (see, e.g., Piven and Cloward 1988). More conservative commentators, on the other hand, tend to see the problem more as one of "hyperinvolvement," often coupled with insufficient trust in leaders (see, e.g., Huntington 1981) rather than apathy. As I have indicated previously, these analysts point to the proliferation of advocacy groups and demands as the source of such involvement, and they believe it accounts for the "overloading" or "stalemating" of government policymaking.

Those who explicitly or implicitly operate under the legitimation-crisis paradigm are to be commended for discerning that the fourth pair's alternatives may coexist in the same overall system. Yet those outside the paradigm provide more flexible analyses that better appreciate the complex ways in which citizens simultaneously funnel demands *and* confidence to the state as well as keep this issue distinct from the problems of political legitimacy. Such flexibility permits us to consider the possibility that the vagaries of contemporary political participation tell us something about political success and failure that cannot be reduced to questions of either state capacities or legitimacy.

In short, the legitimation-crisis paradigm has proven incapable of providing anything like the kind of inclusive theoretical framework needed for a more empirically open understanding of these four common pairs of citizen laments. It has *neither* done justice to the diversity of the underlying issues these diagnoses raise *nor* forged a satisfactory conceptual vehicle for probing the possible linkages among them. This failure goes beyond an insufficient grasp of the myriad relatively concrete problems that the populace sees arising in contemporary democratic politics. Deeper difficulties wait on more abstract levels of analysis.

A scientifically rigorous analysis of the issues embedded in our four pairs of popular diagnoses calls for detailed consideration of several sets of concepts that initially appear tangential to the issues at hand. Certainly, an acceptable paradigm must at least have all of the concepts it embraces denote an unambiguous and consistent system of meanings that those who subscribe to it can use. But, in addition, the matters raised on the preceding pages cannot receive the scrupulous treatment they warrant unless three specific sets of concepts are clarified. The notions of (1) power, (2) political system, and (3) viability are central. These (and cognate ones) receive detailed treatment in Chapter 1, where I present the groundwork for an alternative to the legitimation-crisis paradigm. However, let me briefly point out here how our previous discussion forces us to consider these categories.

"Power," I argue in Chapter 1, is an elemental question for political sociology, focusing our attention on the capacity to make others do things they would not do if left to their own devices. The question of "who does what to whom and why" is important enough for political sociologists in general, but in understanding success and failure the appreciation of "political power" obviously looms as an exceptionally large concern. Some use the terminology loosely and see all "power" as "political," since both terms connote an ability to *impose* one's will on others. I do not think that will do. Not all power is political power; and separating political from other forms of power allows us to address such key issues as the extent of class domination, the mobilization of confidence and demands, and the effectiveness of state capacities as theoretically and empirically distinct subjects. Naturally, they are related in very vital ways, but their interactions cannot be studied unless they are defined so that their meanings do not overlap. Moreover, clearer definitions in this area are essential if one believes that the state may have a special responsibility for political power in the modern world.

Yet conceptual conundrums emerge even if we grant the state a unique role in advanced society. Does the idea of the "state" subsume everything there is to know about political power? Most analysts would say "no"—and so do I. But if the entire system of political power (the political system) is somehow "larger" than today's bureaucratized state, how should we define "political system" and relate it to the "state"? How do we locate and describe the other "political actors" in political systems? These are not idle academic problems. Unless they are clarified, we are unable to separate sufficiently matters of state capacity from issues tied to the mobilization of demands and confidence. Perhaps even more important, we cannot rigorously address such topics as the vulnerability of the state to "outside" pressures (such as from the capitalist class) and the degree of autonomy of modern states.

Once we have clarified the notions of "state" and "political system," we can begin to inquire more precisely about political success and failure. This topic is at the nub of my book. Legitimation-crisis theorists have made this question their core problematic. Neo-Marxist critics always deal with it in terms of "crisis." Others often face it under the rubric of "political stability." Both terms carry heavy ideological baggage and hence I prefer the label "viability." Selection of an alternative name, as we observe in Chapter 1, is more than a cosmetic exercise. The move beyond "crisis" or "stability" makes it easier to break free of the restrictive binary formulation of state-effectiveness-and-legitimacy that plagues the legitimation-crisis paradigm. I argue that an adequate understanding of what goes into an authentically viable political system requires a knowledge of additional elements.

Plan of the Book

This book is primarily an effort to construct a more theoretically comprehensive and empirically open alternative to the legitimation-crisis paradigm's approach to political success and failure. It is predominately a work of synthesis, summation, and generalization and not a theoretical or empirical exercise in the sense of generating or testing falsifiable hypotheses. True, it stresses the importance of a solid theoretical grounding and developing propositions capable of facing empirical scrutiny, and it attempts to incorporate the results of previous scholarly research. Ultimately, however, it is mainly a set of sociological reflections about the assumptions brought to the study of the state and the polity rather than a historical or comparative study per se. This approach has a number of privileges. In particular, it permits a more wide-ranging search for supporting evidence and examples. Thus readers will find citations to Russell Baker, Flora Lewis, and *Time* magazine side by side with references to Lipset, Skocpol, and Skowronek. This is perfectly appropriate in the enterprise of paradigm building and summation rather than of hypothesis testing. Certainly, it allows us to draw more liberally on the political wisdom that exists outside of the academy than conventionally permitted in detailed empirical inquiries.

This book is divided into five chapters. The first of these proceeds directly to the consideration of the essential elements of a more acceptable paradigm. The other four chapters apply the lessons from Chapter 1 to the issues embedded in our four pairs of lamentations. The opening chapter argues that the "right" kind of paradigm makes sociopolitical analyses of "crisis" and "stability" more theoretically and empirically comprehensible than the legitimation-crisis approach has. It suggests that a paradigm's underlying assumptions should be judged by how well they manage the trade-off between a need for both multidimensionality and parsimony. The chapter then considers these fundamental assumptions and says that they must especially include presuppositions and models.

Power and viability are political sociology's pivotal *presuppositional topics*, it argues. A model of the political system with four intrasocietal levels is also presented in this chapter. The highest of these, the state, is modeled as a complex organization. A sociological view of the state-as-organization assumes a "contradiction model" of state effectiveness with the prospect for persistent conflict among inevitably plural government goals. Most important, Chapter 1 provides a firmer ground for talking systematically about political success and failure than the legitimation-crisis paradigm. It argues that the dimensions of viability are a state's capacity to pursue goals effectively, the political system's ability to mobilize participation efficiently, and prospects for rendering the rules of the political game legitimate.

The next three chapters are organized around the factors that foster and check ineffective goal attainment, inefficient participation, and "crises of legitimacy"—particularly as these are manifested in the contemporary United States. In a sense, Chapter 2 brings us back to the query contained in the first pair of citizen laments: Are today's states too strong or too weak? It suggests that this formulation remains too simpleminded and argues that enhancing state effectiveness may become counterproductive. It does this by examining *why* (1) effectiveness is the prime ingredient of viability; (2) states always have multiple goals; (3) authorities and potential partisans focus especially on economic growth; (4) overemphasizing any one goal—most commonly, economic growth—may diminish a state's capacity to pursue other goals effectively; and (5) such overemphasis also weakens the political system's overall viability through adverse effects on political participation and possibly, in the long run, on legitimacy.

Chapter 3 signals that the study of political inefficiency within capitalist democracies raises issues separate from those associated with either the pursuit of state effectiveness or the maintenance of legitimacy. The chapter demonstrates that the world of political participation is considerably more complex than earlier approaches envisioned. It explores why political participation in the contemporary United States is marked by both *apathy* and *overload* or *hyperparticipation*. It returns us to the problems within the third and fourth pairs of diagnoses. That is, it examines under what circumstances the proliferation of special interests leads to an overload in demands that could stalemate state policymaking and under which conditions apathy persists. The chapter suggests that a refurbished, more macrosociological version of the classic "cross-pressures" approach explains a good deal about how these inefficiencies are plaguing participation in the United States.

Chapter 4 concerns the second pair of diagnoses and focuses on the heart of the legitimation-crisis paradigm. It maintains that the rise of rational-legal doctrines in Western societies has helped foster an endemic "confidence gap" regarding officeholders but not a rejection of the moral worth of the system, and that what has passed for lowered political legitimacy in the United States, in fact, may be some minimal erosion in the core values of our more general culture. Paradoxically, then, moral commitment to American political institutions remains high amid distrust of incumbents and some possibly lingering "cultural malaise."

Chapter 5 sums up the empirical statements that have been made in light of this developing paradigm. It questions whether we have achieved the "end of history" or the "end of the state," as some theorists have recently speculated, and it reviews the key factors that are blocking viability in advanced democracies. This chapter distinguishes between the impediments that are more or less unique to the American polity and those that are more widely shared by liberal democracies. It concludes with an examination of the prospects for rational political change.

Conclusions

For over a quarter of a century various sectors within the American public have been telling us that the modern democratic state is somehow in trouble; many citizens and scholars have even applied the diagnosis of "crisis." Neither the apparent triumph of Western doctrines of liberal democracy and capitalist free markets after almost forty-five years of Cold War nor the speedy U.S. victory in the Gulf War has stilled these alarms. Yet social scientists must make more inclusive sense of the diagnoses that citizens have bandied about if they are to detect whether these are more than a congeries of woes. Unfortunately, only one approach has made a concerted effort to provide such theoretical and empirical integration: the legitimation-crisis paradigm.

This way of thinking has proven to be inadequate for the job. Yet, my rejection of this approach should not be construed as a narrow, ideologically inspired polemic against the neo-Marxists who make up the largest and most self-conscious camp within the paradigm. The approach's underlying deficiencies cut across ideological and political boundaries and are shared by neo- and non-Marxists alike. Indeed, non-Marxists who follow in the footsteps of Schumpeter and the early Lipset experience considerably more difficulty because they are often not fully aware that they are working within a paradigm.

The core failure of this paradigm is more formal than substantive—that is, in assuming a simple link between effective state capacities and legitimacy. In fact, these are only two of at least three components of political viability. Thus, for instance, because their binary conceptualizations do not allow for pivotal distinctions, most users of the legitimation-crisis paradigm cannot account for the simultaneous pervasive lack of confidence in political leaders and deep moral attachment to the systems in which these authorities operate. Moreover, seeing state effectiveness as the primordial source of legitimacy, and hence viability, blinds these analysts to the possibility of other, more deep-seated threats to viability.

Both the formal and substantive failures of the legitimation-crisis paradigm in adequately understanding political success and failure—particularly of its neo-Marxist versions—have led to the unwarranted rejection of systematic theorizing about politics in some quarters. Theda Skocpol, for example, in rebuffing the "grand systems theories of the structural-functionalists or neo-Marxists," concludes: "We do not need a new or refurbished grand theory of 'The State.' Rather, we need solidly grounded and analytically sharp understandings of the causal regularities that underlie the histories of states, social structures, and transnational relations in the modern world" (Skocpol 1985a, p. 28). While no one can disagree with her second sentence, a fuller appreciation of the regularities she wishes to analyze cannot occur without some prior clarification of basic assumptions.

It is to a consideration of these assumptions that I now turn.

1 Paradigm Regained
Core Elements of an Alternative Approach

*To its good fortune, political sociology has always been relatively
free of metatheoretical urges—that is, urges to classify the
grounds of other people's arguments rather than pursue
substantive problems. . . . May the good lord protect . . . political
sociologists from wandering into the dead end of metatheory.*
    —Theda Skocpol, "The Dead End of Metatheory"

*When we say "we do not know enough facts" to justify a given
conclusion, we do not mean quantitatively that we cannot make a
sufficient number of verifiable statements about the phenomenon
but rather that we are not in a position to make important
statements which are logically required as premises for the
conclusion. What facts are important is determined by the
structure of the theoretical system.*
    —Talcott Parsons, The Structure of Social Action

The seemingly antithetical quotations from Theda Skocpol and Talcott Parsons that introduce the chapter emphasize that a greater understanding of political success and failure must rely on both perspectives. Skocpol's cautionary statements should be taken to
heart—but in light of Parsons's declaration that facts exist only
within the broader conceptual framework now commonly called a
paradigm. This chapter maintains that paradigm building profits
from the explication of fundamental assumptions that are robust
enough to adduce key theoretical and empirical questions, yet avoid
answering them. But how do we move beyond the tendency of
those within the legitimation-crisis paradigm to talk about "crisis" or
"stability" and begin thinking more satisfactorily about what success
and failure mean in modern politics?

This chapter rejects the idea that a single variable or even a pair can validly render the issues buried in such notions as "crisis" and "stability." Specifically, I offer a multidimensional image of "viability" in the hope of fostering more theoretically comprehensive and empirically open inquiry into state and political-system performances over different stages in their histories, with a special eye on modern democratic systems, particularly the United States. I contend that all political systems, as they struggle to be viable, face three prospective sets of adversity that are potentially independent of one another: (1) their states' ineffective pursuit of goals, (2) the inefficiencies these systems encounter in the incorporation of political participation, and (3) possible challenges to the legitimacy of the prevailing "rules of the game."

The chapter is divided into two main parts. The first section discusses the requisites of a more fruitful paradigm and identifies two of its key components as presuppositions and models. The second section focuses on the presuppositions and models that help us transcend the formulations of political "stability" or "crisis." Power and viability, I argue, are political sociology's fundamental presuppositional questions. This book's special concern with political success and failure obviously makes viability the more central of the two concepts, although each must be more clearly understood to fully appreciate the other. The empirical and theoretical issues clarified by multidimensional analysis of both concepts are discussed. The chapter concludes with an examination of the models that arise from such analyses and how these enlarge our understanding of political viability. Models of the state and political system are given especially close attention.

My goal is to elucidate the appropriate fundamental assumptions or "first principles" for plumbing political success and failure. As we set about building a more satisfactory paradigm, differences between theory and metatheory move to the core of the discussion. In a nutshell, my purpose is to provide a more rigorous and explicit set of "first principles" for the standard theorizing and hypothesis testing of political sociologists. I want to codify the presuppositions and models that many of us who find the legitimation-crisis paradigm uncongenial have been employing for a long time—often unreflectively—so that we can speak about success and failure more precisely. Some of the particular points have been noncontroversial for some time and may even be derived in other ways. But just because many political sociologists may have been "speaking prose" without knowing it does not invalidate an attempt to elucidate their underlying grammar. Moreover, articulating an explicit alternative to the legitimation-crisis paradigm guarantees that we are less likely to slip back into an implicit adoption of its misleading binary formulations as we try to make sense of the empirical world around us. Chapter 1 is not "theoretical" in the sense of furnishing a conceptual apparatus that directly accounts for concrete differences in political success or failure. It develops the key components of a paradigm that will provide a firmer foundation for such analyses. My focus then is on the metatheoretical section of a paradigm, namely, on the portion that provides the criteria for shaping new arguments or hypotheses as well as for assessing the relevance of potential evidence.[1]

Requisites for a Paradigm

If political sociology aspires to be a social science (and not a branch of political philosophy), it must certainly offer "solidly grounded and analytically sharp understandings of causal regularities that underlie the histories of states, social structures, and transnational relations in the modern world" (Skocpol 1985a, p. 28). Yet, as Parsons noted more than half a century ago, arguments cannot be formulated nor evidence marshaled without a broader context of relevance and plausibility. Facts do not exist outside of such a conceptual framework, and sociologists proceed at their own peril if they pursue "data" but fail to make their frameworks explicit (Parsons 1937, pp. 27–42).

Parsons called this broader framework "theoretical"; yet since Kuhn (1970) we have labeled this phenomenon a paradigm. We do so because the broader conceptual context Parsons spoke of also contains statements beyond propositions that are immediately amenable to empirical study. Scientists who work within the same paradigm are guided not only by a common set of theories and methods, but also by a set of fundamental assumptions shaped by metaphysical, epistemological, ideological, and aesthetic factors. The term "metatheory" has commonly been applied to such assumptions or first principles. Metatheory is disparaged in some quarters because it "often gets bogged down in weighty philosophical matters and immobilizes theory building" (Turner 1991, p. 9). However, since these fundamental assumptions affect the kind of theories, hypotheses, and findings we ultimately develop—and are in turn shaped by them—their more precise formulation is hardly a waste of time nor simply a matter of idle speculation or personal prejudices. There are a few minimally acceptable objective criteria that we can use in judging the adequacy of metatheoretical categories. I consider what these criteria are before moving on to ask about the key ingredients that make up the fundamental assumptions for studying political viability.

CRITERIA FOR METATHEORY: PARSIMONY AND MULTIDIMENSIONALITY

All scientific work is governed by Occam's Razor, the principle of parsimony holding that when two conceptual schemes account equally well for observable variations one must always prefer the scheme that contains the fewest concepts and assumptions—all else being equal. On the other hand, Alexander (1982) argues that multidimensional fundamental assumptions are preferred to one-dimensional ones. As we proceed to construct an alternative paradigm, how do we reconcile these two exigencies?

Let us begin with multidimensionality. What precisely does this notion mean? Alexander's usage is somewhat elusive, but close reading yields two core features. First, multidimensionality indicates an acceptance of a "two-directional flow of scientific work." Figure 1 is a diagram of Alexander's (1982) continuum of scientific work. The totality of the continuum may be regarded as containing the essential elements of a paradigm. The continuum is bounded on the left by the more general pole beyond which lies the "metaphysical environment"; to the right is the more specific pole just this side of the "empirical environment." The former consists of possible scenarios about the "ultimate nature" of reality; the latter compromises all "facts" potentially knowable through direct or indirect sense observations. Science thus falls into that sector between metaphysical speculations and "fact finding," affected by both, the result of neither exclusively, but consisting of much more as well. Between these poles (as one moves from left to right or from the general to the

Metaphysical environment   Empirical environment

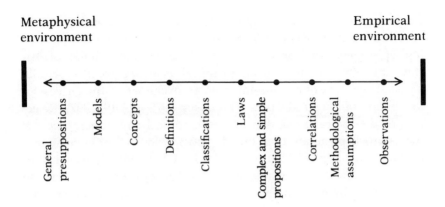

Figure 1
Alexander's Continuum of Scientific Work and Its Components
Source: Alexander (1982, p. 3).

specific) Alexander places presuppositions, models, concepts, definitions, classifications, laws, propositions, methodological assumptions, and observational statements.[2] Each component is relatively autonomous but influenced by all the components on either side. The continuum is asymmetrical only in the sense that a left component has the potential (although probably never the complete ability) to subsume totally the ones to the right (as the general incorporates the specific) but not vice versa.

Thus a multidimensional science moves both ways along the continuum between metaphysical and empirical environments. In the center portion of the continuum this means that research may generate theory but theory may also generate research. One-directional approaches, in contrast, argue that science always moves from the general to the concrete or from the concrete to the general.

How does this first meaning of multidimensionality assist us in selecting the "right" fundamental assumptions? It helps us because we are able to locate a starting point that is relatively noncontroversial, presuming we accept the notion that science is always a two-way street that moves from both specific to general and general to specific. In the process, two extreme positions are rejected: a vulgar idealism that holds that facts are merely the emanations of theories or ideologies; and various brands of positivism that postulate an unbreachable chasm between facts and theories, with the former having epistemological priority. E. P. Thompson's critique of Althusser's effort to reduce all historical evidence to ideologically based theories is often presented as an exemplar of the successful demolition of vulgar idealism (Thompson 1978, pp. 193–397). Rejection of the radical separation of the empirical and nonempirical is the bedrock postulate of a broad, "postpositivist" movement that contains such diverse figures as Michael Polanyi, Thomas Kuhn, Gerald Holton, Imre Lakatos, and Paul Feyerabend. (For a concise overview of the main themes of this movement, see Alexander 1982, pp. 18–35.)

The second usage of multidimensionality entails a preference for two or more parameters in the generation of analytical categories and skepticism about "first principles" that build on only a single factor or binary formulas. Thus, for example, Alexander rejects both idealistic and materialistic presuppositions about social action in favor of multidimensional approaches that synthesize symbolic and objective elements (see below). Closer to our concerns, Lipset ([1960] 1981, pp. 4–9) implicitly makes a similar choice when he argues that political sociology should begin by rejecting the Marxian polarity of conflict *or* consensus in favor of a Tocquevillian approach that sees political life as the interpenetration of conflict *and* consensus.

Parsimony would seem to propel a would-be paradigm builder in an opposite direction from that mandated by multidimensionality. A single-minded zeal for the simplest acceptable formulation, after all, may incline the analyst toward monistic theorizing (at least, in terms of the second usage of multidimensionality). If one feels that the two criteria should complement each other, how does one harmonize their imperatives? In the final analysis, I am going to focus on the need for multidimensionality and employ parsimony mainly as a brake on its potential excesses. I intend to provide a multidimensional outline of "first principles," but on each step of the way I show how the addition of a new dimension increases our theoretical or empirical understanding.

When one is engaged in paradigm building, the risks associated with stressing parsimony in splendid isolation are especially pernicious. The temptation to caricature the social world in the name of abstracting its underlying theoretical "essence" is irresistible for many. Such endeavors, notably in political sociology, gravitate toward bipolarities in which one pole is regarded as the antithesis of the other. The all-too-common result is political analysis that treats the world in black-or-white terms, sometimes with apocalyptic overtones. The classical Marxist formulation of the ruling class's total domination of the state is probably the best example of an unproductive one-directional approach (see Carnoy 1984, pp. 44–64). We have seen that neo-Marxist and non-Marxist adherents of the legitimation-crisis paradigm are only slightly less immune to one-dimensionalism as attested to by their preferences for binary formulas, particularly ineffective state capacities versus legitimacy.[3]

Good metatheory, therefore, is sufficiently robust to allow us to generate appropriate criteria for analysis, yet restrained enough not to dictate results. Piven and Cloward's (1971) *Regulating the Poor* provides useful cautionary lessons on how one-dimensional assumptions can distort the full analysis of the evidence. Piven and Cloward's "first principles" posit a narrow social control interpretation of public relief in which elite self-interest is the pivotal factor driving state action. The authors are concerned with explaining the welfare explosion of the 1960s in the United States, although they cover welfare history from the New Deal onward as well (and even discuss pre–twentieth century Great Britain). In the process, they skillfully present an array of data on such diverse topics as elite uses of humanitarian or moralistic ideals; the poor's varying ability to sustain organized pressure on the state; the ideology and interests of the mass of nonpoor Americans; and the changing capacities of federal and local authorities to balance the claims of elite, poor, and nonpoor constituents. Unfortunately, this rich evidence is framed by rigid fundamental assumptions that do not permit the testing of alternative hypotheses. Many of their data take on the character of "anomalies" (in the Kuhnian sense) in the face of their one-dimensional elite-interest, social control model. (For a fuller critique see Muraskin 1975.)

When parsimony is enriched by multidimensional formulations, we have a greater chance of fostering hypotheses that are empirically open enough to permit the examination of all analytically possible alternatives. Fred Block's (1977) essay "The Ruling Class Does

Not Rule" stands as an exemplar of multidimensional metatheorizing while remaining appreciative of its Marxist roots. Capitalist rational self-interest is not presupposed to determine state actions automatically. "The alternative framework being proposed," Block (1977, pp. 7–8) says, "suggests that the capacity of capitalism to rationalize itself is the outcome of a conflict among three sets of agents—the capitalist class, the managers of the state apparatus, and the working class. Rationalization occurs 'behind the backs' of each set of actors so that rationality cannot be seen as a function of the consciousness of one particular group." This framework opens the way for an authentically empirical political sociology that can ask decisive questions about the interactions of the state and other societal actors as well as about the state's possible range of autonomy while permitting the collection of facts with the potential to provide valid answers.

Lipset's (1963a) use of differences in the core values of the four largest English-speaking democracies to account for variations in their political institutions is another instructive example. He explicitly adopts a set of "first principles" on the interaction of values, broader cultural factors, and political structures derived from the works of Weber, Parsons, and Engels (Lipset 1963a, pp. 530–31). This permits him to reformulate Parsons's pattern variables in such a way that crucial value patterns of the United States, Great Britain, Canada, and Australia can be ranked on four dimensions: elitism-equalitarianism, ascription-achievement, particularism-universalism, and diffuseness-specificity. These rankings, in turn, correspond to concrete differences in political institutions among these four nations. The results allow him to examine how divergent values, despite the constraints of structural and material conditions, help explain some of the political differences among four democratic nation-states that otherwise share a broad cultural heritage.

Skocpol's (1987) attack on metatheory implies that she rejects the pursuit of "first principles" because the enterprise is inherently one-dimensional. "Metatheoretical exercises," she says, "risk creating artificial ideal-typical categorizations that obscure rather than illuminate the more fruitful tendencies in substantial theory and research" (1987, p. 10). The specific object of her criticism is Alford and Friedland's *Powers of Theory* (1985). These authors summarize several hundred studies about the state in advanced capitalist societies. They argue that these studies can be most fruitfully understood and compared when they are classified into pluralist, managerialist, and class perspectives. The result, Skocpol argues, is to cast studies that are potentially multidimensional into a distorting monistic mold. Alford and Friedland's schema, she believes, "obscures the fact that the best work in political sociology has for many years focused" on more than one perspective at a time and been concerned with the interaction among different levels of analysis (Skocpol 1987, p. 10).

Yet, as the foregoing illustrations from Block and Lipset attest, the quest for the "right" fundamental assumptions need not be weighed down by one-dimensionalism. While metatheory has more to fear from some of its practitioners than from its critics, the alleged excesses of those engaged in the study of fundamental assumptions in no way negate the epistemological point that scientific facts exist only within the context of a paradigm of which multidimensional metatheory ought to be a key element. But what are suitable metatheoretical issues for political sociologists interested in examining what lies beyond talk of "stability" or "crisis"? Before we can answer this question, we have to agree on the key elements of metatheory per se.

ELEMENTS OF METATHEORY:
PRESUPPOSITIONS AND MODELS

Presuppositions and models form the heart of fundamental assumptions or metatheory. Figure 1, which presents a diagram of Alexander's (1982) continuum of scientific work (see above), tells us that all activities to the right of presuppositions and models deal with theory and research as they have been more traditionally conceived (see, e.g., Merton 1968, pp. 139–71). Generally speaking, the presuppositions and models of a paradigm provide the standards for developing new arguments or hypotheses as well as for assessing the potential relevance of evidence. Acceptable presuppositions are marked by generality and decisiveness (Alexander 1982, pp. 37–39). Generality means that "all other scientific commitments can be understood as specifications, even while the latter maintain their analytical independence" (p. 37). Decisiveness dictates that presuppositions "must have significant repercussions at every more specific level" and hence "must address fundamentally significant scientific problems" (p. 37). Models, for Alexander, consist of a logically ordered set of concepts that highlight the key features of the subject matter of a scientific discipline. In the realm of general sociology, for example, the principal debate over models revolves around whether or not to treat society as a "system."

Presuppositions and Models

In short, a paradigm's fundamental assumptions consist of presuppositions and models. These constitute a framework that permits the formulation and testing of decisive hypotheses. Presuppositions and models are more scientifically satisfying when they successfully balance the need for multidimensionality and parsimony. In the light of these criteria, which presuppositions and models are most suitable for political sociology?

PRESUPPOSITIONS

Alexander (1982) posits two core presuppositional questions for general sociology: action and order. What do they entail, and why do they lead us to the questions of power and viability in political sociology?

The question of action inquires about the most elementary form of social reality. Armed with the criterion of multidimensionality, Alexander, following Parsons (1937), defines action as simultaneously entailing the enactment of subjective intentions and the adaptation to an objective environment. Action thus is rendered as the capacity to pursue symbolically defined goals in the context of material situations that are also symbolically defined. Sociologically relevant human behavior, in other words, is neither merely the working out of subjectively defined dispositions nor the adjustment to the limits and opportunities imposed by the environment; it is a *synthesis* of a person's symbolically delineated intentions and definitions and the material setting in which these occur. A similar multidimensional view of action has also been formulated by Giddens (1984), who treats it as conduct reflexively monitored by a human actor across time and space. I argue below that power's presuppositional status for political sociology is analogous to the one held by action for general sociology.

A multidimensional approach to order, for Alexander, requires that social life be viewed as the result of both human initiatives and the constraints imposed by emergent sui generis factors. Giddens (1984) states the issue of order more graphically in his call to synthesize human agency and structure: "The constitution of agents and structures are not two independently given sets of phenomena, a dualism, but represent a duality. According to the notion of duality of structure, the structural properties of social systems are both medium and outcome of the practices they recursively organize" (Giddens 1984, p. 25).[4] I regard "political viability" as the presuppositional analog of order in the political sociological domain.[5]

1. Power

General sociology's conferral of presuppositional status on the question of social action is justifiable for its level of analysis. People's conduct makes a difference in the material and symbolic worlds in which they are situated. They are not *just* responding unreflectively to a given environment; rather, the subjective meanings they create and use tell them what to pursue and avoid as well as what they "see" in the environment and how they should react both emotionally and morally to what they "see." A satisfactory multidimensional appreciation of this phenomenon as social action, therefore, seems to be essential for sociological inquiry.

However, the problem of social action is not decisive enough for political sociologists. Our interest in political success and failure leads to a concern with the ability of social actors to achieve ends in their surroundings; but our focus ought to be more specific than people's capacities to pursue their symbolically defined intentions in symbolically defined situations. This additional concern is why political sociologists have been so enamored of the concept of power. While power is an aspect of all social action insofar as both concepts are concerned with intentionality (i.e., with people's ability to formulate and achieve goals), political sociologists should hold power to a higher standard than they do social action. Certainly, we should not equate the two. We tend to be interested in the ability to create and affect the implementation of goals of broader social significance. Moreover, students of power (or at least those in the Weberian tradition) say that this concept (unlike action per se) denotes the probability of making others do what they would otherwise not do. Etzioni (1968, p. 314) captures all this with the following definition: *"Power is a capacity to overcome part or all of the resistance, to introduce changes in the face of opposition* (this includes sustaining a course of action or preserving a status quo that would otherwise have been discontinued or altered)" (italics in original; see also Weber [1924] 1968, pp. 212–99).

Power thus means being able to get something done (or prevent something from happening) even if others may try to stop you. Obviously, such a concept seems quite helpful to those of us trying to talk more precisely about political successes and failures. We can appreciate that the president has power, that Congress has power, that the National Organization for Women has power, that capitalists have power, that political action committees (PACs) have power, that the Republican National Committee has power, that the government of France has power, and so forth. But these actors do not have the same kinds or equal amounts of power. Thus we have to elaborate our definition of power; we have to make it more multidimensional.

How should we go about making the definition more theoretically comprehensive and empirically inclusive? Rather than dashing hither and yon to satisfy the criterion of multidimensionality (and, possibly as a consequence, failing to meet the standard of parsimony), I propose that we construct our multidimensional definition in such a way as to aid us in providing the scientific answers to certain decisive questions about political life without blindly closing off any logical possible empirical option. Our formulations should allow these queries to become more fully rendered as researchable concerns rather than as matters of ex cathedra theoretical assertions. I believe that eight questions about power have loomed as particularly decisive in social science discourse over the past generation. They are:

1. Are actors in a social situation always divided into commanders and commanded, or can they, under certain circumstances, be both simultaneously?
2. When are power relations zero-sum games, and when are they not?

3. Under what circumstances is the power being exercised coextensive with the use or threat of violence, and when do other power bases become important?
4. Is all power equally alienating?
5. What are the historical relationships between the rise of capitalism and the development of the modern state?
6. In which situations are state agencies capable of performing as autonomous actors pursuing their own agendas, and when is the state more likely to act primarily as the instrument of external agencies?
7. What state actions foster substantial societal transformation, and what elements impede such developments?
8. When does the pursuit of societal transformation weaken democratic institutions, and when does it strengthen them?

The first two questions are often tied to the famous debate between Mills (1956) and Parsons (1960) over whether power in America can accurately be described in terms of a virtual monolithic domination by a "power elite" that comprises corporate, military, and federal executive sectors. This debate boiled down to two theoretical issues: Are those with more power always in command, or can those with less power sometimes prevail? Does power inevitably entail the notion of a fixed quantity so that gain by one actor must imply a loss by others?

A multidimensional rendering of power as both subjective (symbolic) and objective (material) allows us to treat both these queries in an empirically open way. Power shares this dualistic feature with social action in general. Those of us defining power within Weber's general framework find ourselves including symbolic and material elements when we use such terms as "chance," "capacity," or "potential." Unless social scientists see power as a prospect for the control of future events, they have to be satisfied with ex post facto analyses, that is, with the study of power as past dominations. Power's potential comes from its wielder (ego) and from the subjects of commands (alters). Ego's power potential or prospect rests on the likelihood of being able to attain or prevent change in the future, even if alters have to be brought into line. This potential has two sources, which have been variably called potential for power versus power as a potential (Rose 1967, p. 47), the objective versus symbolic bases of power (Etzioni 1968, pp. 338–42), and possible power versus latent power (Wrong 1980, pp. 6–10). Ego's own source of power is based on the control of resources. Alters provide ego's symbolic basis for power. Alters are sources of power when ego is attributed some right or ability to issue commands. In fact, power, like all social action, depends on both objective factors (resources at hand and material constraints) and subjective definitions (symbolic attributions).

This duality means that power need not necessarily be lodged in a single social unit. It flows simultaneously from beliefs, reputations, resources, and social positions but always differentially in light of the historical circumstances. Thus the world is not automatically divided into power wielders and subjects. It is empirically possible for social actors to be both at the same time. Moreover, the duality of power dictates that power need not be a zero-sum game on a priori grounds. Power springs from diverse objective and subjective roots. These potentials do not necessarily exist in fixed quantities. The amounts of each may increase, decrease, or remain constant in the course of power relations. Thus, that one actor's capacities grow more at one time does not inevitably determine that other actors have less.

A multidimensional perspective is also essential even when one highlights the resource bases of power. An appreciation of the possible diversity of resources that power wielders may have at their disposal helps us to ask more clearly about the relationship between power and violence and between power and alienation (by which I mean simply a commander's tendency to generate either passive or active resistance; see Etzioni 1968, pp. 373–81). These questions may be traced back to Weber's initial treatment of power (in the absence of legitimacy) as somehow ultimately rooted in violence.[6] If violence is at the root of power, do all commands provoke resistance equally?

In fact, at least three analytically distinct types of resources have been noted, and each lends itself to a distinctive mode of domination (see Etzioni 1968, pp. 350–81; Lehman 1977, pp. 47–48). *Coercive* resources are material objects capable of doing violence to alters' bodies or psyches. Examples from the microsociological level are guns, whips, and knives. On the macro level, coercive resources include weapons stockpiles, military installations, and military, paramilitary, and police personnel. Coercive resources are used most effectively when constraint is the desired mode of domination. Constraint is the common goal of custodial mental hospitals, prisons, and totalitarian regimes. The aim here is to add disadvantages to alters' external situation in order to constrict their options in an encounter with ego.

Utilitarian resources, often referred to as "economic resources" in everyday usage, are material rewards such as goods, services, property, and income. This type of resource is most congruent with domination through inducement. Ego gets alters to comply in exchange for the prospect of positive changes in their external, material situations. Inducement is probably the primary mode of domination in management-worker relationships in advanced capitalist democracies.

Normative resources are malleable symbols rather than material rewards or physical threats. The most universal normative resources are prestige, esteem, acceptance, and love. Examples from the macro level include a state's control of information, the U.S. president's special access to the mass media, a profession's capacity to monopolize certain technical knowledge, and the pope's ability to excommunicate dissidents. Normative resources are especially effective for domination via persuasion, which is the gaining of compliance through the change of alters' interior dispositions (the ways they think and feel) rather than their external conditions. Gamson (1968) notes that complimentary as well as pejorative terms have been used to describe persuasion: "The approving words include education, persuasion, therapy, rehabilitation, and perhaps more neutrally, socialization. The disapproving words include indoctrination, manipulation, propaganda, and 'brainwashing'" (Gamson 1968, p. 125).

The acceptance of a plurality of resources enhances the empirical study of politics in two ways. First, it prevents us from equating power with violence. Power can derive from the manipulation of at least three kinds of assets, of which the coercive is but one type. *Nor should coercive resources, defined as the means of violence, be confused with coercion, seen as the potential for overcoming resistance.* The latter is an integral part of any exercise of power; the former is not. Second, the recognition of multiple resource bases allows for differences in the amount of alienation caused by different power operations. All else being equal, normative resources are the least alienating, coercive are the most, and utilitarian are somewhere in between. Consequently, not all power fosters the same kind of compliance nor the same opposition to commands.

Giddens (1984, 1985) offers an alternative classification of resources, which in its own way makes a distinctive contribution to the multidimensional definition of power. He distinguishes between allocative resources, or control over material objects, and authoritative resources, or control over human beings. This comparison helps him deal with the question about the relationship between the rise of capitalism and the development of modern states. In contrast to the normative-utilitarian-coercive classification, Giddens's categories ask us to inquire about the principal sites of resistance. Some power wielders focus primarily on the control and processing of standardized inanimate objects exemplified by industrial production. The focus for others is the monitoring, control, and processing of people. Marxists, Giddens argues, collapse the latter into the former and hence treat political power as a derivative of class. Giddens's multidimensional use of allocative and authoritative resources permits study of the relation between class and politics, and hence ultimately the interaction of capitalism and the state, to remain open and capable of unbiased empirical study.

But what kinds of changes do power wielders intend to introduce? This issue is embedded in our sixth and seventh questions, which inquire about the state's prospects for autonomy as well as its potential for promoting societal transformation (by which I mean simply the implementation of significant—and not just incremental—changes). Of course, Giddens's distinction between allocative and authoritative resources has already unlocked the door for a more empirically open investigation of state autonomy, since it permits us to study the relationships between capitalism and the rise of the modern state without restrictive preconceptions. More precisely, however, a grasp of the capacities needed to bring about change requires us to acknowledge that intended outcomes can take two directions: as the result of intermember power or of political power.

Power's intermember dimension focuses on the pursuit of members' particular goals. Analysis centers on the members of a system (they can be individuals or groups) and their competition over valued, scarce resources. Yet this competition does not exhaust the topic of power's intentionality. At times, power is exercised for collective purposes (and only secondarily, if at all, to enhance the privileges of particular members). This capacity is not mindless; systemic change is more than the unintended backwash of intermember struggles. Some potential to set, pursue, and implement collective goals exists in all groups. Its generic name is systemic power, but it is most commonly manifested on the societal level, where it is called political power. A hallmark of advanced societies is the structural separation of political power from intermember power (see Lehman 1977). Intermember power reminds us of the immemorial struggle for valued and scarce resources and privilege that has marked all human societies. The concept of political power raises the empirical possibility of specialized agencies with the capability to penetrate the network of intermember power and change the society. This multidimensional conceptualization, which sees power as both intermember and political, gives the notion of collective goals theoretical credibility and makes state autonomy and societal transformation authentic empirical prospects.

Yet political power itself is more fully understood in a multidimensional framework. A distinction between despotic and infrastructural aspects (Mann 1984, 1986) permits us to study whether the pursuit of societal transformation is inescapably inimical to democratic institutions. The despotic dimension makes us examine the degree to which one actor (individual or collective) is empowered with ultimate responsibility without the need for extensive institutionalized negotiations. Premodern empires, such as Rome and China, as well as twentieth-century totalitarian regimes, such as Nazi Germany and the Stalinist Soviet Union, are instances of high despotic power. Today's capitalist democracies, on the other hand, tend to be lower in this regard but to have relatively high infrastructural power. This dimension refers to political authorities' ability to penetrate civil society. Such penetration entails both scope and intensity. All modern bureaucratic states (democratic and nondemocratic alike) have steadily increased the number of domains they are involved in, as well as how deeply they reach into most of these.

Despotic and infrastructural powers have not coincided neatly throughout history, however. In our own time totalitarian regimes and democratic ones have tried alternate routes to societal transformation: The former have "traded off some loss of infrastructural penetration for high despotic powers" (Mann 1984, p. 191); democratic regimes have relied on infrastructural strategies in lieu of despotic control. Thus, a multidimensional rendering of political power helps us to recognize that myriad processes are involved in the modern state's pursuit of societal transformation. Moreover, it suggests that mobilization for a more decent society is not inevitably the "road to serfdom."

In sum, the use of multidimensional presuppositions regarding power paves the way for the formulation and valid investigation of pivotal political hypotheses. Specifically, at least eight key questions become more fully rendered as empirical concerns via a multidimensional definition of power that acknowledges its subjective and objective bases, its multiresource potential, its dual loci of resistance, its intermember and political thrusts, and the despotic and infrastructural aspects of political power. The ability to deal more objectively with the issues of the state's autonomy and transformative potential are perhaps the two most important of these questions at the moment but, as we have seen, hardly the only ones.

2. Political viability

The problem of order in general sociology, I previously noted, asks about what Giddens (1984) has called the duality of structure (or how we reconcile the twin realities of human initiative and systemic constraint). As with the notion of action, order per se lacks the specificity to provide a presuppositional focus for political sociologists. In a general sense, a definition of the sociopolitical analog of the problem of order has been the special preserve of all those who explicitly or implicitly employ the legitimation-crisis paradigm. More specifically, however, the non-Marxists who use the rubric of "political stability" have been the most active members of this camp in trying to define the political significance of the question of agency and structure.

I have argued previously that the quest for multidimensionality in this regard mandates that we follow Lipset's lead and focus on *both* consensus and conflict in order to understand and study political stability (Lipset [1960] 1981, pp. 4–9). Yet the volumes of quantitative, historical, and speculative work on the topic cannot transcend the pervasive murkiness in the basic definition of this concept. Lipset's highly influential opening paragraph to chapter 3 of *Political Man* manages to capture most of the conceptual problems. He says:

> The stability of any given democracy depends not only on economic development but also upon the effectiveness and the legitimacy of its political system. Effectiveness means actual performance, the extent to which the system satisfies the basic functions of government as most of the population and such powerful groups within it as big business or the armed forces see them. Legitimacy involves the capacity of the system to engender and maintain the belief that the existing political institutions are the most appropriate ones for the society. The extent to which contemporary democratic political systems are legitimate depends in large measure upon the ways in which the key issues which have historically divided the society have been resolved. ([1960] 1981, p. 64)

To begin with, this quotation spotlights Lipset's tendency to conflate the question of stability with the issue of functioning democracy. What should be an empirical question—how democratic practices interact with political stability—is lumped into a single conceptual construct, "democratic political stability," thus closing the door for authentic explanatory analysis of the issue. Lipset further complicates matters in that his quotation suggests that economic development, effectiveness, and legitimacy are *either* determinants of political stability *or* dimensions of that concept. In fact, it turns out to be a little of both. Careful reading of his chapter and the preceding one (on economic growth and democracy) demonstrates that Lipset regards economic growth as a causal factor, while effectiveness and legitimacy are his key ingredients of stability. The problem does not end here, since (as I will argue) Lipset's binary formulation omits at least one important aspect of a more fully multidimensional description of stability.

Finally, the entire notion of stability carries needless ideological baggage. I prefer the term "viability" to the more often used "stability" because it is less burdened by connotations of rigidity and resistance to change. Stability carries the unnecessary onus of the seemingly endless and ultimately fruitless debates about homeostasis and equilibrium that plagued structural-functionalism a few decades ago. "Viability" is also preferable to the concept of "crisis," which is the obverse of stability but which shares its penchant for simplistic or foggy definition. (Different factions within the legitimation-crisis paradigm, we observed in the Introduction, are drawn to one or the other of these terms.) A truly successful political system is more than one that is "stable" or avoids "crises." It aims beyond maintaining or overthrowing the existing contours of state institutions. A political system is viable to the degree that it can adapt and transform itself and the entire society in the face of multiple and potentially contradictory constraints.

Although the question of political viability shares with the issue of order the problematic of reconciling agency and structure, it removes the question from a generic concern with social life. Instead, it zeroes in on the interaction of political and social factors (see especially Etzioni 1968, pp. 60–93). On this level of analysis, the assumption of a simple duality of agency and structure proves inadequate.

Political viability is more than a binary equation of agency and structure. To begin with, agency and structure each has two faces. In the sociopolitical realm they both have been analyzed from a pair of alternative perspectives: (1) from the point of view of the parts that make up an overall system (i.e., its *units* and *subunits*), including their actions and interactions; and (2) from the perspective of the overall system (i.e., the *supraunit*), either as a governor of its internal and external environments or as a "context" or "totality" that constrains its units and subunits. Hence four possible types of approaches are available to political viability: unit voluntaristic, supraunit voluntaristic, fragmented structural, and collectivistic structural. Our multidimensional mandate prescribes that we consider all of them when we examine political viability.

Unit voluntarism is the approach that stresses agency and focuses on interventions by units and subunits while ignoring the potential initiatives or even reality of a supraunit actor. Those who impute the ultimate capacity for significant change to entities such as revolutionary political movements employ this perspective (see, e.g., Selznick 1960). Others who feel that the student movement of the 1960s was decisive in American history also operate within such a unit-level agency perspective. (For a concise overview, see Hamilton and Wright 1986, pp. 3–11.)

Supraunit voluntarism posits agency in the larger system and tends to see it as an actor who can call the tune. Many in this camp adopt what Gamson (1968) has labeled a "social control perspective." Theorists who are inclined to give state actions some form of ultimate causal priority subscribe to this approach. Etzioni (1968, p. 68) calls this approach "voluntaristic" in the sense that it "focuses on a societal actor who, in principle, is able to remold his world at will. Limitations on his freedom are recognized but these are viewed as abnormalities. . . . Most voluntaristic theories are a-structural." Nordlinger's (1981) conscious application of the "state-centered model" to account for the autonomy of the modern democratic state provides a clear example of the supraunit voluntaristic approach. Applications of rational-choice theory, game theory, and cybernetics to societal and international problems also assume such a approach when they posit a supraunit actor.

Other approaches make structure rather than agency pivotal. When the condition of a political system is accounted for solely in terms of the relationships among its parts, the full potential of an analysis is rarely achieved. Structure becomes exclusively a matter of part-to-part linkages, and little or no attention is given to whole-part relationships. Variants of Marxism that stress class conflict to the exclusion of total system factors use this approach. Veto-group explanations of the inefficiencies of democratic politics provide another set of examples. I call these fragmented structural approaches.

A collectivistic structural approach is often invoked to compensate for the reductionist tendencies of fragmented analyses. The collectivistic approach assumes that "the units under study hang together and are tied to each other with powerful bonds. The resulting entity has a 'structure,' or 'character,' or provides a *'gestalt'* or a 'context'" (Etzioni 1968, p. 65). Theories of this kind often use biological analogies even while proclaiming the distinctiveness of social facts. Change is possible, and even likely, but a collectivistic structural approach makes it a "mindless" process by omitting effective agency from all levels of the system. Political theorists who unduly emphasize the constraints and opportunities imposed by state structures are part of this approach. Birnbaum's (1988) effort to explain most differences in the forms of political mobilization among European societies in terms of variations in their overarching state structures is a good recent example here.

In sum, a multidimensional approach to political viability ought to include more than a vision of the interpenetration of conflict and consensus. It must also reconcile two aspects of agency—unit and supraunit voluntarism—and two dimensions of structure—the fragmented and the collectivistic. A satisfactory multidimensional rendering of viability demands that an analyst consider all four of these approaches as pointing to possible empirical realities. Compared to the problem of order, the issue of viability fixes attention on specifically political questions, especially in the modern world. For example, in the twentieth century the problems of "nation building" as well as the growth and uncertainties of "supranational" communities—that is, the prospects for combining previously disparate subunits and units into larger supraunits, as well as for transforming the new entities for collective purposes—have become key to the study of relative viability.

But how should we define political viability? Once we visualize the reconciliation of agency and structure as too empirically and conceptually intricate for any binary formulation to handle, additional doubts arise about the adequacy of Lipset's binary definition of viability. Effectiveness, defined as system authorities' (most likely, the state's) capacity to pursue collective goals successfully, certainly introduces activism into the analysis. Legitimacy apparently represents a more passive element in the equation, since it changes only in response to variations in effectiveness.

Unfortunately, Lipset's definition of legitimacy (see above—and usage throughout *Political Man,* notably the second and third chapters) leaves much to be desired. Two strands pervade his treatment. The dominant—and more appropriate—one has Weberian roots (see Weber [1924] 1968, pp. 212–99). In this light, legitimacy is part of a society's political culture and points not to the networks of relations produced and reproduced by political actors but to the beliefs, values, and sentiments they use to orient themselves to political events. Political culture includes both "rules of the game" and political legitimations (Lehman 1977, pp. 21–42). Political authorities and potential partisans must know how the game is played, but viability is enhanced when they regard the rules as legitimate, that is, if they believe the rules are integrated, plausible, and morally appropriate (see Berger and Luckmann 1966, pp. 47–123; for further discussion, see Chapter 4).

Lipset's other use makes legitimacy part of the political system rather than the political culture. Here he parallels the trend that later became common in the legitimation-crisis paradigm. In this mode, legitimacy concerns "upward" participation processes in a political system, in contrast to the "downward" control processes associated with effectiveness (see Gamson 1968). Legitimacy here is more or less equated with political confidence. The latter is accorded separate analytical status by many writers, including Lipset in other contexts (see, e.g., Easton 1965; Lehman 1985; Lipset and Schneider 1983; Parsons 1967). Confidence refers to citizens' general endorsements of specific political authorities, particularly the national executive. Together with "demands" (i.e., petitioning authorities to enact certain policies), confidence is conceptualized as the principal channel along which lower, normally more passive, levels of the political system exert influence on the higher, more active ones. (For a fuller discussion, see Chapter 3.)

When confidence and legitimacy are defined separately and the latter is confined to the realm of political culture, multidimensional analysis of viability is enhanced. More is at stake than theoretical hairsplitting. In the 1970s, an emerging legitimation-crisis paradigm incorporated Lipset's (and Schumpeter's) binary approach to viability. Often the results were diagnoses of an imminent legitimation crisis for democratic capitalist states. A principal defect in this approach lies at the presuppositional level. The failure to distinguish the analytic, and hence possible empirical, separation of confidence and legitimacy has led this paradigm's adherents to conflate distrust of incumbents (the "confidence gap") with loss of faith in the system (a "legitimation crisis"). In fact, a rise in the former has so far had little effect on the latter (see Chapter 4). A potentially powerful tool for political analysis was reduced to an empty slogan.

3. The relationship of power and viability

As I indicated earlier, although our primary concern in this book is with political viability, power also deserves close examination, because these two presuppositional questions are related and a fuller understanding of one helps illuminate the other. To begin with, treatment of viability is affected by how power is regarded (analogous to how decisions about social order are influenced by but remain distinct from presuppositions about social action. See Alexander 1982, pp. 64–112). "Power," Giddens notes, "is one of several primary concepts of social science, all clustered around the relations of action and structure. Power is the means of getting things done and, as such, directly implied in human action" (1984, p. 283). In other words, political presuppositions that attempt to synthesize agency and structure inevitably draw on power to bridge activism and passivity. One-dimensional assumptions about power tend to foster one-dimensional thinking about viability. However, the exact nature of the monism is not easy to predict. Idealistic formulations about power, when focused on the knowledge and subjective intentions of the power wielder, may encourage a supraunit voluntaristic conception of viability. Conversely, when idealism is expressed in terms of the shaping of power by the patterns of culture, the tendency may be to overemphasize a more passive, collectivistic structural view of viability. Similarly, since a materialist view focuses on a power wielder's command of tangible resources (as in Mao's aphorism equating guns with power[7]), such an analysis is likely to adhere to a unit-level voluntaristic version of viability that says particular actors with superior resources always get their way. Yet a materialism that concentrates on the distribution of tangible assets throughout a system tends to produce a fragmented structural outlook because concern shifts to the presence of interunit constraints and underplays the possibility of agency. Marxist theories that give priority to economic power and that stress the hegemonic impact of economic structures are classic examples here.

How we think about viability affects the way we think about power and vice versa. That is, the interaction between presuppositions is not one-way. Multidimensional formulations about viability, for instance, encourage multidimensional approaches to power. An appreciation of the dialectics of agency and structure helps sharpen analysis of the eight empirical questions (which, as I noted above, are also clarified by a multidimensional strategy toward power). It also encourages a more imaginative selection of research agendas and sites. The growing, albeit implicit, acceptance of multidimensionalism during the past two decades is one factor behind the recent rich harvest of historical studies of the state.

The contributions of a multidimensional conception of viability to political sociology extend beyond questions of defining power, however. Perhaps the most critical added contribution here is to a *multilevel* image of political life. We have seen that a synthesis of four approaches to viability tells us that political life must be thought of as having several levels—i.e., supraunit, unit, and subunit—rather than being strictly horizontal or just two-tiered (as in such formulas as state versus society, public versus private, the autonomy of the state versus the relations of production, etc.). The multilevel imagery means the political sociologists do not have to choose between active agency or structural constraint to capture a particular historical moment; a polity can be active and passive simultaneously. These contradictory tendencies may occur in the same overall space and time because the system is vertically as well as horizontally variegated. That is, a political system involves whole-part and not only part-part interactions. Various modes of activity and passivity are distributed differentially throughout the polity. I argue, for example (in Chapter 3), that in the contemporary United States, political participation is characterized by a relatively passive public as well as by "hyperactive" interest groups. Consequently, the empirical question shifts from "Is political system X active or passive at time Y?" to "Where are the pockets of activism in the polity at this time, where is apathy likely to be lodged, and what are the implications for societal transformation or entropy?" This is as far as multidimensional presuppositions take us, however. The more concrete features of a multileveled view of political life require us to inquire about appropriate political models.

MODELS

Do models for a political sociological analysis of success and failure suggest themselves in light of this discussion of power and viability?

I believe the outlines of particular models are readily available, although a final overall model is not yet at hand. A comprehensive model ultimately must contain both multilevel and organizational features. The former remind us to include structural elements; the latter make us recall the issues of agency and the ramifications of the multidimensionality of power.

1. Multiple levels

The use of multilevel imagery does not mean that society "determines" political life, although society is seen as a supraunit that contains many smaller units such as the political system. Society, however, does limit the forms that political institutions can take. But the latter may also shape society. While the whole may affect its parts, the parts can sometimes have an impact on the whole. Indeed, Giddens (1985) argues that the state, via its capacity to create defensible borders and provide internal peace actually brought society as we know it into existence, and not vice versa.

A multilevel imagery also clarifies the relationship of the political system and the state. The political system—or polity, for short—is society's overall system of political power. It includes both "upward" participation processes through which nonstate actors seek to convert intermember power into political power and "downward" control processes through which state authorities use political power to dominate intermember power. *Any study of political viability that is exclusively concerned with state performances and ignores the larger political-power network in which it is located fails to live up to the standards of multidimensionality.*

The state is only one part of the polity, although it can be visualized as its highest and most encompassing level. In fact, this model of the polity contains four intrasocietal levels of participation and control: public, organization, party, and state. They form a hierarchy, with the public at the bottom and the state at the top. Political life is portrayed more fully when this multilevel model of politics is invoked. Conversely, the more a researcher concentrates on a single level, the greater the risks of one-dimensional analysis. Indeed, each level in the past has been associated with its own distinctive research tradition—for example, voting and public opinion, social movements and interest group politics, political parties, and government and public administration.

Bureaucratization, political consciousness, and capacity for concerted action increase as one moves from the public to organization to party to state levels, while size decreases. The public level is described by Richard Hamilton (1972, pp. 49–63) in terms of a "theory of group-based politics." It is the tier of the general population; voting studies and opinion surveys employing explanatory variables taken from social stratification are often used in analyzing it. However, the explanatory language is not simply class—or occupationally—inspired but ought to take into account a "wide range of local, regional, familial, ethnic, or religious traditions" (Hamilton 1972, p. 62).

The greater the web of affiliations spun by voluntary associations, the greater the public's cohesion. Voluntary associations are part of the organization tier. Yet insofar as their roles are expressive (as in the case of lodges, fraternal orders, churches, etc.), they are not the decisive units on this level. Interest groups—that is, organizations *deliberately* using significant portions of their assets to exert political influence—are the pivotal forces. Examples include not only the National Rifle Association, Common Cause, National Association for the Advancement of Colored People (NAACP), the National Association of Manufacturers, and the Right to Life, but also most big business corporations and labor unions. Of course, the distinction between voluntary associations and interest groups is an analytical one. Many concrete organizations are mixtures of the two. Moreover, interest groups tend to be more successful when they are able to use established voluntary associations by appealing to the pecuniary or symbolic interests of their members. *Social movements* represent a very visible and possibly potent type of interest group in our times. They share with other interest groups the bureaucratized core that is a defining feature of the species (although the levels of bureaucratization in social movements are sometimes lower than in more "established" interest groups). But a social movement also includes a periphery of fervent adherents who are not part of the core organization's formal structure but who are capable of mobilization for limited, yet often intense, tasks such as demonstrations, letter-writing campaigns, distributing announcements, etc.

The modern mass political party is at the interface of the state and the public and organization levels. Several kinds of political units use the label of "party." Some groups calling themselves parties are really organization-level actors and do not engage in electoral politics (such as the Black Panther party in the 1960s). Some parties are elite agencies of polities (the Communist party in China, ruling cliques in one-party states in developing nations). Others are revolutionary groups and are not interested in garnering votes. Still other entities represent elite elements in societies where the franchise is circumscribed (the Whigs and Tories in England before the Reform Acts of the nineteenth century). None of these, strictly speaking, is a party in the sense of the mass political party in multi-party democracies. Parties of this type are the prime vehicles for converting public and organization preferences into institutionalized mechanisms for filling state positions and influencing state policies. Only this last kind of party falls unequivocally on the third level of the polity.

The fourth level or tier of the polity is the state. It too can be thought of in multilevel terms. That is, the state can be fruitfully conceived of as a supraunit that encompasses more particular units (e.g., the executive, judicial, and legislative branches). Moreover, I suggest in a moment that in the analysis of the modern state both the supraunit and its units are most productively treated as *complex organizations*.

This four-level description of the polity is not intended to be a "closed" model. No intrinsic barriers exist to the addition of more tiers. Transnational levels culminating in a global state-system are not precluded. "Nation-states only exist in systemic relations with other nation-states," Giddens reminds us. "The internal administrative coordination of nation-states from their beginnings depends on reflexively monitored conditions of an international nature. 'International relations' is coeval with the origins of nation-states" (Giddens 1985, p. 4). Thus, while the modern state continues to be the hub of agency in the study of politics, comprehensive analysis requires that "larger systems" be considered as well. At the very least, these exogenous components constrict and channel a state's options; at most, in the future, they may increasingly be the sites for transnational "communities" and transformative potential. The European Economic Community (EEC) seems to have moved into this phase.

But what precisely is "the state"? Most contemporary uses of the term are based on Max Weber's definition of the state as the social agency that successfully claims a monopoly of the legitimate means of violence over a given territory (Weber [1924] 1968, pp. 56, 65). The following definition incorporates modifications suggested by Birnbaum (1980), Giddens (1985), Mann (1984), Skowronek (1982, pp. 19–23), and Runciman (1969, pp. 35–42). The key point is that each of six items in the definition is regarded as a *variable*. Therefore, the question becomes not whether a particular collectivity is or is not a state but the degree to which different collectivities meet the criteria of statehood at any given time. Statehood, in other words, is a multidimensional variable. (For an earlier treatment of the state as a variable, see Nettl 1968.) The six criteria are:

1. There are specialized personnel and agencies;
2. There is a division of labor and centralized coherence among personnel within agencies as well as among the agencies;
3. These actors have administrative reach over a territorially demarcated area;
4. The territory's population is imbued with a national identity that leads it to attribute to these personnel and agencies the moral (i.e., legitimate) right to wield political power;
5. These actors are attributed the primary responsibility to set, pursue, and implement collective goals for the society;
6. This ability is backed up by a legitimated monopoly of the means of violence.

In this formulation the distinction between polity and state is especially critical. Polity and state are never synonymous. A political system's potential for self-sufficiency (and, hence, its prospects for viability) depends to a considerable extent on how closely its "state" meets the six criteria. Yet many participants in these processes (particularly those who are the subjects of political power in the last four criteria) are not part of the official state apparatus. The multilevel model of polity permits one to designate actors and their actions as "political" even though they are not state officials.

The distinction has two immediate benefits. First, as I remarked earlier, we are alerted to the fact that an organizational analysis of the state—regardless of how multidimensional (see below)—never exhausts the subject of political viability. Second, it calls our attention to the expanding "gray zone" that has grown up at the interface between the state and the rest of the polity. This emerging sector contains actors variously labeled "quasipublic," "semigovernmental," and the "quasipolity." At the core of this zone are agencies with some formal link to the state that remain legally outside the state's official perimeter, although they regulate or administer a public benefit. The British Broadcasting Corporation and the United States' Securities and Exchange Commission are often-cited examples. The number of such agencies has been increasing as authorities seek to escape the alleged costs and inefficiencies of democratic political bargaining. Moreover, in advanced capitalist polities the large corporation's role as employer and generator of societal wealth blurs the state-polity boundary still further. Hence big business also may play a part within this "gray zone" (see Poggi 1978, pp. 127–32).

Once we see the state as a variable and the polity as larger than the state, the need to locate semipublic actors as either unequivocally inside or outside of state boundaries disappears. Rather, the expanding "gray zone" can be treated as a common feature of most modern democracies, and its causes and consequences become matters for empirical inquiry free of distracting classification disputes.

2. Organizational features

Some collectivities are more likely to meet the criteria of statehood than others. Moreover, a model of the political system becomes more general and decisive and our picture of the state more complete when the latter is analyzed as a *complex organization*. This concept refers to a social unit deliberately constructed and reconstructed for the pursuit of specific goals (Parsons 1960; Etzioni 1975).

The treatment of states as complex organizations is not so commonsensical as it may seem at first glance. After all, human groupings are ranged on a continuum from those on one end marked by deliberate creation, conscious planning, structuring and restructuring, and routine change of personnel (through recruitment, dismissal, promotion, demotion, and transfer) all the way to the other end where social units possess none of these traits. Social scientists have historically dichotomized this continuum into "such established classifications as primary and secondary groups, in-group and out-group, *Gemeinschaft* and *Gesellschaft*, formal and informal group, etc." (Merton 1968, p. 371). A recognition of the modern state's un-equivocal *Gesellschaft* features sharpens awareness of its distinctive-ness from the more "spontaneous," localized, communal, and even associational units that fall under its aegis. Moreover, it reminds us that the concepts of "state" and "political system" are not coexten-sive and that while the latter entity is more inclusive, the former is more thoroughly bureaucratic. Thus the multilevel model of the po-litical system presents us with an image of the state as a bureaucratic overlayer struggling to control the myriad of nonstate actors (both bureaucratic and nonbureaucratic) across the territory it seeks to en-compass. This image illuminates four additional issues for the study of political viability: (1) the state is both a supraorganization and an organization; (2) organizational analyses of states assume a potential for autonomy; (3) the state, like all organizations, may be both effec-tive and ineffective at any given time; and (4) political viability never rests on effectiveness alone.

Supraorganization and Organization. The state is a supraorganiza-tion in the very general sense that most other organizations in a society exist within its context. Thus many other bureaucracies (in-cluding businesses, schools, hospitals, labor unions, and so forth) fall under this supraorganization's administrative reach—although it is possible that they retain some autonomy.

Perhaps more critically (as I have noted previously), the state is defined as a supraorganization vis-à-vis its particular components. We see the state as a supraorganization when we treat it as a *supra-unit* that is more than the sum of its parts (see Etzioni 1968, pp. 106–7). This supraorganization in turn includes the state's principal *units* (i.e., its branches, such as the national executive, legislature, and judiciary; for a detailed specification see the discussion below) and *subunits* (i.e., the specific agencies within particular branches, such as the National Institutes of Health, the Federal Bureau of Investiga-tion, and the New York City Office of Consumer Affairs). Like all organizations, this supraorganization is normally guided by a writ-ten charter, by-laws, or constitution heavily imbued by rational-legal doctrines (see Chapter 4); marked by a systematic division of labor among the units (branches) and subunits (agencies); and linked hier-archically and laterally by lines of authority, decision making, and communication among units and subunits.[8] The relationship of the American state to its executive, legislative, and judicial components is supraunit-unit (i.e., whole-part) interaction. Skowronek's (1982) inquiry into why America's "awkward and incomplete" state system restricted the potentials for the professionalization and bureaucratization of the United States Army provides a more concrete example because it focuses on how a supraunit property (being an "awkward and incomplete" overriding state) affects unit properties (the army's relative incapacity to become professional and bureaucratic). (For a more detailed analysis, see Skowronek 1982, pp. 85–120, 212–47. His book is discussed more fully in Chapter 2.)

The state as a supraorganization always contains more than one major branch. It is never correct to equate the state with the national executive, regardless of the latter's power. Ralph Miliband (1969, pp. 49–53) argues that the typical state has six branches: the national executive, the administrative, the military and police, the judiciary, subcentral government, and the national parliament. This list is a useful antidote to the conflating of state and national executive, but it is not logically exhaustive nor does it tell us how these six branches are linked to constitute a supraorganization. The state may contain other elements, such as the party in one-party regimes. Moreover, the "organizational character" of a state derives less from the elements taken singly than from the network of relations among them. Merely knowing which elements are present tells us little about the form of the supraorganization. States range from monocratically organized entities in which one of the parts (usually the national executive but sometimes others such as the military) is decisive in shaping the supraorganization all the way to a "state feudalism" in which the branches are only loosely coordinated.

On the other hand, the state also may sometimes be treated as just one organization among other organizations. We have observed that it possesses most of the key traits normally associated with a complex organization (e.g., formal rules, a systematic division of labor, hierarchy). Certainly there are times when the interaction of the state and other actors is rendered satisfactorily in organization-to-organization terms rather than as supraorganization-organization (supraunit-unit or whole-part) coordination. This is probably true when we examine state-church relations in confessional societies.

The language of organization-to-organization is also usually appropriate when interstate exchanges are examined. The relations of the United States to its "peers" (China, Germany, Japan, etc.) and even to its "clients" (South Korea, Israel, etc.) reflect networks among actors on the same level of analysis. Under such circumstances little theoretical benefit normally derives from employing the language of supraorganizations.

Finally, an organization-to-organization approach is also profitably exercised when we are concerned about the actions of one state agency that is more pivotal than performances of the overall state. For example, Skocpol and Finegold (1982) demonstrate how the prior public planning, unique administrative capacity, and practical experience of federal agricultural experts in the early New Deal fostered autonomous state contributions to agricultural policy. While their general argument is about state autonomy, their research focuses on the relationship between a particularly "strong" organization within a relatively "weak" supraorganization and nonstate actors linked to American agriculture.

Organizations and Autonomy. When we treat the state as a complex organization, our appreciation of its potential for autonomy is enhanced regardless of whether we employ a supraorganizational or an organizational framework. The decision to take seriously the state's responsibility for collective goals entails accepting the possibility that these goals are not simply a reflection of the demands or interests of other powerful actors. Little contention exists over the fact that states are able to adopt and pursue goals despite internal (unit and subunit) resistance. Yet organizational analysts go much further: They are able to balance the potential for organizational initiative and the likelihood of environmental constraints and to see reality as encompassing both. If political sociologists consciously adopt this model, it should strengthen our capacity to resist polarization of the issue and hence to entertain the simultaneous possibility of state autonomy and external pressures. The implications for empirical research are significant. The model permits us to study the varying capacities of states over time to set, pursue, and implement collective goals in the face of actual and potential opposition from within as well as from other societal and extrasocietal actors or in the face of inauspicious economic or social conditions.[9]

The "Contradiction Model" of Effectiveness. Since organizations are entities deliberately created for the pursuit of specific goals, the question of their effectiveness is by definition decisive. We have seen how Lipset pinpointed the importance of this question in his inquiries into the viability of political systems. Yet, despite the importance of goal attainment, complex organizations can seldom be univocally categorized as effective or ineffective. This has been understood by organizational analysts for some time; political sociologists have still not recognized this fact as fully. "A realization of the contradictory nature of effectiveness," Hall (1982, p. 296) notes, "is essential if organizational analysis is to proceed." He proposes a "contradiction model of effectiveness" (Hall 1982, pp. 271–74, 294–307). He says:

> Put very simply, a contradiction model of effectiveness will consider organizations to be more or less effective in regard to the variety of goals which they pursue, the variety of resources they attempt to acquire, the variety of constituents inside and outside of the organization whether or not they are part of the decision making process, and the variety of time frames by which effectiveness is judged. (P. 271)

Treatment of modern states as complex organizations subject to such a "contradiction model" clarifies why political success cannot be readily equated with the satisfactory attainment of any single goal. Neo-Marxist and neoconservative adherents of the legitimation-crisis paradigm are particularly mindful of the contradiction model (even when they haven't heard of it). Both camps within the paradigm fault today's democratic capitalist state for failing to pursue economic growth and social entitlement effectively at the same time.[10] While a binary image of state goals distorts political reality, neo-Marxists and neoconservatives are to be commended for focusing our attention on how multiple goals create potential conflicts for a modern state and thus pointing out the complexities in assessing the latter's effectiveness.

Effectiveness, Efficiency, and Legitimacy. On the other hand, students of organizations have long rejected the position that success or failure hinges only on effectiveness. In political analysis such a view is implicit in the "managerialist perspective" (Alford and Friedland 1985, pp. 161–268). Lipset clearly saw the benefit of a more multidimensional approach in his treatment of effectiveness and legitimacy as the bases for political viability. Lipset's definition also forces us to recognize that viability is not only a matter of state performances but entails operations of the overall polity as well. In other words, relative viability is a polity-level property and not a characteristic of the state, even though state effectiveness is one key dimension of such viability. The previous discussion has shown that his definition of viability is not yet sufficiently multidimensional, however. I have argued (above) that the dilemmas of political participation are theoretically distinct from the problems of legitimation. Effectiveness' reciprocal concept in organizational analysis is *efficiency*. This cardinal concept is defined by Chester I. Barnard (1938) and his most celebrated follower, Herbert A. Simon (1957), as the social and economic costs of inducing members to participate in the organization. Efficiency, in other words, can and should have a different focus from legitimacy.

Our primary spotlight is, therefore, on a viable political system rather than just a successful (or failing) state. Political viability has at least three main ingredients. First, it needs an effective state that is able to impose political control. Effectiveness speaks of a state's ability to attain collective goals. Second, the overall polity must efficiently incorporate political participation. Efficiency points to the fact that a state depends on contributions from key societal actors, but at an acceptable cost. In the realm of politics, effectiveness focuses on "downward" processes through which binding decisions are made and enforced, whereas efficiency points to the "upward" mobilization of confidence and demands (see Chapter 3). Third, a viable polity must possess legitimate rules of the game (see above). While the concepts of effectiveness and efficiency focus on activities within political systems, legitimacy is a theoretically *extrinsic* element. Legitimacy does not point directly at the properties of intrapolity relationships but to shared meanings about the morality of political rules. Legitimacy, as noted previously, is an aspect of a political culture, not of a political system.

The effectiveness-efficiency-legitimacy formulation is enhanced by our having modeled the polity as multileveled and the state as a complex organization. Indeed, it is now multidimensional enough to permit research on viability to let the chips fall where they will. To begin with, it allows us to see that "viability" has several facets that *are* analytically—and *may be* empirically—distinct. A "crisis" along one dimension may or may not bespeak a downturn in fortunes along the other dimensions. Moreover, each of the three dimensions is best conceptualized as a continuous rather than a categorical variable. Polities are never simply effective or ineffective, efficient or inefficient, legitimate or illegitimate. The issue is instead usually one of degree. Thus the assessment of relative viability requires an intricate model that allows for precise location of a polity at any point in time on a three-dimensional grid. Finally, this model allows us to examine the empirical interaction among the three ingredients. For instance, as noted above, this model rescues the diagnosis of "legitimation crisis" from a defective paradigm and political sloganeering and returns it to the domain of scientific inquiry.

Summary and Conclusions

This chapter has undertaken the construction of a new paradigm for the treatment of political success and failure by emphasizing presuppositions and models. We have focused on two distinctive presuppositional issues: power and viability. Although viability is the more central, power (and especially political power) also must be studied because the two topics are closely related. A multilevel imagery and the notion of organizations are key features for any ultimate overarching model. The former is helpful for talking about: (1) the interaction of society, polity, and state; (2) the relationship between the state and other actors in a polity; and (3) how the overall state encompasses its several branches.

The state itself is best modeled as a complex organization. While the state is one organization among others, it is also a supraorganization with administrative reach over organizations inside and beyond its official boundaries. Such a treatment of the state sharpens our capacity to deal empirically with questions about its potential autonomy. Moreover, the topic of its effectiveness, by definition, assumes a pivotal role. Like all other organizations, the state is subject to the contradiction model of effectiveness. In the final analysis, however, even a multidimensional approach to effectiveness will not define the success or failure of a political system. The degree to which a polity is viable must be judged along three dimensions: How effective is its state? How efficient are the mechanisms for political participation? How legitimate are the rules of the game?

The next three chapters focus on these dimensions. Armed with the framework I have provided here, they clarify three pivotal anomalies of modern democratic life: (1) why enhancing effective state capacities in one sector can undermine overall effectiveness and even foster inefficient participation and perhaps declining legitimacy; (2) how polities can be simultaneously racked by the apparently contradictory inefficiencies of extensive public apathy and widespread moralistic participation; and (3) why high political legitimacy actually goes hand in hand with pervasive lack of confidence in government leaders. While state effectiveness can never be equated with viability, it plays such a singular role in shaping a modern polity's prospects that I examine its unique characteristics first. Clarification of this matter also aids our subsequent analyses of efficiency and legitimacy.

2 | Predicaments of State Effectiveness

*The first and almost the last rule is that the rulers must deliver
the goods, that they must share some of the winnings of the game
with their clients, with the great mass of the American people,
and that these winnings must be absolutely more than any rival
system can plausibly promise. I have used the word "clients"
advisedly, for the rulers of America have not the advantage
of some of their European brethren, the advantage of a patina
of age.*
                    —Denis W. Brogan, American Themes

A predisposition to make effective state capacities the ultimate causal
factor and to deal with legitimacy as the singular outcome of effectiveness is a pivotal defect that runs through the works of those who
explicitly or implicitly operate within the legitimation-crisis paradigm. In other words, there is a inclination to zero in on how the
state's proficiency in achieving its goals affects faith in the system—
to the virtual exclusion of other major considerations. Yet, despite
this flaw, this binary formula harbors a critical empirical insight:
While effectiveness is hardly the only ingredient of political viability
nor always the prime causal factor, both state authorities and potential partisans now treat it as the most important component of success or failure. Moreover, for modern states, effectiveness has come
to mean one thing above all else: delivering the economic goods.

The binary formula that is at the heart of the legitimation-crisis
paradigm fails to recognize that the study of political viability must
touch evenhandedly on three broad processes—state capacities, political participation, and legitimation—and this failure prevents the
paradigm's adherents from fully developing the implication of their
empirical insight. Our alternative paradigm offers the tools to make

greater sense of the distinctive role of effectiveness in modern polities without slipping back into either binary or one-dimensional frameworks.

Specifically, this chapter begins by arguing that all three of these processes have helped make effectiveness the prime ingredient of viability. The unique position of state effectiveness has not been without costs, however. For one thing, it has made the liabilities of the contradiction model of effectiveness (discussed in Chapter 1) all the more acute. This chapter advances our paradigm's organizational yet "nonmanagerialist" approach by arguing that three organizational features of the modern state are especially important in explaining why it is so subject to intergoal conflicts. In particular, these three traits push states to multiply their goals. This proliferation not only increases the likelihood of conflict among goals; an appreciation of its inexorable nature also clarifies why contemporary states can never be univocally effective or ineffective.

Moreover, not all state goals are equally important. This chapter considers why economic growth is the modern state's paramount goal. Once this is accomplished, we can see that the clashes between the quest for economic growth and other state goals are probably the most decisive political manifestations of the contradiction model of effectiveness. Yet an analysis that probes only goal conflict remains incomplete, since viability has three dimensions. Consequently, the chapter concludes with a discussion of how the state's penchant for emphasizing economic growth may have adverse effects on efficient political participation and perhaps even on the degree of legitimacy attributed to political institutions.

In short, this chapter asks why: (1) effectiveness is regarded as the prime ingredient of viability; (2) states always have multiple goals; (3) economic growth is considered the paramount goal by both authorities and citizens; (4) a special zeal for any one goal—most commonly, economic growth—exacerbates the goal conflicts inherent in the contradiction model of effectiveness; and (5) such zealousness also raises special problems for other components of viability. These effects can occur in all modern systems. They assume special urgency for capitalist democracies, including the United States.

The Primacy of State Effectiveness

Generally speaking, we would expect the state to be preoccupied with effectiveness insofar as it is a complex organization. But, more specifically, can our alternative paradigm account for the modern state's special responsibility for delivering the goods effectively? We have mentioned that aspects of three broad processes—state capacity, political participation, and legitimation—encompass political viability. A focus on the contemporary forms these processes have taken provides a more detailed understanding of the state's expanding concern with successful goal attainment. Specifically, the increasing bureaucratization of state capacities promotes the centrality of effective payoff; the nature of contemporary political participation stimulates the public or its representatives to press more claims; and the doctrines of legitimation most used today encourage polity members to see the state as a rationalized "delivery system."

STATE CAPACITIES

When we speak of the modern state in organizational terms, we are in effect saying that it is more bureaucratically organized than its premodern forbearers. At a minimum, bureaucratization means that a state is more often: guided by a written charter, by-laws, or constitution heavily imbued by rational-legal doctrines (see below); marked by a systematic division of labor among its branches and agencies; and linked hierarchically and laterally by lines of authority, decision making, and communication among similarly organized branches and agencies. Moreover, the notion of bureaucratization suggests that, like other modern organizations, a state mobilizes personnel, knowledge, and material resources to master its environment rather than just becoming the creature of external forces (see Skocpol 1985a, p. 9).

The greater a state's coherence and administrative reach—that is, the more bureaucratic its capacity—the more important effectiveness is. Why should this be so? Two answers suggest themselves, one focusing on the nature of the "technically competent" actors who inhabit modern bureaucracies and the other zeroing in on how they are judged by others. First, the more bureaucratic states are, the more government personnel and agencies will see themselves as specialists and define their responsibilities in terms of rational goal delivery. They are particularly prone to adopt a policy style I call "instrumental consciousness" that stresses rational and technical criteria and depoliticizes issues (see below). Second, the more a state, its agencies, and personnel are accepted as service deliverers, the greater the probability that others (e.g., "clients," pressure groups, public interest advocates) will invoke effectiveness as the prime criterion by which to judge state actors. The need to raise taxes to sufficient levels to subsidize warfare, a development well under way between the late fifteenth and late seventeenth centuries, may have been pivotal in starting this process (see, e.g., Giddens 1985; Mann 1986; Poggi 1978; Tilly 1986), but it has long ago spread to other sectors as well.

As Skowronek (1982, p. 287) notes, "the American Constitution has always been awkward and incomplete as an organization of state power." Does this mean effectiveness is less important here than for other capitalist democracies? Historically, the United States' centralized capacity has been limited by the division of authority between central and subcentral governments and the "separation of powers" among the branches of national government. The result, however, has not meant less concern with effectiveness. Rather, the American polity employs more concrete, goal-by-goal assessments of effectiveness and is leery of grand designs. The view that politics is the "science of 'muddling through'" is a distinctly American response to our special circumstances (see Lindblom 1959, 1977).

Yet, even in this allegedly "exceptional" polity, state capacity and a concern with effectiveness have grown hand in hand during this century. Skowronek's (1982) study of federal administrative capacities shows how reform of the civil service, the army, and business regulation shifted from "state building as patchwork" between 1877 and 1900 to "state building as reconstitution" between 1900 and 1920. The pivotal features of the latter period were the strengthening of the executive branch and the expansion and professionalization of the bureaucracy, coupled with the weakening of the judiciary, the Congress, and political parties. Yet, these state-building processes proved incomplete, hampered by renewed constitutional stalemate and bureaucratic confusion. Nevertheless, the history of the twentieth-century United States has been one of the relentless (albeit uneven) development of the federal bureaucracy and its goal-delivery capacity. Thus, while the growth of America's state capacity has lagged in effectiveness, no "exceptions" exist among today's states in the sense that the United States is a "unique" state characterized by "singular" variables. It is far more accurate to speak of different cases along the same variables and then to account for these differences.

POLITICAL PARTICIPATION

By definition, political viability includes the need for the efficient incorporation of citizen participation. Broadly speaking, this means that modern polities work better when their citizens are not totally apathetic or hostile. These systems benefit from two different kinds of citizen contributions or inputs to the state: confidence, or trust in the incumbent state authorities, and demands, or the pressing of petitions and claims on the state by partisans (Easton 1965; Parsons 1967). These inputs do not come from a single location. The multi-level model of the polity presented in the previous chapter suggests that degrees and kinds of confidence and demands flow from diverse sites among the public, voluntary associations, and interest groups through political parties to the state.

When a state is perceived as responsive to at least some demands, its ability to garner confidence is enhanced. Although confidence and demands can be mutually reinforcing, a potential tension also exists. One is concerned with delivering trust to authorities; the other involves the prospect for contentiousness among partisans and between partisans and the state.[1] The balancing of confidence and demands is further complicated by the fact that citizen contributions need not necessarily be expressed in overtly political ways. While confidence and demands are articulated most directly through political involvement, citizens may sometimes communicate via economic performances. The low productivity of workers in the formerly Communist regimes of Eastern Europe and in the Soviet Union may be interpreted as an expression of both low confidence and inchoate demands.

Tensions between confidence and demands are most visible in democracies. Institutionalized political competition regularly provokes new claims, particularly from the more organized and influential sectors of civil society (see, particularly, Schumpeter [1950] 1975). "A good case can be made for occasional Government inaction," Russell Baker observes, "but no party ever swept to glory by promising, if elected, to do nothing" (1976, p. 39). Both elite and nonelite actors must be considered. State policies must respond to big business because, at least in capitalist democracies, this sector directly manages society's economic performances, although the state is held ultimately accountable for the results (see Block 1977; Lindblom 1977). Yet authorities must also periodically respond to nonelites' claims since their numbers are crucial for electoral support (Block 1977).

Despite the surge in demands, democratic polities are plagued simultaneously by chronic manifestations of apathy. (This phenomenon is discussed in detail in the next chapter.) Moreover, neither escalating claims nor disaffection with payoff is merely a "democratic distemper," as Huntington (1975) suggests. Demands and the authorities' reliance on confidence are universal because political mobilization of the citizenry is now universal too; discontent with payoff and officeholders occurs everywhere.

Nondemocratic regimes do not confront the problem in the same way since they are not subject to authentic periodic electoral review, although they too are pressured to appear receptive to claims and solicit citizen confidence. Indeed, in totalitarian polities the causal link between demands and an emphasis on effectiveness has often been reversed. Such systems have typically been more activist and claimed an exemplary effectiveness. Activism and a cult of effectiveness require extraordinary mobilization of nonstate actors (i.e., people from the public and organization levels), and this is difficult to accomplish without stimulating new petitions. Old-guard Communist party leaders in China were stunned to discover this fact in the spring of 1989. Mikhail Gorbachev's policy of *perestroika* was premised on the inevitability of this reversed dynamic, although he too was constantly astonished until August 1991 by the magnitude of demands that his "restructuring" had unleashed.

DOCTRINES OF LEGITIMATION

The legitimation process is also an integral feature of political viability. Put simply, *whether* and *how* a polity receives diffuse moral support are essential aspects of how successfully it functions. Most modern political systems rely heavily on rational-legal doctrines in an effort to legitimate their rules of the game. That is, contemporary political practices tend to be rendered moral, integrated, and plausible by invoking broad themes stressing the rationality of a set of abstract criteria, seen as the logical bases for all lower-level rules (Weber [1924] 1968, pp. 212–99).

I suggest that the invoking of more fully rational-legal (as opposed to traditional) doctrines promotes the centrality of effectiveness. Specifically, this tendency is enhanced when both a state and its citizens employ such doctrines.[2] Such themes justify activism by authorities, spur an "instrumentally conscious" policy style among them (see below), and encourage them to extend state capacities. Among citizens, this frame of reference both champions the moral appropriateness of pressing new political claims and stimulates grueling, short-term judgments about how well incumbents are pursuing them—often resulting in a "confidence gap." (For an explication of these issues, see Chapter 4.)

The relationship between legitimacy and effectiveness is more complex, however. While rational-legal doctrines push rational goal attainment forward, a zeal for effectiveness (especially in the matter of economic growth) may also influence the degree of legitimacy. The final section of this chapter considers this scenario that looms so large in the legitimation-crisis paradigm.

The Multiplicity of Goals

The bureaucratization of state capacities, spiraling demands, and the bond between rational-legal legitimation and goal attainment do more than move effectiveness to center stage. The processes we have just discussed increase the number of state goals as well and so may intensify the conflicts suggested by the contradiction model of effectiveness. Economic growth is usually the most important state goal, but it can never be the only one. An organizational approach points to three features of modern states that further encourage goal multiplication: internal structure, external constituents, and array of resources. This section examines how these three features encourage goal multiplication. The special roles of economic growth and competing primary goals are considered in the following section.

INTERNAL STRUCTURE

The modern state is not a seamless cloth. We observed in the last chapter that advanced states have at least six major branches: the national executive, the administrative, the military and police, the judiciary, subcentral government, and the national parliament (see also Miliband 1969, pp. 49–53). Each branch is further subdivided into more specialized personnel and agencies (e.g., the various units of the Department of Health and Human Services). States vary considerably in the degree of centralized coherence among and within agencies, branches, and the overarching state. Regardless of these variations, the mere existence of diverse parts guarantees that a state will always have several goals on the table. Internal diversity breeds plurality of interests, which in turn fosters goal multiplication.

The American state is not confined to fewer kinds of goals than other advanced states simply because its internal structure is more fragmented. However, its goal attainment is more *incremental, dispersed*, and *localized*. It is incremental in that policies are more often made in a piecemeal fashion rather than as part of a larger agenda, so that American goal attainment has indeed become the "science of 'muddling through.'" It is dispersed in that the goals of one state agency are at best loosely coordinated with those of others. Incrementalized and dispersed decision making are not uniquely American phenomena, although they are more pronounced here. Localized goal attainment is not unique either, but it is the most distinctively American of the three. No other major modern state encourages so much policymaking below the national level. If one expands the notion of localization to include the privatization of the delivery systems (notably in the areas of health, education, and welfare), then the United States' goal attainment is all the more localized despite recent European forays into privatization.

EXTERNAL CONSTITUENTS

States must always take into account forces beyond their formal perimeters. These environmental factors are referred to here as "constituents" (see Hall 1982, pp. 299–301, for a similar approach). While this term normally points to the electorate in a legislative district, I apply it to all strategic external actors who interact with a state. The prefix "external" limits the discussion to actors beyond the state's own personnel (since I have previously focused on intrastate factors). External constituents include actors in the "gray zone" that has grown up between the state and the rest of the polity (discussed in Chapter 1), explicitly nonstate actors on the public, organization, and party levels, and actors located outside the given polity.

All states are situated in a bundle of environments, each composed of multiple actors. This heterogeneity drives a state to goal multiplication, since it must respond to varied and potentially contradictory pressures. For example, throughout much of late 1980s, Western democracies were working at cross-purposes in dealing with Khomeini's Iran: on the one hand, seeking international stability by applying pressure to compel it to end its war with Saddam Hussein's Iraq; on the other, pursuing domestic economic advantages by selling it arms that encouraged the continuation of that war.[3]

A state's external constituents are domestic, foreign, and multinational, as well as transnational. Economically powerful actors appear in all four categories, and they warrant the extensive attention they have received. However, they are far from the entire story. Domestic constituents are normally treated under the rubric of political participation. Yet this should not lull us into equating the phenomenon with public-level activities or electoral politics. All modern states—whether democratic or not—must take domestic constituents into account. As with effectiveness, the impact of democratic polities on goal multiplication represents the most visible instance of the genre—but hardly the whole story.

Other states have historically been the most important foreign constituents, but firms located in their territories play a potentially key independent role as well. Moreover, the United States' and Soviet Union's concern over Western European public opinion during the Cold War illustrates how foreign constituents, who singly are neither economically nor politically powerful, are sometimes taken seriously.

The term "multinational" highlights the significance of large-scale corporations that are not wholly domestic or foreign. These enterprises pose problems for a state because their rise accelerates the divorce of national from corporate economic priorities that had been more fused at the beginning of the capitalist world economy.

Finally, transnational constituents have only recently become pivotal. They are international organizations that seek to provide coordination or guidance to member states. Older (less strategic) transnational organizations play a mediating role in such sectors as postal, customs, and health services. Newer ones often have a more ambitious agenda: the formation of international political communities. Both the United Nations and the EEC were founded on such hopes.

No state is immune from external-constituent pressures toward goal multiplication. Regardless of how autonomous a state is, it must cope with and respond to some environmental demands made on it.

ARRAY OF RESOURCES

Students of organizations have long known that the relationship between resources and goals (between an actor's means and ends, if you will) never goes only one way. True, an organization often scurries after resources mandated by its operative goals; but the opposite also occurs. Its repertoire of accessible assets pushes an organization toward new goals (see, e.g., Cohen, March, and Olsen 1972). The rise of research universities that use their faculties' specialized knowledge to seek both educational and research objectives is perhaps the most frequently cited example of this process. Blau (1955, pp. 99–179) found a similar tendency in a federal regulatory agency where the desire to employ staff expertise and interests productively led to an expansion of its mandate.

States are not immune to the predilection to multiply goals to "justify" resources they actually possess (e.g., weapons, the ability to deploy financial resources, classified information) or to which they have ready access (e.g., a society's transportation and communications facilities). An enormous breadth of human and nonhuman assets are at the disposal of the modern state. Hence, states, since they control a greater cornucopia of resources than most other organizations, are especially inclined to goal multiplication. Further, state resources are more likely not only to be plentiful but to range more across types: The state has both more goals and a wider array of them. In the contemporary world, only the state controls significant quantities of coercive (e.g., military hardware), utilitarian (e.g., financial and technological capabilities), and normative (e.g., loyal and skilled officials, means of propaganda, administrative capabilities) resources. Consequently, today's political authorities are able to set goals that permit domination via constraint, inducement as well as persuasion. No other collective actors have such capacities.[4]

Giddens (1985, pp. 172–81) has argued that the modern state's goal expansion is rooted in consolidation and availability of three main resource-related processes: "the mechanization of transportation; the severance of communication from transportation by electronic media; and the expansion of the 'documentary' activities of the state, involving an upsurge in the collection and collation of information devoted to administrative purposes" (p. 173). The last two are of particular importance because they greatly enhance the technical possibilities to code, store, and transmit the information capable of expanding the scope of domination and goal attainment.

States also differ in the structural arrangements conducive to goal multiplication. While I have treated this issue primarily under the heading of "internal structure," what some scholars call "policy instruments" may sometimes be profitably seen as a variable *resource capability* with the potential to increase a state's range of goals. Whether or not a state possesses a long-standing centralized bureaucracy is often mentioned in this regard (Skocpol 1985a, pp. 11–18). The presence of such a policy instrument is generally regarded as a facilitator of goal multiplication. For example, Heclo's (1974) study of the formation of innovative unemployment and old-age assistance policies in Great Britain and Sweden found that these were especially due to the presence and concerted actions of professionalized civil services; the interventions of political parties or interest groups cannot alone account for the inclusion of these goals.[5]

As I have noted previously, the United States (particularly if one focuses only on the national level) has fewer effective policy instruments than most advanced systems.[6] I have also suggested that the fragmented internal structure of our state has incrementalized, dispersed, and localized decision making. Yet, while these factors may have blocked the American state's capacity to coordinate its goals, let me reiterate that there is no evidence that they have reduced the sheer number of its goals.

Economic Growth versus Other Goals

THE PRIMACY OF ECONOMIC EFFECTIVENESS

A national executive tempted to focus exclusively on any single goal is severely constrained by the state's multiple responsibilities. But when overemphasis does occur, economic effectiveness is the most likely site. No regime—even one committed to a neoconservative ideology—can rationally pursue national prosperity to the exclusion of other goals for long. Moreover, immoderate enthusiasm for any other goal (such as national security) soon comes up against the special role of domestic prosperity in modern politics. As Daniel Bell (1974, p. 42) reminds us, growth "has become the secular religion of advanced industrial societies: the source of individual motivation, the basis of political solidarity, the ground for mobilization of a society for a common purpose."

The pursuit of economic growth has become the state's core responsibility everywhere, even when the state might be expected to assume a formal hands-off policy, as in a polity that officially embraces a free-market ideology. Indeed, it is not without irony that this responsibility crystalized in Western history precisely at the time when laissez-faire ideology was at its zenith. Today neoconservatives and monetarists in the West as well as "liberal" reformers in the republics that comprised the Soviet Union insist that the state's primary policy objective should be to enhance the economy's effective delivery of goods and services. Other goals (even national security) that result in the "costly" outlay of capital should be relegated to secondary status, they say, and unflinchingly rolled back if they are shown to erode economic effectiveness.

Those who explicitly adhere to the legitimation-crisis paradigm also place economic growth at the hub of the democratic capitalist state's quest for viability, but they have more gloomy prognoses. They argue that the pursuit of economic growth (or, in the eyes of their neo-Marxist camp, of "capital accumulation") must conflict with other goals, notably those normally linked with the welfare state. We have observed that a legitimation crisis of the capitalist state is a possible outcome. However, disagreements exist within the paradigm about the exact character of the goals in conflict. Neoconservative adherents put the blame on welfare-state goals; neo-

Marxists steadfastly place the onus on the pursuit of economic growth. (For a fuller discussion of the potential for a legitimation crisis, see Chapter 4; on the convergence in the neoconservative and neo-Marxist positions, see Mishra 1984, pp. 26–100.)

Lipset ([1960] 1981, pp. 27–86) recognizes the operation of a virtuous circle here: Economic development, all else equal, fosters "democratic political stability"; yet the state's capacity to promote economic effectiveness is itself a key ingredient in Lipset's binary formulation of such "stability" (see Chapter 1). One is tempted to argue that, over and above the other liabilities of the legitimation-crisis paradigm, Lipset perpetrates a tautology here; but the temptation should be resisted. Lipset's independent variable focuses on how the economy's infrastructure (particularly such factors as levels of wealth, industrialization, education, and urbanization) leads to the emergence of viable political formations (i.e., "democratic political stability"). One strength of his analysis is its appreciation that political formations can "feed back" and shape the economic base. His insights into how a state's contributions to national prosperity can substitute for legitimacy in the short run and generate it in the long run (discussed below) thus assume a deeper significance.

In other words, economic factors play separate and pivotal roles in the independent and dependent variables. This alone signals their importance and indicates why the state's ability to be effective in these matters looms so large in the minds of authorities and partisans alike. Yet, while national prosperity is paramount, it can never be a state's sole goal nor the only one to receive strong emphasis. Undue zealousness in pursuit of economic growth—or any other goal—undercuts the achievement of all goals.

What are the modern state's other goals, and how do they conflict with the zeal for economic effectiveness? Advanced states have at least four other categories of goals: (1) social entitlements or services (or the welfare state), (2) internal order, (3) national security, and (4) "quality of life." While one should not rely totally on the overused term "contradiction" to describe each one's interaction with economic effectiveness, I intend to show that a *potential for conflict* exists in all four situations. At this particular moment in "world-historical time," economic effectiveness is often stressed to the detriment of social entitlements and quality of life. On the other hand, a single-minded zeal for internal order and especially national security has also been seen as a threat to economic growth in our times.

ECONOMIC EFFECTIVENESS VERSUS SOCIAL ENTITLEMENTS

Neoconservatives and neo-Marxists who lean on the legitimation-crisis paradigm frequently render their binary formula as the conflict of state goals—that is, a clash between economic effectiveness and social entitlements as if these are strictly antithetical. Yet, although economic expansion contradicts some of the requisites of a more generous welfare state, the events of the past twenty years also suggest an urgent need to reconcile these two goals. Since the welfare state has always been conceived of as the mechanism to compensate for the more egregious inequities spawned by the pursuit of economic effectiveness, the pressure for more entitlements will not disappear.

The dilemmas facing Eastern European regimes in the 1990s highlight the strain between economic effectiveness and social entitlements with an extraordinary intensity. These states, having shed Communist domination, are struggling to make the transition to market economies. To accomplish this, they have also felt the need to eliminate cherished features of the Communist welfare state and not just the despised Communist leaders and ideology. "In dismantling rigid economic structures inherited from four decades of Communism," Greenhouse (1991, p. A1) reports, "Eastern Europe's governments removed price controls, legalized layoffs, slashed budget deficits and eliminated most subsidies to consumers and companies." The distresses experienced by workers and consumers led to a surge of strikes and protests in Czechoslovakia, Poland, and Hungary in 1991. Political leaders face acute pressures in trying to foster economic effectiveness while remaining responsive to welfare-state needs; in effect, they want "to carry out economic transitions as fast as possible but [are] worried that public dismay with the resulting pain could throw them out office" (Greenhouse 1991, p. A1).

Yet capitalist democracies with developed market economies also endure a conflict between these two goals (albeit not so dramatically). Why should this be so? To begin with, economic growth in such systems requires the accumulation of capital by business elites. Government policies further this goal when they sponsor the expansion of such infrastructural assets as technological hardware and software, buildings, factories, and transportation facilities, all of which may directly generate revenue. While every sector of society may benefit from such policies ("a rising tide lifts all boats"), business tends to gain disproportionately more.

The classical rationale for this has been that special incentives are necessary to promote entrepreneurial risk taking. As a result, few people today question the manipulation of the tax structure or the use of outright government subsidies to encourage business initiatives such as the opening of new plants or the expansion of research and development capabilities. However, those who use this rationale tend to equate economic effectiveness with the policy preferences of business leaders. It is not clear how parallel these preferences actually are with genuine, long-term economic effectiveness, and this connection must always be a matter for empirical research rather than mere ideological assertion. Fred Block, for example, has argued that "consistently failing to understand that what is good for corporate profitability is not necessarily good for the economy as a whole" has led authorities "to mistaken and irrational policy prescriptions" (1987, p. 111).

Other segments of society look to the welfare state's programs of entitlements to redress this "imbalance." Hence economic growth versus entitlements has become a crucial basis for political division in the modern world and the core of what is commonly referred to as "class politics." Advocates of economic growth tend to contest for office with those who emphasize more social services. Conflict is particularly intense in the debate over ways to overcome recession and unemployment, with some arguing for the stimulation of capital accumulation and others calling for improved benefits.

Economic growth, however, is closely linked to entitlements. Capital formation fuels social services by providing the revenues (through surpluses and taxation) that pay for improved education, welfare, and health care. Moreover, an argument can be made for the long-range economic advantages of a better educated, healthier, and happier public. But, in the short run, social service expenditures are more difficult to justify economically because they yield no direct profits; schools and hospitals, for example, do not pay for themselves on corporate or government ledgers the way factories or dams do. Thus when inflation and recession slow capital accumulation, more than economic growth is impeded. The commonly accepted fiscal basis for the welfare state is also weakened.

Why has the modern democratic state's pursuit of welfare goals been under such intense attack over the last two decades? As I have just indicated, the slow economic growth in advanced societies, in general, and the United States, in particular, provides a generally satisfactory answer; but our understanding is furthered by inquiring about more specific concomitants of tepid growth. Closer inspection reveals that weaker economies have undermined the justification of social services in two related ways. First, and more directly, they have threatened the revenue base on which the welfare state had come to depend. Second, authorities and many partisans are now less willing to pay for entitlements because they believe that these programs cost "too much." Yet there is no ready way to cap social service outlays while retaining their effectiveness. Freidson (1987, p. 13) suggests two reasons for the intrinsically expansive nature of such costs: These services have a tendency to become professionalized and they are labor intensive. Professionalization is intrinsically costly, since it entails the recruitment and retention of technically trained personnel who can command relatively high incomes in their respective labor markets. The labor-intensive dimension refers to cost savings derived from the reduction of personnel (a practice that often works successfully when the resources being processed are standardized, inanimate objects) but generally undercuts successful goal delivery when provider-client contacts are at the core products.[7]

In the current political-economic climate, political leaders in the United States (as well as in Western and Eastern Europe) who give policy priority to the stimulation of capital accumulation have the upper hand. The partisans of the welfare state have continued to insist on an expansion of social benefits, but the advocates for cutbacks currently enjoy a number of advantages in this debate. Not the least important edge is that they possess a clear-cut priority of goals. Their unequivocal purpose is to foster economic productivity and operating efficiency, at the expense of other goals, if need be. The position of welfare-state advocates is more ambivalent.

While the general political interests of the advocates for entitlements are no less clear, their legitimating principle and ultimate objectives are more ambiguous. Just like their opponents, they claim to counter the effects of low growth or recession and chronic unemployment. Some of their number suggest that their proposed policies are mainly an economic stimulant; others suggest that their main objective is to provide public welfare particularly as a "safety net" for needy citizens during hard times. This ambiguity over the principal operative goal of social programs is keenest in America. The persistent dominance of the "ideology of individualistic capitalism" (Farer 1982, p. 40) in the United States is one basis for Americans' profound ambivalence toward goals linked to programs in welfare, health, and education. This ideology holds that individuals must, in the final analysis, be responsible for their own actions; it remains a critical feature of America's so-called exceptionalism. As a result, the welfare state has been only grudgingly accepted. As Farer notes:

> The peculiarly American System of "welfare capitalism" . . .
> has never quite transcended its image as a suspect deviation
> from the true, free enterprise faith. It may have been useful
> in coping with certain practical problems, such as what to do
> with the very poor and retired, but was vulnerable to attack
> by economic fundamentalists and was never able, by the
> power of its moral vision, to summon passionate enthusiasts
> for its defense. (1982, p. 40)

Yet, since the need for neither goal will disappear, the reconciliation of economic growth and the welfare state remains key for all modern polities. Mishra (1984, pp. 101–20) sees the problem as most urgent in those capitalist democracies that have subscribed to a Differentiated Welfare State (DWS) planning model as opposed to an Integrated Welfare State (IWS) one. The DWS entails a Keynesian solution to economic growth questions and a Beveridgian solution to issues of social entitlements. More specifically, the DWS relies only on macroeconomic demand-side policies both to regulate the economy and to respond to interest group pressures for entitlements. Since DWS policies, however, are bifurcated and ad hoc, economic expansion and public welfare are not dealt with comprehensively; they are certainly never coordinated. The incremental and dispersed pursuit of both goals exacerbates the demands of narrow-based interest groups and leads to intergroup conflict and political "overload." The democratic left in the United States and the other English-speaking democracies still tends to advocate DWS strategies. The declining credibility of this model is one reason for the rise of neoconservative forces, especially in Britain and America, with supply-side agendas.

The IWS is a neocorporatist model. Mishra believes it is employed in certain European countries, most intensely in Austria, but also strongly in Sweden, West Germany, and the Netherlands. Skocpol (1985b, p. 309) summarizes Mishra's IWS model, which "regulates the economy from both demand and supply sides, affecting investments and labor markets as well as macroeconomic parameters. Social policy is closely coordinated with economic management, and this happens through centralized bargaining and trade-offs among major economic groupings and the government." Clearly, Mishra wants all Western democracies to adopt the IWS model, as he calls it "a pragmatic approach to the integrative problems of the political economy of advanced capitalism" (Mishra 1984, p. 102).

States, however, could not convert to the IWS paradigm overnight even if authorities became convinced of its superiority. Structural constraints limit a state's capacity for more comprehensive guidance in economic and welfare matters, including (according to Mishra): the availability of a long-standing, legitimate, centralized state bureaucracy; the presence of strong Catholic or Social Democratic parties or labor movements; and a polity's substantial dependence on international trade. These factors lead Skocpol to conclude that no reason exists "to believe that Britain or (especially) the United States, with its decentralized pluralism and relatively small dependence on international trade, could suddenly generate . . . an Integrated Welfare State in the style of Austria or Sweden" (1985b, p. 311). Thus, finding appropriate mechanisms—and not just the political will—to reconcile economic growth and the welfare state is likely to prove vexing for authorities in many nations for some time.

ECONOMIC EFFECTIVENESS VERSUS INTERNAL ORDER

Economic growth versus social entitlements hardly tells the entire story, however. Internal order was one of the earliest responsibilities of emerging states, and this goal often has been linked closely to the quest for national prosperity. Indeed, the growth of a state's capacity for internal order and the rise of industrialism have been intertwined in all modernizing societies, both capitalist and noncapitalist. Yet it is a gross distortion of the historical record to assume that internal order and the exigencies of industrialization are always congenial (see particularly Giddens 1985, pp. 181–92).

In fact, the modern state's capacity to provide a social climate conducive to industrial growth entails a paradox. Internal order depends heavily on a state's ability to impose constraint (rather than just the capacity to induce and persuade); coercive resources (the threat or use of violence) are the most effective means to achieve constraint. Although authorities throughout history have sought the right to monopolize the means of violence, only in modern or modernizing states has this become regularly possible. The growing effectiveness of internal police powers yielded the compliant populace and pacific climate suitable for the labor contract, in general, and large-scale industrial enterprise, in particular.

Thus emerging states' success in constraining the populace has helped foster an economic system inimical to this mode of domination, since police powers are not congruent with economic stimulation. These states' capitalist economic order relies instead heavily on self-interest and inducements (via utilitarian resources) and, to a lesser degree, persuasion (via normative resources) to gain citizens' cooperation. Considerable evidence exists to show that coercive compliance undercuts utilitarian compliance in the quest for effective and efficient economic performances (for an overview, see Etzioni 1975). That is, workers' performances respond better to material or moral incentives than to threats. The former Communist states of Central and Eastern Europe and the Soviet Union are now struggling to implement this lesson.

In the final analysis, effective police power is a precondition for economic development, but its excessive application is counterproductive. Consequently, the potential for conflict between economic-growth and order goals is high. Modern economic systems operate more effectively when they rely heavily on noncoercive resources for compliance. On the other hand, the need for internal order, and hence the state's necessary continued monopoly of the means of violence, remain. Ask yourself, for example, what is the better way to bring order and greater economic responsibility to our crime-ridden inner-city ghettoes. In the past generation we have tried both social programs (that lean on the dispensing of normative and utilitarian resources) and "law and order" approaches (that stress police powers). The two strategies seem to have canceled each other out because they have been employed separately. Yet we have failed to come up with a plan that recognizes the need to persuade and induce as well as constrain such groups and that also appreciates that the mustering of coercive power is inherently alienating.

ECONOMIC GROWTH VERSUS NATIONAL SECURITY

We have noted at several junctures that social science writings about politics often cast critical problems in binary (either-or) terms even when matters are actually much more complex. The explicit adherents of the legitimation-crisis paradigm are particular malefactors, relying on a contradiction model of effectiveness that boils down to the clash between economic growth and social entitlements.

Yet they are not alone in framing the potential contest of state goals in binary terms. In the 1960s and 1970s, the popularity of the legitimation-crisis paradigm's binary formula undoubtedly influenced debates raging over the appropriateness or effectiveness of Great Society programs. By the mid-eighties, however, the binary slant more often took the form of controversy over economic effectiveness versus military costs. This shift was influenced by a new set of decisive policy debates. The arms race's increasingly onerous burden on both the United States and the Soviet Union (by then apparent to even the more unsophisticated observers in each nation) was the principal impetus for the new debate.

One book that in particular crystalized the issues of the moment is *The Rise and Fall of the Great Powers* by Paul Kennedy (1987). It manages to capture the strengths and weaknesses of this newest tendency to analyze the clash between state goals in binary terms by someone seemingly far removed from the concerns of the legitimation-crisis paradigm. The subtitle, *Economic Change and Military Conflict from 1500 to 2000,* might give one the impression that this book can be read as merely a straightforward history of five hundred years of military ascendancy and decline among key (mostly European) states. But the book also contains a simple (one might say too simple) yet bold sociological thesis that remains provocative today despite the fact that the sudden end of the Cold War has eliminated much of the overt political controversy that flared up at the time of publication.

For Kennedy, the ultimate predicament that states face is the choice between economic effectiveness and military expenditures. As states aspire to the mantle of "great power," he argues, they divert larger and larger proportions of their available economic assets to military purposes. In their zeal for international dominance, they foster relative economic decline, because they begin to neglect a prudent balance between national prosperity and military spending. When this diversion of national wealth becomes too great, a polity is endangered. National success hinges finally, he believes, on economic effectiveness.

Kennedy points especially to the histories of Spain, the Netherlands, France, and Great Britain to prove his point. His treatment of Britain and early-twentieth-century Germany is instructive, for it demonstrates that his thesis need not be read as a rigidly deterministic one. Specifically, he argues that in these two instances the "skill and experience" of political authorities account for differential outcomes. Today the skill and experience of American and Soviet authorities are being tested, he writes; they now had to ponder their national imbalances between the creation of wealth and the zeal for military expenditures. "Great Powers in relative decline," he declares, "instinctively respond by spending more on 'security,' and thereby divert potential resources from 'investment' and compound their longterm dilemma" (Kennedy 1987, p. xxii). He concludes: "If they neglect to provide adequate military defenses, they may be unable to respond if a rival Power takes advantage of them; if they spend too much on armaments—or, more usually, maintaining at growing costs the military obligations they had assumed in a previous period—they are likely to overstrain themselves, like an old man attempting to work beyond his natural strength" (p. 540).

Kennedy's book failed to anticipate how rapidly both the Soviet Union's successor states and the United States would abandon the Cold War and its most exhausting burdens. Yet the book's pivotal defect, as I have asserted previously, lies in its binary image of state goals, an image that is as intrinsically incomplete as the one embedded in the legitimation-crisis paradigm.[8] However much the analysis of economic effectiveness versus military expenditures illuminates the predicaments of modern states, in general, and the rise and fall of great powers and late-twentieth-century geopolitical developments, in particular, the formula remains inadequate because it fails to give proper analytical weight to other state objectives. Modern states always have more than two goals. Thus the struggle for primacy among goals is invariably more intricate than is envisaged in Kennedy's analysis.

A second problem in Kennedy's treatment of state goals is nearly as severe as his clinging to a binary formula to analyze conflict. In effect, he is unclear about the principal rival of economic growth: Is it "military expenditures" or "national security"? More specifically, Kennedy's work remains confused about what constitutes an *operative goal*. The typical operative goal of most states is "national security," not "military expenditures." To confuse the latter with the former is to equate means with their ends.[9] "National security," of course, has a euphemistic ring to it. This harmless-sounding label has been used to disguise not only aggressive but genocidal designs. Nevertheless, the label "national security" directs our attention to a complex bundle of phenomena of which military prowess and diplomacy have historically been the two most important dimensions. Analytically, these two activities have been the principal *means* for the *goal* of national security. Yet, empirically, the relationship between these two means—particularly military prowess—and the more general end has always been difficult to disentangle.

Nationalistic politicians have been especially inclined to conflate national security and military strength. Sociologists of organizations call this "goal displacement": the substitution of means for ends (Merton 1968, pp. 253–55). This tendency is common in both the state and nonstate sectors of modern bureaucratic life.[10] Yet the particular goal displacement under consideration here has accelerated in the post–World War II era, as military strength was increasingly treated until the late 1980s as an end in itself. Cut off from the official goal of national security, it did more than sow bewilderment as to a state's actual foreign policy agenda; it exacerbated the drain of resources from other pivotal goals, notably economic effectiveness (but others, such as social entitlements, as well).

The "costs" of the displacement of national security by military prowess have been nowhere more visible than in the United States. America's official national security goal after World War II may best be described as "anti-Communist internationalism"; military prowess has generally resulted in a "military industrialism" here. Both goal and means were backed by a broad national consensus until the close of the Eisenhower years. After that, each became the subject of intense, continuous debate. While many factors accounted for this, I would suggest that the uncoupling of one from the other via goal displacement is a key element in the debate. In other words, anti-Communist internationalism became a less compelling objective and for many Americans has been replaced by the building of military power that is "second to none."

It is not surprising that the anti-Communist internationalism became a displaceable goal even before the Berlin Wall was razed in October 1989. It initially represented a compromise capable of achieving bipartisan support and was held together more by what it opposed (viz., communism) than by a positive vision of America's role on the world scene. Yet, while it lasted, the compromise fostered such initiatives as aid to Greece and Turkey in 1946–47, the creation of the North Atlantic Treaty Organization (NATO) in 1949, intervention in Korea in 1950, restoring the Shah to the Iranian throne in 1953, the overthrow of Arbenz in Guatemala in 1954, sending troops to Lebanon in 1959, and forcing Soviet missiles out of Cuba in 1962. Regardless of how appropriate one may judge any of these actions, they do reflect a capacity to intervene decisively on the world scene with broad domestic support. After Vietnam this capacity diminished precipitously.[11]

Military industrialism is a relatively recent phenomenon. "Hawks" have sought to treat it as the prime national security objective in light of the absence of a more fundamental consensus on foreign policy goals. "Doves" have regarded it as the prime subverter of all of our domestic goals. Under the impact of two World Wars and the Korean and Vietnam wars, the United States has constructed a permanent military establishment unimaginable in the nineteenth century. This means-masquerading-as-goal became the principal rival of economic growth and social entitlements for governmental appropriations, a tension that has survived beyond the Cold War. Some have argued that the existence of a military-industrial complex serves as an underpinning for economic growth, so that defense and capital accumulation go hand in hand rather than being antagonistic goals. A number of analyses over the past two decades, however, suggest that ties between the military and business are far from monolithic. A small segment of the corporate elite profits excessively from swelling military appropriations, but the overall economy does not. In particular, a military budget bloated by high-tech, high-cost hardware pushed by military-industrial lobbies may threaten economic growth (Kennedy 1987; Lieberson 1971; Rothschild 1984; Szymanski 1973; Tucker 1971; Weidenbaum 1969). Big-ticket spending is not only inflationary but when excessively stressed can undermine efforts at international accords by fostering new destabilizing weapons systems. It can also injure military prowess itself by deflecting funds from the maintenance of troop strength and conventional weapons.[12]

Thus the end of the Cold War forces us to think more deeply about what national security really ought to signify as we move toward a new century. Ironically, while Kennedy's conflation of national security and military spending remains serious as a theoretical and practical oversight, it has also become something of an anachronism. The United States and other advanced capitalist democracies are now focused on national security much more as an outcome of international economic growth and less as the product of military spending. This may well signal that political analysts concerned with explicating their fundamental assumptions will have to worry more about a conflation of national security with economic growth, and less about the tendency to substitute military spending for national security.

Yet, as the Gulf War has demonstrated, the reshuffling of the cards in world-power poker (and the appearance of new players) mandates that the United States, as the last great power, will have to play a greater military-security leadership role for some time. How we define and combine the military and nonmilitary elements of that role *and* how we relate these to domestic and global problems of economic effectiveness will go a long way in determining America's relative standing on the world scene in the coming decades.[13] (On this issue, see Nye 1990.)

ECONOMIC EFFECTIVENESS VERSUS QUALITY OF LIFE

Quality of life is the latest entry into the national goals sweepstakes. The past twenty years have witnessed the rise of a myriad of "environmental" issues, such as opposition to nuclear power plants; cries for pollution and toxic substance controls; demands to check the "greenhouse effect"; concern for forests, parks, and wildlife; demands for automobile safety; and the advocacy of "animal rights." Business and financial circles cast a wary eye on this movement. Over a decade ago, the Chase Manhattan Bank claimed that the quality-of-life agenda would cost at least $100 billion per year (Butcher 1978). This estimate would probably be more than doubled today. Quality of life obviously poses a challenge to the advocates of economic growth, because the costs of items such as automobile safety and pollution equipment are potentially inflationary as well as "nonproductive" (in much the same way as social entitlements are). Moreover, quality-of-life goals may drain funds away from investments in new plants and equipment needed for national prosperity. But to pose the question as quality of life *or* economic growth may not be the most useful approach. Just as we need both social entitlements and national prosperity, we must repair the damage we are doing to our environment while pursuing economic effectiveness.

Robert Reich's comments on the unproductive debate between free marketeers and environmentalists over the benefits of enforcing the Clean Air Act are instructive here (Reich 1987, pp. 224–27). In effect, he argues that pollution should be reduced within the context of economic effectiveness. Rather than debating over the value of clean air versus the inefficiencies of state regulation, Reich believes we should ask: "How can government better organize the market to attain the cleanest possible air at the lowest possible cost?" (Reich 1987, p. 226). Mishra, no doubt, would regard this as an IWS approach to the issue of quality of life versus that of economic growth.[14]

In short, national prosperity is never pursued in a political vacuum. Rational-legal legitimations, modern political participation, and the bureaucratization of the state including its internal structural diversity, heterogeneous external constituents, and multiple resources all operate to guarantee that a state always has more than a single goal and that the relations among these goals can never be rendered fully in binary terms. Despite the importance of economic growth, modern states must also grapple simultaneously with the delivery of social entitlements, internal order, national security, and quality of life. Yet, although binary formulas are blatantly inadequate, conflicts between certain "paired" goals have been visible as loci of concern. For example, entitlements and quality of life have both been vulnerable to a zeal for economic effectiveness; on the other hand, economic growth itself is likely to suffer from an overemphasis on either national security or internal order.

Economic Growth versus Efficient Participation and Legitimacy

A multidimensional analysis of the contradiction model of effectiveness moves us beyond the question of effectiveness itself. Thus we now shift attention from how the modern state's zeal for one goal handicaps its effective pursuit of others to how this factor affects the efficient mobilization of political participation and the legitimation of the rules of the game. The stress that both authorities and partisans place on economic growth is so central that the following discussion zeros in on its impact on these other ingredients of political viability.

ECONOMIC GROWTH AND PARTICIPATION

The modern state's zeal for national prosperity undercuts a polity's capacity to process demands and confidence in two ways. On the one hand, it further encourages an already dominant policy style of "instrumental consciousness" that strives to render all problems as strictly rational or technical ones. On the other hand, the stress on economic growth gives rise to the "political business cycle," that is, a fusion of previously incommensurate political and economic time frames to the potential detriment of each sector. Both instrumental consciousness and the political business cycle impede the efficient mobilization of participation on every level of the polity. They differ, however, because instrumental consciousness tends to originate on the state level and ramifies "downward," while the roots of the political business cycle are below the state and its effects tend to work their way "upward." The two sets of effects are most likely to conflict on the state level; yet their impacts on lower tiers of the polity are actually more reinforcing than contradictory.

Instrumental consciousness

Instrumental consciousness is a policy style employed by state authorities in coping with their mandates, particularly with pressures for economic growth. It is probably strongest among the professionals and bureaucrats who inhabit the administrative branch, although its influence has grown in the state's other branches as well. Policy styles "are distinct clusters of images, symbols, rhetoric, and techniques that an individual or group can use in thinking about public problems, developing solutions, and persuading others" (Jasper 1990, p. 11). Instrumental consciousness is a general style that promotes the belief that societal problems have become increasingly depoliticized and are capable of being solved by the application of rational or technical criteria alone. Habermas (1975) calls this outlook "technocratic consciousness" and sees it as the tool of a state dependent on popular support while it advances policies that contradict the real interests of the majority of citizens.

Poggi believes that the state's pursuit of economic effectiveness has intensified its propensity to drape its actions in technical garb:

Around the middle of the twentieth century . . . the political process in Western countries begins to revolve around . . . how to promote "industrial development," "affluence," and so forth—this being seen as the only large issue (other than war, hot or cold) that might provide the basis for a reconciliation of societal interests. . . . This development . . . is said to be ultimately a "technical" rather than a political one. (1978, p. 141)

Both Habermas and Poggi argue that authorities employ instrumental consciousness to head off opposition to their economic planning. But the ascendancy of this policy style is more than a clever ruse. The experts who staff the modern state's burgeoning administrative branch are devotees of the cult of rational and technical efficiency who are faithful to and use "scientific" standards to think about, define, and solve problems—especially economic ones.

"Competence, prudence, and above all balance are the characteristics" that most distinguish the inhabitants of the administrative branch of advanced polities (Aberbach, Putnam, and Rockman 1981, p. 241). It is hard to believe that their reliance on instrumental consciousness has not made the state generally more effective. Nevertheless, this policy style poses dilemmas for efficient mobilization of participation.

The bearing of instrumental consciousness on political efficiency tends to work "downward" through the polity. This policy style emerged as an integral part of the bureaucratization of state capacity and the state's unique responsibility for monitoring and fostering national prosperity. As a result, it has helped alter the relationship between administrative and elected personnel. In particular, Poggi suggests that, as instrumental consciousness has grown in this century, elected officials in general and parliaments in particular have lost many of their prerogatives in the processing of demands and confidence. Bureaucrats, who tend to be leery of the "irrational" turmoil of electoral politics and who feel more at ease with the policy styles of powerful interest groups and the way they package their demands, increase in power. "In the eyes of ministers and top civil servants," he says, "legislation has become too important to be left to legislators" (Poggi 1978, p. 143). The net result has been "to shunt parliament away from the effective center of a country's political life, leaving in control the state's executive organs, and especially its administrative apparatus, now thoroughly 'interlaced' with . . . various controlling nonstate forces" (Poggi 1978, p. 144).

Yet the pervasiveness of instrumental consciousness has not totally standardized how different modern states elicit participation or respond to it. For one thing, this policy style has not resulted in uniform relations among administrative and elected personnel. For example, a comparison of bureaucrat-politician linkages in six nations (the United States, Great Britain, West Germany, Italy, the Netherlands, and Sweden) found two major patterns (Aberbach, Putnam, and Rockman 1981, pp. 209–37): mediated linkages— where bureaucrats have fewer contacts with parliamentarians and forge closer ties with ministers because cabinet solidarity, ministerial responsibility, and party-centered parliaments prevail (as in Britain, the Netherlands, and Sweden); and direct linkages—where bureaucrats' links with parliamentarians are more frequent and decisive than with ministers because cabinet solidarity, ministerial responsibility, and party-centered parliaments are weak or absent (as in the United States, West Germany, and Italy). The first pattern reduces the need for bureaucrats to become involved in overt politics outside the national executive arena; the second one compels them to do so. Aberbach, Putnam, and Rockman found that the United States has developed a unique variant of direct linkage, which they term the "end-run model":

> Institutions and history have pushed American bureaucrats toward more traditionally political roles as advocates, policy entrepreneurs, and even partisans, and have led congressmen to adopt a more technical role. American bureaucrats are more polarized ideologically . . . and therein they resemble politicians more. They are much like congressmen in their conceptualization of policy matters and in the consistency of their partisanship and ideology. This pattern of bureaucratic-legislative contact is very special in the United States. (1981, pp. 243–44)

Moreover, the impact of instrumental consciousness on how the state elicits and responds to participation is far from monolithic, because this policy style has distinct subspecies. Jasper (1990), for instance, distinguishes between cost-benefit and technological-enthusiast policy styles. Adherents of the former style "typically propose, in market settings, to change relative prices (or let the markets change themselves) and, in non-market settings, to perform cost-benefit analyses that mimic market prices" (Jasper 1990, p. 25). Advocates of the latter style "are skeptical about the rationality of uncoordinated individual choices, feeling more comfortable with physical structures whose behavior can be predicted with the certainty of the natural sciences" (Jasper 1990, p. 25). I expect that states today are still more likely to give greater weight to the cost-benefit policy style in light of the special role of economic growth in modern politics and the apparent triumph of market-oriented economics throughout the world.[15]

Thus, despite palpable differences, instrumental consciousness has fostered the relative power of state bureaucrats along with an overall tendency to frame political issues in rational or technical terms. This "depoliticization" reverberates on all the other tiers of the polity and affects the formation and efficient processing of political participation.

On the party level, instrumental consciousness encourages parties to be less ideological. Mass democratic parties have become more prone to present themselves to the electorate as "sensible managers" who can solve economic problems efficiently rather than as "true believers" or the representatives of "special interests." Insofar as American parties have been less overtly ideological and disciplined than most, political leaders here have found this style particularly congenial. It is worth recalling in this context that Tocqueville found lawyers, the first modern political "experts," playing a decisive role in nineteenth-century U.S. party politics at a time when aristocrats still held sway on the European scene (Tocqueville [1835–40] 1954, Vol. 1, pp. 282–90).

The rise of instrumental consciousness, however, has exacerbated the problems of parties. Their slackened ideological stance has weakened their moorings to permanent constituencies. This factor has accelerated "party decomposition" (Burnham 1970, 1975) that, as I detail in Chapter 3, has had two major concomitants: the individuation of issues and the particularization of elections. The net result has been to give the appearance that parties are merely opportunistic and the electoral process is chaotic. (For similar tendencies in Western Europe, see Panebianco 1988.)

By the time instrumental consciousness gets to the organization level, a good deal of the collectivity orientation has been peeled away. In the chambers of elected officials and especially state bureaucrats the rational pursuit of economic effectiveness is still discussed in terms of "national growth," "industrial development," and "affluence." For a growing number of today's interest groups it has become almost entirely a question of enhancing or preserving the incomes of their constituents. Powerful interest groups who can congenially shape their claims in terms of the prevailing policy style are more likely to receive a sympathetic ear from likeminded bureaucrats. This no doubt reinforces the strong preference among state bureaucrats to "mediate narrow, focused interests of organized clienteles [viz., interest groups]" (Aberbach, Putnam, and Rockman 1981, p. 9). Hence, instrumental consciousness encourages the contemporary trend toward single-issue interest groups and away from multi-interest groups (Etzioni 1984, pp. 171–218). In particular, it fosters single-issue, pecuniary groups. These special interests are often as passionate and uncompromising as any "status politics" group because of the parochial, even communal, character of their economic claims (see Chapter 3).

When instrumental consciousness reaches the public level it tends to have conflicting effects on participation. On the one hand, if the optimal democratic polity is marked by a moderately involved majority whose participation dampens the impact of apathetic and ideological minorities (Berelson, Lazarsfeld, and McPhee 1954, pp. 305–23), then this policy style fosters suboptimal functioning by cutting into the middle majority. Instrumental consciousness encourages citizen apathy and a deference to experts because it stresses "scientific" criteria and "depoliticizes" issues. Perhaps the clearest empirical indicator of this proclivity is an indirect sign: One would expect that as people's educational levels rose they would feel more politically competent and get more involved; but in the United States an increase in the public's level of education has failed to increase their sense of political efficacy (Lipset and Schneider 1983, pp. 19–24).

On the other hand, side by side with extensive apathy, single-issue zealotry will become more common on the public level. This zealotry may take the form of particularistic economic demands (e.g., bailing out a local industry), or it may take a manifestly "moral" direction (e.g., protecting the right to life). The formation of these pockets stems from both a growing inability or disinclination to develop broad political interests (fostered in part by a sense that most "big" problems should be handled by "experts") and the emergence of single-interest pressure groups who are able to step into the breach and mobilize very specific segments of an otherwise apathetic public.

The political business cycle

David R. Cameron delineates the impact of economic growth on the political business cycle succinctly:

Voters have tended to provide short-term electoral rewards to incumbents who can effect, through their tax, fiscal, and monetary policies, increases in real personal income . . . [B]ecause incumbents are aware of this relationship, most adopt policies in anticipation of elections which stimulate the economy and increase personal income by pumping funds into the economy. As a result, periodic electoral competition frequently produces a long-term cyclical effect into the economy. (1978, p. 1246)

The political business cycle thus tends to have its roots in the economic interests of nonstate actors and to flow in the opposite direction from instrumental consciousness. Yet, except for the state level, the two factors are most commonly mutually reinforcing.

As Cameron indicates, the political business cycle stems from the public's concern with economic effectiveness, which they are inclined to equate narrowly with their real personal incomes. This is why questions of inflation, recession, and taxes are so central in their political calculus during election campaigns (Hamilton and Wright 1986, pp. 289–325; Lipset and Schneider 1983, pp. 153–59). Incumbents know they are being judged by the "What have you done for me lately?" test and so try to have a special delivery of goods as close to election day as possible. During nonelection periods constituents are likely to remain apathetic.

These effects on the public level help sustain narrowly based single-issue interest groups and party decomposition on the next two tiers of the polity. Both phenomena are furthered by the political business cycle's fragmentation of constituent demands. Interest groups and parties find it difficult to articulate a broad array of consistent interests at a time when they lack recognizable and coherent bases. PACs are probably the most pernicious manifestation of these tendencies in the United States over the past two decades (Drew 1983; Etzioni 1984; Neustadtl, Scott, and Clawson 1991).

Finally, on the state level the effects of the political business cycle and instrumental consciousness appear to contradict each other. The latter, we saw, increases the power of bureaucrats over elected officials; the former tends to do the opposite. The responsibility and capacity of elected officials to deliver economic benefits, seemingly on short notice, creates a special bond with constituents that bureaucrats are not able to replicate. Bureaucrats are more at ease with organized groups who speak the same "depoliticized" language of instrumental consciousness. The prescribed periodicity of elections adds a special urgency to bonds between incumbents and voters. Overall, the peculiar dependence between incumbents and the electorate enhances the power of both, and it gives executives and legislators a political leverage that is not accessible to the administrative branch.

In the United States, where bureaucratic state building has proved incomplete, the administrative branch (following the end-run model) is at times an accomplice in the political business cycle. Skowronek points out:

> The New Deal turned bureaucracy itself into the extra-constitutional machine so necessary for the continuous operation of the constitutional system. Like party patronage in the old order, bureaucratic goods and services came to provide the fuel and the cement of the new institutional politics. They became something valuable for Presidents to offer and for congressmen to support. They articulated a new set of concrete institutional ties between the state and the citizenry. (1982, p. 289)

Overall, however, the political business cycle and instrumental consciousness work at cross-purposes on the state level. Yet, as far as political participation is concerned, their countervailing impacts are not likely to yield a synthesis or balance. Elected officials who value short-term responsiveness to voters' manifest economic interests will continue to generate the political business cycle with its emphasis on the electoral process. Instrumental consciousness will still be more congenial to bureaucrats who take the "longer view," are disturbed by the "irrationality" of electoral politics, and feel more comfortable dealing with powerful interest groups with whom they share this policy style. It is hard to see how these tendencies might mutually support each other. The result is more likely to remain one of confusion and conflict over how to deal with citizens' claims on the state.

The two tendencies do have three points in common, however. First, they are both fostered by the stress on economic growth in modern politics. A policy style of instrumental consciousness represents a state-level response to this emphasis, especially in the administrative branch; the political business cycle is the result of non-state actors looking "upward" for a solution mainly via the electoral process and pressuring politicians for short-run answers. Second, both tendencies contribute to similar outcomes below the state level: general apathy or a focus on narrow pecuniary advantage among the public; the rise of narrowly based single-interest groups on the organization level; and the acceleration of decomposition on the party level. Finally, both tendencies (singly and in combination) guarantee that the contemporary drift to political inefficiency (discussed at length in the next chapter) is exacerbated.

ECONOMIC GROWTH AND LEGITIMACY

Ironically, the case for a legitimation crisis—the most celebrated alleged liability of the zeal for economic effectiveness—is the least compelling. As noted previously, the interaction between economic growth and legitimacy has been the special domain of legitimation-crisis analysts. Not everyone within this broad tradition has predicted an imminent collapse of political faith, however. The thesis that the democratic capitalist state's inevitable failure to achieve economic effectiveness guarantees such a crisis has been most commonly associated with the paradigm's neo-Marxist camp. Other adherents, such as Lipset ([1960] 1981), reject the prognosis because they are more optimistic about the state's involvement with economic effectiveness. Yet both approaches are based on at least one of three possible types of conflation. These cast a cloud over the prospects for empirically open inquiry into how the pursuit of economic growth might shape faith in the system.

Conflating legitimacy and confidence

The first type of conflation is shared by virtually all followers of the paradigm, whether or not they see a legitimation crisis looming on the horizon. This conflation confuses legitimacy and confidence. The former, as I said in Chapter 1, refers to moral approval for the system, the latter to support for particular incumbents. Thus when legitimation-crisis analysts tell us that a decline in economic effectiveness helps erode political trust, we remain perplexed as to from whom or from what trust is being withheld. The legitimacy of a system and confidence in the particular people running it are theoretically distinct issues. Although these phenomena have often been fused empirically in the past, the rise of rational-legal doctrines has led to more frequent separation in modern times (see Chapter 4).

Thus we must remain wary of binary formulas that conflate legitimacy and confidence. Yet this vigilance must not lead us to reject the possibility that under specified circumstances the quest for economic effectiveness may influence legitimacy. It is likely, for example, that while most polities are affected in some way, new ones encounter interaction of the two factors with special urgency. "All claims to a legitimate title to rule in new states," Lipset (1963b, pp. 45–46) argues, "must ultimately win acceptance through demonstrating effectiveness. The loyalty of the different groups to the system must be won through developing in them the conviction that this system is the best—or at least an excellent—way to accomplish their objectives."

In other words, Lipset is suggesting that effectiveness may sometimes substitute for legitimacy in the short run and generate it in the long run. However, our alternative paradigm alerts us that confidence, in all likelihood, must serve as the intervening variable in such equations. Weil (1989) has offered an empirical demonstration of the inadequacy of studying effectiveness and legitimacy in isolation, as practitioners of the legitimation-crisis paradigm are wont to do. He demonstrates, by comparing survey data from France, Great Britain, Italy, Spain, the United States, and West Germany, that *in the short run* economic effectiveness does not affect the legitimacy of democratic institutions but does have an impact on confidence in authorities. He suggests that economic effectiveness's only influence on legitimacy occurs via the mediation of confidence.

Lipset's celebrated analyses of Germany and Austria in the interwar years and of the birth of the United States achieve greater plausibility in light of Weil's corrective. Lipset ([1960] 1981, p. 69) suggests that the republics established in Germany and Austria in the wake of World War I survived through the 1920s, despite a lack of legitimacy, because they were seen as economically effective. Conservative elites went along with despised democratic institutions so long as the leaders of the new states delivered the goods. He also argues the fledgling United States—the prototypical "first new nation"—coped with an absence of pervasive legitimacy partly because the Union provided an economic payoff to potential critics (Lipset 1963b, pp. 45–60). Tangible effectiveness allowed the new state time to sink its moral roots and build a reservoir of legitimacy. Lipset's German and Austrian examples can be reinterpreted as arguing that economic effectiveness bestowed sufficient confidence on incumbents to allow their systems to function in the absence of legitimacy but that the Depression destroyed this more concrete form of trust. His U.S. case can be rephrased to say that sustained confidence nurtured by long-term growth ultimately fostered legitimacy.

Conflating legitimacy and social entitlements

A second conflation equates social entitlements with legitimacy. Here, the welfare state becomes essentially a mechanism for purchasing faith in the system (see, e.g., O'Connor 1973; Offe 1984), and analysis centers on the binary conflict of state goals. Legitimacy, however, is a distinct ingredient of viability and is not to be confused with a government's social entitlement goals. As a goal, the welfare state is best treated primarily in terms of effectiveness. Acceptance of the distinction between legitimacy and delivering social entitlements does not mean that the study of their interactions is unimportant. In fact, such research is possible only if the two concepts are kept distinct.

Conflating legitimacy and economic growth

The third conflation fuses cause and effect. I have argued that economic effectiveness may substitute for legitimacy in the short run and be its indirect cause over the longer haul, with confidence serving as the intervening variable. This process has led some to claim that economic effectiveness has usurped the legitimation role of classical rational-legal doctrines, especially in capitalist democracies (see, e.g., Habermas 1975; Poggi 1978). Poggi, for instance, declares that "in the long run, the state found a new and different response to the legitimacy problem: increasingly it treated industrial growth per se as possessing intrinsic and commanding political significance, as constituting a necessary and sufficient standard of each state's performance" (Poggi 1978, p. 133). He believes that the rhetoric of economic growth is now "utterly self-justifying, and . . . validating whatever burdens the state might impose" (Poggi 1978, p. 133).

This last conflation is not just theoretically unacceptable but methodologically and empirically unsound. Methodologically, it transforms an independent variable (economic effectiveness) into the variable whose variance it has been used to explain (legitimation). Explanatory analysis, in effect, has been converted to descriptive statements behind our backs.

Perhaps more crucially, no systematic data exist to substantiate a latter-day shift in our doctrines of legitimation. Yet this line of argument rests in the reality of such a shift. While the prevailing doctrines may have remained formally rational-legal, it has been suggested that we are experiencing a move away from popular compliance captured in Weber's classic formulation of obedience based on abstract rational criteria. The new doctrines are said to be crudely economistic. The pursuit of domestic prosperity, it is alleged, has become the state's principal justification. Consequently, we are led to the unwarranted conclusion that the economic turmoil of the past two decades might translate directly into an impending legitimation crisis.

Anecdotal data abound purporting to describe how the rise of capitalism and industrialism has altered political legitimation. It is possible that the state's special responsibility for economic growth has added justifications based on conditions of prosperity to the moral grounding for political authority. Yet such anecdotal evidence is matched by equally plausible anecdotes that appear to refute claims for a legitimation shift. For example, if shared national rituals are valid indicators of legitimacy, then the collective euphoria induced by the bicentennial celebration in 1976, the Statue of Liberty centennial in 1986, and the plethora of Desert Storm victory parades in 1991 suggests more than the fact that legitimacy is pervasive in the United States. These compelling rituals also tell us that the doctrines that continue to inspire vast numbers of Americans retain significant noneconomic themes.

Moreover, ample evidence alerts us to the fact that America's doctrines of legitimation retain more than classical rational-legal elements (such as extensive respect for the rule of law). They still include significant traditional strands as well. The importance of "civil religion" in America's avowedly nonsectarian political culture provides vivid testimony in this matter (see Bellah 1975).[16]

Nevertheless, extensive practical and scholarly concerns over the impact of economic policy on legitimacy—coupled with the need for more systematic comparative data—suggest that this topic warrants further scrutiny. Weil (1989) has shown that the contemporary state's zest for economic effectiveness may help to erode legitimacy only over the longer run and then always via a loss of confidence. Whether or not such an event ultimately occurs depends on either of two problematic developments. First (and more directly), a withdrawal of citizens' confidence from a series of political leaders (because of their perceived inability to deliver economically) would have to set off a gradual loss of faith in the system. Yet no one is certain how long a "confidence gap" would have to last before we would experience a "legitimation crisis." In the United States, the years from Lyndon Johnson through Jimmy Carter proved insufficient. Second, the time span between "confidence gap" and "legitimation crisis" might be shortened if doctrines of legitimation begin (or continue) to incorporate economic justifications and lose their deeper, "moral" grounding. However, I have noted already that this scenario lacks solid supporting data.

Summary and Conclusions

The foregoing analysis flows directly from treating modern states using categories drawn from the sociological study of complex organizations. As I stressed in Chapter 1, it would be incorrect to see this as a one-dimensional "managerialist perspective" (Alford and Friedland 1985).

Rather, the analysis assumes that the state faces multiple, complex, and possibly contradictory pressures that require a multidimensional framework to be understood. Some of these pressures are located inside the state, but others come from other (nonstate) actors and forces as well as from actors and forces outside the polity. In particular, the bureaucratization of state capacities, modern forms of political participation, and rational-legal doctrines of legitimation heighten the state's already strong interest in effectiveness. Moreover, these factors, along with the state's inherent structural diversity, its multiple constituents, and the array of resources over which it has command, guarantee that the authorities will have to pursue several goals. When a system such as the United States gives undue weight to economic growth or national security, the results are self-defeating. I have focused especially (but by no means exclusively) on how a single-minded zeal for the most important of these—economic growth—can undermine effective pursuit of the other goals as well as effectiveness generally. Moreover, a multidimensional perspective allows us to see that this same zeal may have repercussions for the nongoal exigencies of polities—especially for how participation is mobilized and even possibly for whether institutions are rendered legitimate.

The special position taken by state effectiveness in modern life justifies discussing it first. Let us remember, however, that it is not the only component of political viability. Moreover, effectiveness is not necessarily always the basis of our independent variables; in the opening section of this chapter, for example, I suggested that effectiveness in turn may be influenced by efficient participation and by doctrines of legitimation. Thus we move on to consider the efficiency of political participation and the question of legitimacy as components in their own right. Only then can we assert that the dimensions of political success and failure have been covered satisfactorily.

3 Anomalies of Inefficient Participation

If there is an organization which controls . . . [the] concentrated means of coercion, it is a government *. . . any group that collectively applies resources to influence the government . . . is a* contender *for power. Some contenders have routine means of making claims on the government that are accepted by other contenders, and by agents of the government; collectively, such contenders make up the* polity *related to a particular government; individually we call them* members of the polity *. . . Contenders that do not have routine, accepted means of making claims on the government are not members of the polity; they are* challengers.
—*Charles Tilly, "Town and Country in Revolution"*

A political system's success or failure depends on more than the interaction between its state's effectiveness and the legitimacy of its institutions. Viability also hinges on how well state authorities deal with a welter of nonstate actors in the polity on whose "contributions" they have come to rely. The concept of efficiency helps us focus on how adeptly the political system does this. Just as states are never unequivocally effective or ineffective in goal attainment, so advanced polities cannot be judged as univocally efficient or inefficient in the incorporation of participation. The question of relative efficiency poses unique problems for democratic polities, but it is now especially problematic for the American system.

Political participation in the contemporary United States is being buffeted by an array of inefficiencies that initially appear to be more acute than in other advanced democracies and, at the same time, seem at least partially contradictory. We see, on the one hand, apparent signs of *apathy*: disappointing voter turnouts, an erosion of party identification, and a "confidence gap" vis-à-vis authorities. On the other hand, there are signs of "overload" or "hyperparticipation," especially in the allegedly growing influence of powerful "special interests" and the return of a self-congratulatory "new patriotism." Despite the lack of an obvious fit among these factors, they all have been invoked to account for the long-term decomposition of our two-party system in particular and the American polity's inefficiency in general.

Can our alternative paradigm provide the tools for making greater sense of these apparently anomalous tendencies and arriving at a more comprehensive picture of how well or poorly our polity is incorporating participation? This chapter argues that, once the various "pathologies" are analyzed macrosociologically within the framework of a multitiered polity outlined in Chapter 1, there is in fact greater continuity than first meets the eye. Specifically, I suggest that (1) outwardly incompatible inefficiencies can occur at the same time because they originate on different levels of our polity; (2) these inefficiencies have the most pivotal ramifications on the political party tier even when their initial sites are elsewhere; and (3) a refurbished, more macrosociological version of the classic "cross-pressures" approach explains a good deal about why participation in the United States is currently so inefficient.

The Stigmata of Inefficient Participation

Who is a political participant? What is political participation? What do we mean when we speak of participation as relatively efficient or inefficient?

The term "political participant" may be applied to all the polity's nonstate members. Actors (both individuals and collectivities) are polity members when strategic portions of their role performances occur within the circumscribed territory over which the state has operative administrative reach, and when a state is able to command significant role performances from these actors. Both criteria must be met before we call a person or a group a polity member and a participant. The modern state's responsibility for internal order as well as its penetration of economic, health, education, and welfare sectors guarantees that most adults inside a demarcated territory are polity members in this generic sense. Gamson (1968) refers to such members as "potential partisans." They become actual "partisans" when they struggle to affect a state's policies rather than serving merely as the recipients of its dictates. Thus, while, along with the state, both potential partisans and partisans are members and participants broadly speaking, only the latter actively participate in the political realm.

Political participation (or involvement) refers to the processes through which the polity's nonstate members try to influence state actions. In the most general terms, participation in a polity is efficient when the influences exerted help state authorities to anticipate and respond to societal problems and to guide the polity more effectively; it is inefficient to the degree that the processing of influence fails to achieve such objectives. As noted earlier, effectiveness focuses on "downward" political processes through which the state authorities seek to make binding decisions, while efficiency refers to "upward" processes initiated by those who seek to influence the decisions of these authorities.

Participation is a multifaceted phenomenon. Not only can involvement in the polity take place in multiple ways, but opportunities for participation also exist on every level of the polity below the state. For example, voting under some circumstances may be a crucial way to exert influence, but we should not equate it with all participation nor assume that all political actions are public-level phenomena.

Olsen (1982) identifies six types of participation that occur on nonstate levels of the polity: cognitive, expressive, electoral, organizational, partisan, and governmental. This typology provides a handy vehicle for analyzing the multidimensionality of political participation; it also serves as a tool for showing that there is an overall pattern to the phenomenon, notwithstanding diversity. To begin with, Olsen's typology implicitly acknowledges the multilevel nature of participation. The first three types are essentially public-tier practices; the remaining three for the most part fall on the organization and party levels.

Cognitive and expressive participation focus mainly on public opinion formation. The former concept captures the public's capacity for political awareness, particularly through its ability to digest information from the mass media. The latter also concerns the formation of the public's political consciousness but highlights the interpersonal and communal bases of public opinion (e.g., the role of influentials, the frequency of political conversations with relatives or friends).

Electoral participation means voting. Social scientists generally agree that voting regularly is the minimal requirement for transcending the label of "politically apathetic" (i.e., turning from a potential partisan into a partisan). Approximately 63 percent of Americans report voting regularly, leaving about one-third of the public inactive or apathetic (see, e.g., Milbrath and Goel 1977).[1] Voting is a low-intensity public-level activity; that is, it requires little effort from participants. Nevertheless, it represents the principal—albeit imperfect—corrective to unequal influence in democratic polities. Although their turnout rates remain lower (Piven and Cloward 1988), the less privileged members still provide a plurality of the electorate in most elections. Thus, elections have a populist tilt. Since suffrage is universal, politicians are commonly forced to compete, however unenthusiastically, for support from some of the less privileged sectors of the public.

Elections also benefit the less privileged because the act of voting is itself relatively "cheap." Elections occur only periodically, and casting a ballot is free and takes relatively little time. On the other hand, the costs of electoral participation mount the farther back from election day one moves. As we go back from casting a ballot, to being active in the campaign, to raising and contributing funds, to shaping platforms, to selecting candidates, and to keeping party structures alive between elections, "expenses" jump sharply. Only at the very end of the process does the democratizing effect of one person–one vote prevail. Privileged members have greater leverage over the more remote events. Moreover, these events tend to be orchestrated above the public tier.

What Olsen (1982) calls "partisan"[2] and "governmental" participation seems to take place mostly on the organization or political party levels. Partisan participation refers to activities of a considerable range of intensity and influence. A common feature, however, lies in selecting or advancing the cause of candidates for office. The lowliest of these efforts, such as wearing a campaign button, are still usually public-level actions. The most pivotal forms of partisan participation—raising funds or managing a campaign, for instance—have lodged historically on the party tier. The fact that interest groups (from the organization level) now play such a central role in these matters stands as vivid testimony to intensifying party decomposition (discussed below). Governmental participation, for Olsen, concerns mainly lobbying activity. It, like partisan activities, ranges across levels and may even contain low-intensity public-tier actions (e.g., signing a petition). Yet, I would argue that the very nature of lobbying and pressure group behavior dictates that governmental participation rather than partisan participation will be more heavily concentrated on the organization level.

But what are citizens trying to accomplish when they decide to participate? While the ultimate aim of participation is to influence state decisions, political involvement often entails more than socially approved "within-the-system" behaviors. It also includes "unruly" political conduct (Gamson 1975) by both "contenders" and "challengers" (Tilly 1974, 1978). Unruly conduct consists of actions that are disdained by "decent folks" as well as others that are patently illegal and even insurrectional. Unruly involvement is thus a possibility within all six of Olsen's categories and may manifest itself on the public, organization, or party levels.

In the final analysis, people participate in order to influence a state in two ways: to offer generalized trust or support to authorities or to withhold it; and to press the state apparatus to recognize certain "problems" and to redress them via binding decisions. All advanced polities operate more efficiently if their states receive both types of influence. It is in this sense that political participation may be considered a contribution civil society makes to a state as well as to an overall polity. Social scientists tend call the first type "confidence" and the second "demands" (see, e.g., Easton 1965; Parsons 1967).

Confidence refers to polity members' broad endorsements of incumbents, particularly (although by no means exclusively) the national executive. When granted, confidence confers a "zone of indifference" so that officials do not have sell each directive or deploy resources to ensure compliance.[3] Commentators touch on this factor when they say that a new administration has a "mandate" or is in a "honeymoon period." Such notions suggest that confidence is greater early in a government; later trust is tarnished by repeated political combat. As I suggested in Chapter 1, multidimensional analysis prospers when confidence is not confused with legitimacy. The two concepts are theoretically distinct, and their real-world referents are often empirically differentiated as well, particularly in the modern world. (See Chapter 4 for a more detailed analysis of the implication of these points.)

The concept of demands focuses attention on how partisans channel claims on the state "upward" and whether they succeed in having them converted into policies. Electoral participation has been the most commonly studied mechanism for making such claims in U.S. social science. But this form of involvement is also a statement about confidence. Moreover, demands can be expressed by acceptable and unruly nonelectoral means (and from above the public tier), as I noted in our discussion of the aforementioned types of participation.

Demands themselves have been frequently classified as either "class politics" or "status politics" (see, e.g., Lipset 1968). This terminology has been used in a number of ways, the most useful of which points to the alternative strategies partisans employ to "package" their petitions. Some partisans call on authorities to change or preserve the distribution of utilitarian (i.e., economic) resources (class politics); others use a moralistic rhetoric that focuses on a change or preservation of basic values, religious symbols, styles of life, or patriotic concerns (status politics). Some groups press both class-politics and status-politics claims, while others focus on one set and even on a single issue. Specific demands are not either essentially "economic" or "social" in content but are socially constructed to fit into class-politics or status-politics molds. This means that the social orchestration of demands into class and status rhetorics is inevitably a multilevel experience, because public-level actors by their very nature are incapable of accomplishing such a feat on their own. (For a fuller analysis of the concepts of class politics and status politics, see Lehman 1977, pp. 160–69.)

Although expressions of confidence and demands may be mutually reinforcing, a tension also exists between the two. One is concerned with delivering trust or support to authorities; the other necessarily involves the prospect for conflict, since it has to do with pressuring a possibly recalcitrant state. This strain between confidence and demands has proven a handy vehicle for delving more deeply into the nature of political inefficiency, especially in advanced democracies. The polity's capacity to achieve a balance between the two exigencies is the core of efficient participation processes.

Classic analyses of democratic involvement have argued that, although potential partisans with blocked access to authorities generally do not bestow enough confidence on leaders, efficiency requires that their demands must be sufficiently broad and flexible so that confidence does not rest on meeting a particular petition. Political participation works more smoothly, it was assumed, when confidence slips only after a group senses that many of its claims are being evaded or rejected (see, e.g., Berelson, Lazarsfeld, and McPhee 1954). This mode of analysis suggests two elementary—and seemingly contradictory—types of inefficiency: *overload* and *apathy*. The first of these is a situation in which demands outstrip the available reservoirs of confidence, thus overwhelming a state's ability to process claims in an effective manner; the other is one in which looming problems are obscured by a pervasive trust in authorities that outpaces rather insipid demands. In fact, the past generation has witnessed the simultaneous exacerbation of overload via the proliferation of powerful "special interests," and the rise of apathy as signaled by mediocre electoral participation and a persistent "confidence gap" in major American institutions, including the state and political parties. These trends have continued into the 1990s and alongside the recent rise of a "new patriotism" in which people are "feeling good again about America."

The Cross-Pressures Perspective

A revised version of the cross-pressures perspective helps us to understand why the American polity can be apathetic and hyperactive at the same moment. What is this perspective, and why and how must we modify it before use?

The final chapter of *Voting* (Berelson, Lazarsfeld, and McPhee 1954, pp. 305–23) inspired a generation of political sociologists concerned with how efficient democratic participation is achieved and understanding its wider ramifications (see, particularly, Lipset [1960] 1981). It is often erroneously assumed that this celebrated chapter is primarily about the *social-psychological* paradox that ignorant and apathetic Americans often provide our polity with an unexpected source of vitality and flexibility. Actually, its major thrust is to explore implications of the fact that political formations flow primarily from a society's *social structural* bases. *Voting*, along with its predecessor studies (notably Lazarsfeld, Berelson, and Gaudet 1944), found that party identification, political opinions, and voting decisions are most significantly shaped by people's familial, communal, and other primary groups and much less by the issues per se.

What forces, Berelson, Lazarsfeld, and McPhee wondered, can check the rigidities and polarization that arise because group affiliations have a decisive impact on people's political preferences and conduct? They argued that rigidity and conflict are attenuated when a polity is capable of balancing the competing requisites of confidence and demands (especially of indifference versus involvement and consensus versus conflict) via a "heterogeneous public." Specifically, Berelson, Lazarsfeld, and McPhee declared:

> In short, our electoral system calls for apparently incompatible properties—which, although they cannot reside in each individual voter, can (and do) reside in a heterogeneous electorate. What seems to be required of the electorate as a whole is a *distribution* of qualities along important dimensions. We need some people who are active . . . , others in the middle, and still others passive. The contradictory things we want from the total require that the parts be different. (1954, p. 314)

Cross-pressured voters—those holding conflicting positions in society—were seen as playing a critical role. The authors of *Voting* found that in 1948 Elmira citizens who were cross-pressured identified less with the two major parties, knew less about the issues, made their election decisions later, and were less likely to vote. Ironically, these marginal political persons were hailed by Berelson, Lazarsfeld, and McPhee as the inadvertent saviors of (what we have called) political viability. Their overlapping affiliations balanced confidence and demands by dampening the polarizing effects of socially structured conflict while providing a flexible social basis for future political alignments. *Voting* presented middle-class Catholics and working-class Protestants as quintessential cross-pressured Americans (of the late 1940s).[4] Lipset summarizes this perspective's core findings:

Cross-pressures resulting from multiple-group affiliations or loyalties account for much of the "deviation" from the dominant pattern of a given group. Individuals who are subject to pressures driving them in different political directions must either deviate or "escape into apathy." Multiple-group identification has the effect of reducing the emotion in political choices. ([1960] 1981, p. 13)

Despite the major contributions of the cross-pressures perspective,[5] it suffers from three key deficiencies: an overemphasis on the polity's public tier, an overly "atomistic" analysis of the interests motivating political participation, and a resulting inability to anticipate the malign effects of cross pressures. As we shall see, adding vertical and macrosociological dimensions to the cross-pressures approach allows us to reinvigorate the notion of cross pressures to explore why both apathy and overload plague the American polity at the same time.

The Vertical Dimension

The concepts of "heterogeneous public" and "cross pressures" are not sufficiently vertical: Because they focus our attention on the polity's lowest rung—the public—they give the erroneous impression that participation is explained adequately by analyzing this tier. While public-level bonds may be most decisive in shaping voting behavior, all four intrapolity levels play a role in the mobilization of involvement: The public, organizations, and parties all create and process confidence and demands; the state, for the most part, is the target rather than the conveyor of influence.[6]

As noted in Chapter 1, as one ascends from the public to the organization to the party levels, bureaucratization, political consciousness, and the capacity for political action increase, while group size decreases. Moreover, voluntary associations, interest groups (including social movements), and political parties are all "gatekeepers" of influence: By restricting, remolding, and editing the confidence and demands that are implicit in the public's mood, they permit some features to move up to the state and hold others back. The risks of distortion are ubiquitous. Organizational interests rather than public needs and sentiments often shape what is finally passed upward. But in a large, complex polity such as the United States the intervening tiers remain essential, for the public in isolation cannot otherwise influence the state directly in any sustained manner.

Political influence is more complex than this upward-flow imagery suggests, however. For one thing, the impetus for confidence and demands can originate at any point: in the "public opinions" of familial, communal, and other primary groups; in the associational webs that bind these groups together; in interest groups and social movements[7] claiming to represent the "public interest" or specific public-tier constituencies; or in political parties seeking to put together agendas capable of winning popular support and electing officials. In the United States, if a form of influence originates above the public tier, the initiators must usually resort to downward consultation. For example, if an interest group presses a claim, it must persuade its "constituents" to support it. Interest groups "have always been concerned about public opinion," according to Everett Ladd (1987, p. 438), "but they now devote greater resources . . . to the measurement of opinion through polls and to efforts to demonstrate through poll data that the people are on their side." Generally, nothing "turns off" political authorities faster than the discovery that an interest group has no constituency base.[8]

Moreover, the upward-flow imagery may obscure influences that skip levels. The direct access of lobbyists to federal decision makers is perhaps the most clear-cut illustration of this pattern. Although the close bond between regulatory agencies and those whom they regulate is the most highly visible manifestation of this, elected officials are also affected. Pressure groups' access to Congress is a long-standing instance of skipping. The explosion of PACs—initially mechanisms to finance election campaigns—since 1974 has probably increased the proclivity to skip levels. Critics charge that PACs not only weaken democratic institutions by subverting the electoral process; they also distort state decision making and encourage the corruption of elected as well as nonelected officials.

A WORD REGARDING THE MASS MEDIA

At first glance, the mass media do not fit neatly into our model of the political participation process. Yet, because it is now fashionable in some quarters to blame the media (particularly television) for many of the major inefficiencies in American political involvement (e.g., the debasement of the electoral process), their role in our polity deserves a closer look. Moreover, critics often treat the media and their alleged inefficiencies as if they were a sui generis phenomenon and a malevolent force "outside" our multitiered polity.

In fact, the media are best considered an organization-level phenomenon. News reporting, it is generally agreed, plays an essential role in shaping confidence and demands for all modern polities. In particular, the day-to-day functioning of democratic influence is heightened through the availability of ample and credible information about political events and actions. The horizontal and geographical dispersion within and among polities and not just their vertical structure dictates that news reporting can no longer operate effectively as a locally based cottage industry. Yet, while the mass media tend to operate above the public tier, they are not (in democratic systems at least) lodged on the party or state levels. Treatment of the media as a unique organization-tier factor permits a more sober assessment of their purported adverse effects on political participation.

The mass media's impacts on participation are very different from those of voluntary associations, interest groups, and social movements. Declarations that the media have replaced these other organization-level actors—and thereby eroded efficient participation—are unjustified. These other entities still thrive and strive to integrate and mobilize constituencies on the public tier as well as to represent them to higher levels. In the course of these activities, they sometimes employ in-house newspapers, magazines, and even radio and television broadcasts. But these are not the core functions of the contemporary mass media: Today's principal mass media actors (the television networks, mass circulation magazines, and highly influential national newspapers) inform the public-at-large rather than speak for particular sectors of the public. Indeed, this informational role is so integral to the mass media's legal mandate that one can readily be led to assume mistakenly that only the public is the target. While public information may be their primary objective, the media also have important consequences for political actors on the organization, party, and state levels.

The provision of information is probably the most obvious effect they have for actors on the same and higher tiers. Cable News Network, for instance, was said to be a pivotal source of information for American military and diplomatic planners during the Gulf War. The mass media's roles in unraveling the Watergate and Iran-Contra scandals are also instructive examples. True, the media were here decisive in rousing a previously indifferent public (which no doubt helped provide congressional leaders with the requisite "courage" to pursue both matters). Yet in each case the media also channeled information directly to state-level actors. How often during both investigations were members of the legislative, administrative, and executive branches (as well as independent counsels) reported as saying something like, "I wasn't aware of *that* until I read it in this morning's *Washington Post,*" or "*New York Times,*" or "heard it on 'Nightline'"? The variegated and complex nature of modern political participation makes it inevitable that even insiders (those on the organization, party, and state levels) cannot depend entirely on routine internal (official and informal) channels of communication.

In short, the mass media are unique organization-level actors. Their main mobilizing role is in all likelihood a downward one: to provide the general public with information about actions on higher tiers. But they have more than a downward thrust insofar as they provide those on higher tiers with vital information.

Have the mass media contributed to contemporary political inefficiency? Current analyses of this question are prone to covertly reintroduce a "mass society" model.[9] Fundamentally, the mass society thesis sees modern men and women as trapped on an atomized public tier, unprotected by intervening groups, and directly manipulable by powerful elites. The elites in question, in the present instance, are the mass media. We citizens are regarded as spiritually and socially naked before our television sets. Most contemporary communications research assumes an "informational hegemony" wherein media blitzes directly shape the political consciousness of individuals. Hamilton and Wright provide a thoughtful and balanced summary of this approach:

> There is an obvious mass media role . . . ; most of those distant events that appear to determine the general con-

sensus about important national problems are matters about which the population would know little or nothing were it not for media coverage. An important implication follows: through their choices in reporting the media have considerable influence on popular views about what are the central or urgent concerns. Theirs is, indeed, an agenda setting function. Some room for error is possible in this process; a mistaken judgment, the easy (or gullible) acceptance of source material, or collective misperception could, of course, lead to a corresponding error within the general population. (1986, pp. 328–29)

Yet mass society approaches systematically ignore the potentially pivotal role of "influentials" or "opinion leaders" so decisively spelled out in an older two-step theory of communication (see, particularly, Katz and Lazarsfeld 1955; Berelson and Steiner 1964, pp. 546–55). This latter tradition claimed to have disproved the mass society thesis, at least regarding the role of the media. Instead, the proponents of the two-step theory found that media signals were refracted through people's affiliations: Groups (mainly on the public level but in voluntary associations and even interest groups as well) and the most influential figures in these groups decode media messages for the average person. Contemporary research too often tends to act as if these studies had never occurred. So, for example, reports of who "won" and "lost" the three presidential and vice-presidential debates in 1988 assumed that Americans made their decisions sitting alone in their living rooms in front of their television sets.

Such omissions are not trivial. They have led to the widespread impression that television in particular is having an increasingly pulverizing impact on the production of confidence and demands. In other words, the telecommunications media's informational hegemony is allegedly undercutting the "classical" contributions of primary relations, voluntary associations, interest groups, social movements, and especially political parties. Such complaints reach a crescendo around the time of presidential elections. In fact, there is not a scintilla of empirical evidence that the two-step flow of communication and the role of intervening group affiliations have any less explanatory relevance now than in the 1940s and 1950s. The allegedly hegemonic impact of today's extensive and sophisticated mass media on the efficiency of political participation has not received the detailed scientific assessment it warrants.

Indeed, other recent researches demonstrate that Americans are hardly a mass society people. They continue to be immersed in intricate networks of familial, communal, and associational affiliations. Moreover, they recognize and value the difference between public and private spheres, and most of their energies and time are devoted to the latter. Politics, by comparison, has a much lower priority in the lives of most citizens. (For a more complete analysis, see Hamilton and Wright 1986, especially pp. 327–73, as well as Gans 1988.) Despite the media's expanded role in shaping confidence and demands, we do not have evidence to demonstrate that they have replaced the polity members who have historically stood between the individual citizen and the state. The mass media may have altered the latter's mobilization roles but probably not these actors' overall input. It is unwarranted to assign to the mass media a single-handed responsibility for lowering political efficiency.

Of course, it would be absurd to argue that the modern mass media have had no impact on the development of political inefficiency. While the media have not destroyed the levels between the public and the state, they have undoubtedly altered their organizational forms. Parties and electioneering have been probably most significantly deformed by the changes in the technology of mass communications over the past generation (Ladd 1987, pp. 478–79). "The biggest single factor," according to Ladd "is the increasing use of television: Candidates can reach far more people through television news coverage, political advertisements, and televised debates than through the most vigorous traditional campaigning" (pp. 478– 79). The Kennedy campaign of 1960 now serves as the "symbolic date" (Panebianco 1988, p. 266) for ushering in these changes—although the success of the famous Nixon "Checkers speech" in 1952 suggests that the process began earlier.

Thus the media's most significant effect is likely to be in fostering political inefficiency on the party level. They have probably accelerated party "decomposition" or "dealignment" (discussed below). How have the changes in communications technology weakened political parties? For one thing, they are "causing an earthquake in party organization: old bureaucratic roles [are] becoming obsolete . . . ; new professional roles are gaining ground" (Panebianco 1988, p. 266). Candidates and party functionaries unfamiliar with how to mount and monitor television campaigns are giving more leverage to so-called media consultants.

Moreover, the media have changed the "terms of political communication" (Panebianco 1988, p. 266). Campaigns increasingly stress personalities over parties, specific issues over party platforms, and expert preparation over grassroots politics. Ladd (1987, p. 555) observes: "The national nominating contests now center not in party committees or conventions but in mass-public-participation primaries across the country. The press has unparalleled resources for covering these campaigns; indeed it is the only institution that can do it." Further, the public looks to the media and not to the parties for up-to-date information about a campaign. Handbills and house-to-house canvasses are seen by campaign experts as quaint anachronisms rather than as reliable techniques. "Political parties," Ladd (1987, p. 555) concludes, "are now ancillary structures in the whole process of communication between candidates and elected officials on one side and voters on the other."

PARTIES AT THE PIVOT

The organization level in all modern polities—via voluntary associations, social movements, interest groups, *and* mass media—has an enormous impact on which expressions of confidence and demands reach the state as well as on how efficiently or inefficiently they are processed. As I have noted, actors from this second tier often penetrate state decision making directly. Generally the mass political party stands at the interface between the state and the public and organization levels in all advanced democracies. The U.S. party system traditionally has been dominated by two great "parties of representation" (Lehman 1977, pp. 151–61; Lipset [1960] 1981, pp. 74–76; Neumann 1956, pp. 403–5) that are noted for their pursuit of heterogeneous bases of support, minimal party intrusion into private spheres, and a greater inclination toward opportunism than to political moralism.[10]

After the Reagan era, we can now see more clearly that Democrat and Republican passions for electoral victory still normally outstrip these parties' zest for ideological purity. Rather than resting on rigidly fixed constituencies, each continues to try to widen its base by drawing adherents from the other's. Both "bargain policies for votes" (Lipset 1968, p. 397). Parties of representation are not capricious, however. In any given election each party struggles "not to try to convert a sizeable number of those disposed to vote for its opponent but to do everything possible to get out the vote among its own supporters" (Lipset 1968, p. 390).

Since the end of the New Deal era, neither Republicans nor Democrats have been able to build the stable coalitions necessary to gain permanent majority status. Instead we have become mired in what Walter Dean Burnham (1970, 1975) has called a period of "party decomposition." He saw this as a necessary but not sufficient step toward "critical realignments" such as occurred in 1896 and 1932. "Critical realignment" refers to "a major change rooted in the behavior of critically large minorities of American voters that durably alters electoral coalitions, the shape of election outcomes, and the flow of public policy" (Burnhám 1975, p. 246).

Despite the expectations raised in 1980,[11] the long-anticipated realigning election does not seem imminent. Further, realignment is not the simple phenomenon it first appeared to be. As Ladd notes:

> *Realignment* is commonly used in three different though related meanings: (1) major social groups changing their partisan loyalties and voting differently than they did in times past; (2) a significant net change in the partisan balance of power; and (3) the emergence of a new majority party. Has the American polity experienced realignment? Yes, if either of the first two meanings is employed; no, if the last construction is the one intended. (1987, p. 489)

The shift of blacks to the Democratic ranks over the past generation and the concurrent movement of southern whites in the opposite direction are unquestionably the most striking instances of the first type of realignment. Other switches have also occurred. In particular, younger voters used to be the most Democratic; in the 1980s they became the most Republican. The erosion of support for the Democrats among northern, blue-collar Catholic "ethnics" is less precipitous but of longer duration and of no less significance. The near equality between those who now identify themselves as Republicans and as Democrats (after unchallenged Democratic dominance since the time of Franklin Roosevelt) is an obvious indicator of Ladd's second kind of realignment.

The long-term absence of a durable majority party (the third kind of realignment) has been labeled "dealignment" by some analysts (see, e.g., Phillips 1982). In terms of the multilevel model of the polity, dealignment points to a fractured linkage between the public and organization levels, on the one hand, and parties, on the other.

How do we recognize dealignment when we see it? Party dealignment has two principal manifestations: an individuation of issues and a particularization of elections. The notion of individuation of issues alerts us to parties' inability to mold diverse claims into broad, consistent platforms capable of mobilizing substantial and durable electoral support. We are faced instead with the seeming paradox of a public that favors the general principle of reduced government and at the same time supports demands for more state interventions (see, e.g., Ladd 1978; Morrow 1987). The central thrust of these claims may vary. At some moments the public and its spokespersons may be more concerned about crime or national security; at other moments their demands may be "kinder and gentler" and give special emphasis to social programs (e.g., education or the problems of the homeless).

The net result of the individuation of issues is that political parties are becoming *more opportunistic* even while they have apparently become *more ideologically differentiated*. At first glance these trends may seem mutually exclusive. In fact, although the two are not reinforcing, they coexist quite comfortably. The individuation of issues forces office seekers to abandon general principles—even more than they might be temperamentally inclined to—in the pursuit of votes. Concurrently, regional voting shifts have made Democratic elected officials more uniformly less conservative while their Republican colleagues have become more consistently less liberal.[12] The Democrats' loss of their erstwhile "solid" bastion in the South is particularly noteworthy. The party's candidates in this region have been compelled to seek black voters aggressively, and consequently the party has produced a brand of "southern moderate" official unimaginable a generation ago. At the same time, new opportunities among southern whites have made Republican conservativism a much more marketable commodity there. In the final analysis, however, the great majority of politicians (of both parties) fall somewhere between the two Jesses, Jackson and Helms; hence opportunism propelled by the individuation of issues is a more potent motive for political behavior than is increasing ideological consistency within one's party.

The particularization of elections refers to a rise in voter discontinuity and means that choices in each election or contest have little bearing on subsequent choices and are themselves relatively unaffected by previous decisions. Candidates are working even harder to "bargain policies for votes" because they feel less certain of a bedrock of group-based support for their party from election to election. Ticket splitting is probably the most frequently mentioned instance here, but the apparent discontinuity in voting decisions across elections is equally important. Tuckel and Tejera (1983) found, for example, that factors that in the past have smoothed out the electoral process—particularly the so-called midterm congressional swing, party strength, and incumbency (apart from the capacity to raise campaign funds)—have far less effect today than they did in the 1950s. The impact of changes in communications technology, above all the growing role of television, have had a similar impact here (as suggested in the previous section).

Despite the inefficiencies of today's parties, they continue to be the linchpin tying the public and organization levels to the state. To begin with, American parties of representation are not embedded in a "polarized plural" party system (Sartori 1966, 1976); there are only two major parties, and neither is antisystem nor in permanent or semipermanent opposition (especially when one includes the local and state sectors of the state). Such a constellation contains fewer built-in impediments to the mobilization of adequate levels of confidence and even legitimacy. In other words, since each party has an authentic prospect for winning key offices from time to time, both Democrats and Republicans have an interest in maintaining some trust in public officials (even when they are from the other party) and certainly in encouraging enthusiastic support for the moral principles undergirding the system.

Yet American parties have lost some key functions over the past generation. Polsby (1982, pp. 6–7) emphasizes their decline as welfare and patronage intermediaries, along with their diminished ability to monopolize the nominating process. Nevertheless, he argues, parties retain two important roles: They still monopolize the "labels which channel the preferences of voters," and they provide the organizational basis for coordinating relations between state officials and legislative bodies. Polsby (1982, pp. 6–8) notes that in playing these roles, parties must provide settings for "the promulgation and elaboration of public policies" and for making nominations and conducting election campaigns. (For a fuller elaboration of these views, see Polsby 1983.)

Since dealignment and its concomitants are particularly decisive forms of inefficiency, it is instructive to inquire about the roles of public and organization-level factors. In other words, if parties are the pivot for the analysis of inefficiency, then the other tiers are profitably treated as their environments. This application of an organizations-environment approach to the study of political participation warns us that the parties' mediation of confidence and demands should not be studied in isolation. Nor should parties be treated simply as "black boxes" whose responses to environmental changes (particularly in the electoral arena) are automatic. Instead, their relative success and failure—indeed, their overall adaptation, growth, and decline—are more fully understood if we see them as complex organizations (viz., deliberately structured and restructured goal-seeking actors) with varying capacities to master pressures from the public, organization, and state levels. (For an overview of the organizations-environment approach, see Aldrich 1979; for an application to parties, see Panebianco 1988.)

The two levels below parties—the public and organization tiers—exert especially crucial pressures toward dealignment. Over the past three decades changes on these two rungs have produced the most turbulent sectors of the parties' environments. That is, significant changes have occurred in the communal, familial, and occupational sectors of people's lives as well as in their associations, interest groups, and social movements. These changes have fostered a good deal of uncertainty for political parties and hence have contributed to dealignment. They have also generated inefficiencies on their primary sites as well. A more macrosociological understanding of cross pressures helps us to describe and explain these inefficiencies more fully.

The Macrosociological Dimension

Over the past twenty-five years or so, the works of Amitai Etzioni, Erik Olin Wright, Norbert Wiley, and Morris Janowitz have made possible a renewed, more macrosociological appreciation of cross pressures. These sociologists have employed disparate presuppositions and models, and they have addressed different concrete problems. Yet a reading of their works demonstrates that (1) cross pressures are group, not just individual, phenomena, (2) critical cross pressures have occurred within the public sphere because of economic changes and growing tensions between economic and community life, and (3) they have also arisen between the public and higher tiers, since interest groups find it increasingly difficult to mobilize the cross-pressured sectors of the public.

Of the four, only Etzioni (1968, pp. 451–560) explicitly seeks to refurbish the cross-pressures perspective. He charges that the tradition paints an unduly "atomized" portrait of the potential partisans in which groups are equated with single ("mono-faceted") social attributes. In fact, collective actors on the public level (such as social classes, ethnic groups, and even local communities) are defined by several attributes (they are "multi-faceted"). Often one of these is economic, but others may be religious, racial or ethnic, educational, territorial, or based on lineage. For example, to be an Irish-American entails being Catholic and in the past implied urban residence, working-class status, a parochial school education, and an allegiance to the Democratic party. It seems likely that national and local collectivities occur at the empirical intersection of two or more social categories, such as class, race or ethnicity, religion, or education.

An atomistic bias distorts our picture of the cross-pressured. Such people are treated as isolated, marginal, and possibly psychologically distressed. Etzioni (1968, p. 452) argues: "The well-to-do Negroes and the Tory workers are often cited as typical examples of persons caught in cross pressures. But there is some evidence that these two groupings are ecologically, associationally, and organizationally segregated from the collectivities that are said to pressure them—poor Negroes and well-to-do whites, labor workers, and the Tory middle class." Thus, such persons are often not marginal but members of emerging subcollectivities or communities with "unbalanced" rankings. Moreover, how people handle potential conflicts is more fully explained with the introduction of sociological—indeed, macrosociological—variables.

Finally, Etzioni notes, traditional cross-pressures analysis treats the attributes of all members of collectivities as if they occur on the same level of mobilization. Many individual traits point to affiliations on the public level. These are bound to such stratification factors as class, religion, ethnicity, education, and community. Other traits are linked to activities in voluntary associations, interest groups, and political parties. Yet these latter factors too are analyzed as if they are "natural" or spontaneous public-tier occurrences. This conflation of levels creates problems for social-psychological analysis because organization and party affiliations are seen as shaping a person's political moods and actions in the same way as public-level ties do. In fact, we know that participation in voluntary associations, interest groups, social movements, and parties entails far greater consciousness and activism than public-level bonds, which tend to function as background factors in shaping political opinions and behaviors.

This conflation has far more serious consequences when the unit of analysis becomes the polity rather than individual citizens. Political analysts often confuse public-level and organization-level groups. They speak of newly aware and active political participants such the elderly, blacks, Hispanics, gays and lesbians, and women as if these are inevitably interest groups. The phenomena they are pointing to are, many times, the opinions and voting shifts of constituencies on the public level. Conversely, the accomplishments of interest groups are frequently confused with the demands of the constituents they claim to represent. Geraldine Ferraro's nomination for vice president in 1984, for example, was explained more fully by the pressures of feminist interest groups and less by the actions of women-as-public.

What are the main macroscopic cross pressures on the public level, and how do these affect the conduct of organization-tier agents? Cross pressures in advanced societies have two public foci: within the economic (or class) nexus itself, and between economic life and residential or community life. Erik Olin Wright (1978, 1985) and Norbert Wiley (1967) have demonstrated that one-dimensional notions of economic position no longer make sense, the former drawing inspiration from Marxist structuralism and the latter from the Weberian tradition.

Wright (1978, pp. 61–110) has developed the concept of "contradictory locations within class relations" to better understand those economic positions that do not have a class identity in the Marxist sense but whose "class character" is determined by their location between such classes. Wright (1978) provisionally identified three contradictory locations: (1) managers who fall between the working class and the bourgeoisie, (2) small employers who occupy a position between the bourgeoisie and the petty bourgeoisie, and (3) semiautonomous employees who are located between the petty bourgeoisie and the working class. Wright (1985, pp. 42–57, 86–98) subsequently discovered a number of theoretical and methodological problems with this formulation. As a consequence he has extended the notion of contradictory locations beyond capitalism to other class systems (feudalism and state bureaucratic socialism) as well. Perhaps more important, he elaborates twelve classes for capitalist society using three dimensions to locate class: ownership of the means of production, organizational position, and skills/credentials. Nine of the twelve are expansions of his three original contradictory locations; eight of the nine are elaborations of the manager and semiautonomous employee categories.

The principal gains from using the concept of "contradictory locations within class relations" are to demonstrate the superiority of multidimensional images of class and to show that actors experiencing conflicting economic interests do not represent anomalies but are strategically lodged in all advanced societies. Wright's treatment of the impact of contradictory locations on political participation remains somewhat elusive, however. Sometimes he seems to see actors in such positions as having distinctive interests and objectives of their own. He argues that the principal contradictory locations under different modes of production (the bourgeoisie under feudalism, managers/bureaucrats under capitalism, intelligentsia/experts under state socialism) often are the prime beneficiaries of revolutions rather than the "oppressed class" (Wright 1985, pp. 86–92). "Most notably," he says,

> It was not the peasantry who became the ruling class with the demise of feudalism, but the bourgeoisie, a class that was located outside the principal exploitation relation of feudalism. A similar argument could be extended to manager-bureaucrats with respect to capitalism and experts with respect to state bureaucratic socialism: in each case these constitute potential rivals to the existing ruling class. (Pp. 89–90)

At other times Wright seems to believe that those in contradictory locations must cast their lots with either the ruling or the oppressed (i.e., the noncontradictory) classes (1985, pp. 124–26). In the matter of "class alliances," he argues:

> Individuals in contradictory locations within class relations face a choice among three broad strategies in their relationship to the class struggle: first, they can try to use their position as exploiters to gain entry as individuals into the dominant exploiting class itself; second, they can attempt to forge an alliance with the dominant exploiting class; third, they can form some kind of alliance with the principal exploited class. (P. 124)

Wiley (1967) provides a more explicit definition for the multipositional bases of class location. Following Weber, he sees three market positions embedded in the class situation: labor, credit, and commodity. The labor market, the most frequently analyzed, divides people into owners or managers and workers; the credit or money market separates them into creditors and debtors; and the commodity market distinguishes between sellers and buyers as well as landlords and tenants. Wiley contends that the presence or absence of cross pressures along these three dimensions clarifies several puzzles in the history of American politics. Moreover, he believes that his multidimensional analysis of class conflicts reduces the need to invoke noneconomic explanatory variables such as alienation, mass society, and status protest.

Wiley applies his framework to three concrete historical issues regarding participation. First, he uses class cross pressures to explain the failure of agrarian and labor protesters to forge an enduring alliance at the end of the nineteenth century. Second, he argues that the often-cited association between small business affiliations and radical right-wing politics is explained more fully by class-based cross pressures than by notions of status protest. Finally, Wiley explains black "unruly" protests of the 1960s in terms of blacks' contradictory locations in the commodity market, again providing a multi-dimensional economic account where nonclass factors have often been used.

Wiley's analysis leaves us unsure whether the pivotal cross pressures are located exclusively on the public level or *also* arise from the interaction between unbalanced subcollectivities from this level and the organizations that seek to mobilize them. Janowitz (1978, pp. 221–63, 300–19) clarified this matter. He obviously preferred the second option, since he made the case that a crucial source of political inefficiency is the growing inability of organization-tier actors to mobilize a more heterogeneous public in a broad and consistent manner. Yet Janowitz was not unaware of the increasing stresses on the public level. In effect, he regarded public-level cross pressures as the necessary but not sufficient ingredient of much of today's inefficiency. Unlike Wright and Wiley, however, Janowitz did not see contradictory public-level locations as simply a class or economic matter. Rather, he pointed to the growing rift between economic and residential (community) spheres as the key locus of conflict. It is now commonplace to assert that a fissuring of work and residence has profoundly shaped the modern world; but wide currency makes this point no less important. (For an overview of this issue, see Bendix 1974. His analysis builds primarily on the works of Max Weber, who used the insight as the basis for the now-classic distinction between classes and status groups.)

Janowitz traced this separation's impact on American political participation from the early 1920s through the mid-1970s. The gulf between where people work and where they conduct their private lives has been widening since the onset of the Industrial Revolution, he noted, but has become decisive in the United States only since the end of the First World War. Political parties must now deal with a "dual system" on the organization level spawned by the separation: organizations that are work-based, and "those embedded in the familial residential setting." The work-based organizations include groupings of "economic entrepreneurs, industrial managers, professionals, and trade unionists" (Janowitz 1978, p. 302). These actors' power and the resources they command now vastly exceed the clout of community-based organizations.

Nevertheless, community-based organizations are not without political leverage. Since the community is the site of elections, political parties cannot afford to ignore local organizations. The residential focus of our electoral system often has encouraged attempts by work-based organizations to penetrate community units. When such efforts succeeded, they fostered the illusion that coordination between work and community interests was a relatively simple matter. The business elite, having found new ways to affect the electoral process, now feels less pressed to gain access to community organizations. "In contrast," Janowitz (1978, p. 304) declared, "the trade union movement in the United States has energetically tried to strengthen its institutional base and expand its political influence by using local community and religious organizations." "However," he continued,

> The long-term trends toward dispersion of industrial plant and the increased length and diversity in the journey to work have weakened the links between trade unions and local community after 1960. The trade union became more and more an occupationally based interest group with less support from the community-based leadership. . . . The task of community leadership falls more upon indigenous personnel with limited external support or to a limited number of political party agents; and thereby such "working-class" localities have few direct linkages with the industrial sector. (P. 305)

The chasm between work and residence has also been widened by the resurgence of racial and ethnic politics. The rise of the welfare state has had an impact too because most new entitlements since the 1960s have gone to citizens by virtue of their age, familial, or residential statuses rather than their occupations. The net result is a citizenry that finds it progressively more difficult to coordinate work-based economic interests with the community's "lifestyle" concerns. "We are in essence dealing," Janowitz (1978, p. 546) concluded, "not with the monopolization of political power by tiny elite groups, but with new forms of dispersion of political influence which lead to the inability to create meaningful majorities which can effectively govern."

Janowitz's analysis is readily applicable to the rise of the gender gap (i.e., the tendency of greater proportions of women than men— notably working women—to support liberal causes; see Goertzel 1983; Klein 1984), "women's issues," and feminist politics generally (although he did not treat these topics). Specifically, his approach sharpens our understanding of the general increase of cross pressures among women in recent times (see also Epstein 1970), the parallel expansion in women's issues, and why women remain divided politically even over a "women's issue" such as abortion (see, e.g., Luker 1984). These developments have been accelerated by both the growing separation of home and work (intensified by an increased participation by women in the latter sector and the coinciding decline of the role of the traditional housewife) and the concomitant multiplication of specialized interest groups for different categories of women.

Families (or households) continue to be pivotal actors in societal stratification. While the family is the vehicle for assigning a common rank to all its members in class- or status-group terms, it has always produced and reproduced internal inequality and conflicts between men and women (Curtis 1986, pp. 168–83). Thus, on the one hand, the structure of the family has ensured that women have continued to share a common lot in the matter of gender inequality; at the same time, it has guaranteed that they have remained divided along such other stratification dimensions as race, class, and religion. It has never been a matter of being a woman *or* being black *or* being poor. Rather, one is, for example, either a white woman *or* a black woman, an affluent woman *or* a poor woman, a Protestant woman, a Catholic woman, *or* a Jewish woman (or, more likely, some combination of all three of these factors).

Moreover, the impact of cross pressures on women has been further complicated by the differentiation of family from occupational life along with women's rapid entry into the labor market. Notably, these factors have altered the nature of the gender inequalities women must face and the intragender conflicts they experience. These inequalities and conflicts no longer unfold exclusively (or primarily) in household and community contexts. The forces that led women simultaneously to be treated as inferior and yet divided among themselves have now spilled over to the labor market. The result has been the growing consciousness of distinctive women's issues related to work (e.g., affirmative action, comparable worth, sexual harassment) beyond those associated with the community and home (e.g., abortion, domestic violence, Aid to Families with Dependent Children). Further, a seeming conflict of interest has arisen between women who are in the labor market and those who are not, with the former far more liberal on both class- and status-politics issues. These developments clarify the ascendancy, tenacity, and political clout of a spectrum of interest groups that claim to organize and speak for this one gender; they also clarify why these groups sometimes disagree so strongly with one another.

In short, Etzioni, Wright, Wiley, and Janowitz has each contributed to a renewed, more macrosociological study of cross pressures. All recognize that the elementary forms of cross pressures appear on the public level, and they see that reverberations from these elementary factors assume a relevance of their own on higher tiers (although only Etzioni and Janowitz give this point the emphasis it deserves). The articulation of the public's interests in modern times, after all, depends on these tiers. The efficient operation of interest groups and voluntary associations is difficult enough in the abstract; but their problems are only exacerbated by the growth of contradictory locations on the public level within the economic, work, or class situation itself (Wright and Wiley) and, perhaps more critically, between workplace and community (Janowitz). Etzioni (1968, p. 452) may have been unduly optimistic in calling today's cross-pressured "atypical minorities." Once we consider contradictory locations within class relations as well as between work and home, this atypical minority swells and may even include the majority of adult Americans—particularly if we take cross-pressured women into account.

Macroscopic cross pressures of the kinds we have been consider-
ing weaken citizens' ability to calculate a consistent set of interests
across sectors and time. They obviously make the efforts of organizations struggling to speak for such women and men particularly
vexatious. Cross pressures of this magnitude do not produce the
benign balancing of confidence and demands envisaged by the authors of *Voting*. Instead, they have given rise to the turbulent environment facing our two major parties. Moreover, they account for
the simultaneous appearance of seemingly antithetical inefficiencies.

The Inefficiencies of Macro–Cross Pressures

Samuel Huntington (1981) hypothesizes that American political inefficiencies have gone through four recurring stages: moralistic reform
(or moralism), cynicism, complacency, and hypocrisy. Each represents a different way of coping with the gap between the ideals of
the American Creed and institutional realities. Moralistic reform be-
speaks a deep commitment to eliminating this gap. "The moralistic
response occurs," Huntington (1981, p. 68) says, "when people feel
intensely committed to American political values . . . and attempt to
restructure institutions and practices to reflect these ideals." Cynicism refers to tolerating this gap. It surfaces because "people can
sustain high levels of moral indignation for only limited periods of
time. . . . Moral indignation is replaced by moral helplessness. All
politicians are crooks, all institutions corrupt. The gap must be accepted—and perhaps even enjoyed" (Huntington 1981, pp. 68–69).
Complacency means ignoring the gap. It refers to a renewed surge
of privatism rather than a disdain for politicians and institutions.
People begin to turn away from the public arena. Privatism becomes
complete only during the hypocritical stage, however.[13] Hypocrisy is
a denial of the gap. "American institutions are seen to be open and
democratic"; under this response, according to Huntington (1981, p.
70), "America is the land of opportunity; the equality of man is a fact
of American life; the United States is the land of the free and the
home of the brave; it is the embodiment of government of the people, by the people, and for the people." In Huntington's theory,
hypocritical phases inevitably generate the discontent that fuels a
new moralistic surge.

Huntington's four stages have been expressed as imbalances between demands and confidence (Lehman 1985). Moralism reflects

rising claims on the state; the other three are related to demand deficits. Moralistic reform entails the kind of increasing demands that leads to *overload;* confidence levels may vary, but the reservoirs available are never sufficient given the growing volume of petitions. Cynicism, complacency, and hypocrisy are manifestations of *apathy.* Each involves declining political demands; the volume of claims never taxes state capacities. Of course, confidence varies. Cynicism means withdrawing significant levels of confidence from authorities. Complacency implies a more "agnostic" stance—it refers to a suspension of new inputs of confidence. Hypocrisy is the coupling of lowered demands with an infusion of higher confidence.

Huntington uses his four responses longitudinally as well as cross-sectionally. His main thrust is in the former direction, since his primary objective is to analyze cycles in American history. I, for the most part, use them cross-sectionally, since my focus is on the concurrent features of today's inefficient participation. Each type has contemporary manifestations, all of which have been mentioned earlier. Moralism is reflected in the proliferation of single-interest groups that threaten to overload the polity. Cynicism is found in the decline in trust in officials and in slipping party loyalties. Complacency is expressed in America's low rates of voter turnout. Hypocrisy is manifested in the rise of a "new patriotism."

A multilevel and macrosociological view of cross pressures clarifies how these disparate inefficiencies are able to occur in the same overall political space and time and foster a "turbulent environment" for political parties. The decisive factors (as indicated previously) are the increasingly cross-pressured character of life on the public level and the concomitant dilemmas faced by interest groups and social movements when mobilizing "unbalanced subcollectivities."

Yet *systematic* study of cross pressures as multitiered, macrosociological phenomena remains neglected. In particular, the impact of "contradictory locations within class relations" on political mobilization deserves close attention. The conflict between work and residence has been studied much more fully, albeit from a distinctly social-psychological perspective (for an overview, see Lipset [1960] 1981, pp. 503–21). In this latter context, two cross-pressured subcollectivities have been assigned critical significance. The first includes the blue-collar workers whom unions can no longer mobilize, alluded to by Janowitz. These people tend to be white Protestants in the South and "ethnics," mainly Catholics, elsewhere. Their class affiliations have kept them relatively liberal in economic concerns (class politics), but their community ties have made them increasingly conservative on lifestyle issues such as family, sex, drugs, crime, court-ordered integration, and national security (status politics). On the other hand, some commentators (mostly those with a neoconservative outlook) have discerned the emergence of a new subcollectivity that they call the "new class" and journalists prefer calling "yuppies" (for "young urban professionals"). The existence and composition of this "new class" as well as its possible political tilt are still matters of considerable dispute (see, e.g., Brint 1984; Bruce-Briggs 1979). Nevertheless, it is generally assumed that its key potential members are highly affluent post-1960s college graduates, many of whom are professionals or managers in the expanding knowledge and service industries. These people still tend to identify themselves as liberals, but they have become increasingly conservative on class-politics issues. Nevertheless, on such status-politics issues as environment and quality of life, abortion, gay rights, and leaner defense budgets, the yuppies continue to hold decidedly liberal (perhaps even libertarian) opinions.

Cynicism, complacency, and hypocrisy spring from cross pressures on the public tier. Both blue-collar whites and yuppies display each of these responses. Moralism, on the other hand, flows from the strain between the organization and public rungs and is articulated by polity members on the former level.

As noted previously, past research shows that political opinions, party identification, and electoral behavior are influenced strongly by public-level affiliations. That is, most people turn to relatives, neighbors, friends, coworkers, and other local "influentials" in making such choices. If an organization-level influence is felt in these matters, it is much more likely to come from community-based voluntary associations than from interest groups or social movements. Thus, the cynical and complacent responses of weakened trust in authorities, lowered identification with parties, and mediocre electoral turnouts are likely to be the products of public-tier cross pressures. These relationships, after all, were identified over thirty-five years ago by the original works on cross pressures. The factors promoting the hypocritical "new patriotism" appear to be more complex.

Is American public-level participation currently more cynical, complacent, or hypocritical? This question is worth asking because it is, in effect, an inquiry about whether the public is withdrawing confidence, has merely suspended new inputs, or has increased trust in political leaders over the past couple of decades. The hypocritical response of "feeling good again about America" is a relatively recent, Reagan-era manifestation. So let us put consideration of it aside for the moment. Cynicism and complacency in their present guises have been among the public much longer, and thus it is appropriate to speculate about which of these two inefficiencies has been more pivotal since the end of the 1960s.

One can gauge the relative tilt between these two forms of apathy by examining whether diminished electoral involvement (an indicator of complacency) has accelerated more rapidly than the "confidence gap" toward authorities and eroding party identification (indicators of cynicism). When the question is framed in these terms, it is clear that we have experienced a considerable withdrawal of confidence by the public during the past three decades (greater cynicism) over and above just the rise of "wait-and-see" attitudes (more complacency). In the seventeen years from the assassination of John F. Kennedy to the election of Ronald Reagan, many observers noted much greater fluidity in party identification and a concurrent rise in the proportions of "independents" (see Janowitz 1978, pp. 106–11; Ladd 1987, pp. 489–510; Milbrath and Goel 1977, pp. 43–85; Nie, Verba, and Petrocik 1976; Piven and Cloward 1988, pp. 122–80) as well as a precipitous drop in trust in officeholders (see Hamilton and Wright 1986, pp. 361–73; Janowitz 1978, pp. 111–13; Lipset and Schneider 1983). Electoral turnouts, on the other hand, although somewhat diminished since the 1960s, are roughly the same as during the New Deal era. In presidential elections, the peak turnout over the past sixty years or so occurred in 1960, when about 63 percent of eligible voters went to the polls. For the last five presidential elections, the comparable figures are 56 percent in 1972, 53 percent in 1976, 54 percent in 1980, 53 percent in 1984, and 50 percent in 1988. The turnout in Franklin Roosevelt's four elections ranged from 52 to 59 percent; the figure for the Truman-Dewey-Thurmond-Wallace race of 1948 is 51 percent (see, especially, Janowitz 1978, pp. 85–111).[14]

There can be no doubt that the Reagan era marked the end of nearly two decades of across-the-board withdrawal of political confidence. This event has often been called the "new patriotism," and it meets our criterion for hypocritical response since it is the unbalanced coupling of lower levels of demands with rising confidence. The label "new patriotism" is something of a misnomer, however, because it conjures up images of old-fashioned flag-waving enthusiasm. To be sure, some recrudescence of traditional nationalistic sentiments is part of the picture, as the euphoria created by the quick victory in the Gulf War attests, but other elements are at least as important. In particular, our recent hypocritical response also includes the bottoming out of the "confidence gap" and the rise of self-congratulatory privatism.

From 1965 through the early 1980s, Americans' level of confidence in their political leaders dropped precipitously (Lipset and Schneider 1983, pp. 13–96). During the Reagan era and through 1991 this steep erosion (particularly in confidence in the presidency) was checked. Yet, in that time no fundamental shift back to pre-1965 levels occurred; cynicism and complacency hardly disappeared. The conclusions voiced by Lipset in a 1985 summary of data on confidence still ring true today:

> The confidence gap still exists. Most Americans remain suspicious of their leaders and of the way their institutions are performing. Good times presided over by a president who is upbeat about the country and its institutions . . . have helped to increase the level of confidence, but it is a change in mood linked to economic effectiveness and presidential performance, not to a sustained conviction that all is well. (1985, p. 60)

Citizens are "feeling good again about America" but in a more special, personal way; these sentiments have taken a distinctly nonpolitical form. The importance of individual accomplishment and privatism took center stage in the 1980s. A 1984 quote in *Time* by former radical Jerry Rubin captures the moment: "People are very patriotic. I'm much more pro-American than I have ever been in my life. It's not that people are optimistic about foreign policy or Government, but about their own power and achievement" (Andersen 1984, p. 16). As Hirschman (1982, p. 129) has noted, "the turn to private life can be viewed as a move toward reality, sincerity, and even humanity." Yet the "ultimate ideological revanche of private over public action," he concludes, "lies in the idea that the creation of wealth (the objective of private action) is fundamentally superior to the pursuit of power, which is seen as the exclusive goal of public action. . . . Total immersion in private life suddenly is felt as a liberating experience" (p. 129).

The flag-waving component of the "new patriotism" has been around a bit longer. Until Desert Storm, the most recent flowering of this more traditional brand of patriotism was among the "hardhats" of the late 1960s. This group has usually been equated with the (previously mentioned) blue-collar whites, and their "new patriotism" has been seen as a reaction to student anti-Vietnam protests. Ironically, the privatistic segment of this impulse blossomed in the 1980s mainly among these same former students, now allegedly transformed into the "new class" or yuppies. In other words, the "new patriotism," like cynical and complacent responses, seems to have significant manifestations among cross-pressured groups. But it tends to take different concrete expressions: Among white workers divided between liberal class politics and conservative status politics, it assumes an old-fashioned "my country right or wrong" rhetoric; among yuppies cross-pressured by an increasingly conservative economic perspective and liberal social positions, the "new patriotism" has emerged primarily as a celebration of their own marketplace achievements. In light of the immense popular support for initiatives such as the Gulf War and invasions of Grenada and Panama, observers have felt little need to disengage the two rhetorics and have been comfortable with the umbrella concept of "new patriotism." Even though the Republican party has been able to capitalize successfully on both in three consecutive presidential elections, the rhetorics actually warrant separate treatment.

In short, we see an American public that, over the past quarter-century, has gone beyond complacency. Mediocre voter turnouts do not tell a complete story; the rising distrust of officials and the drop in party loyalties point toward greater cynicism. Confidence rebounded somewhat during the Reagan years, but this increased hypocrisy was circumscribed. It was limited for the most part to more favorable attitudes toward the presidency, privatistic satisfaction with economic achievements, and more old-fashioned nationalism rather than a broad-scope and decisive turnaround in public confidence.

How can cynicism, complacency, and hypocrisy coexist alongside such contemporary single-issue outbursts as the right-to-life movement, feminism, support for prayer in public schools, animal rights, environmentalism, support for or opposition to gun control, and opposition to nuclear power plants (to name just a few)? The answer lies (as I have indicated) in the fact that moralism is not exclusively a public-tier response; it emerges from the disarticulation between organization and public levels. The key factor is the growing inability of interest groups and social movements to orchestrate a broad self-interest within public constituencies in such a way that work-based interests and family and community concerns come together as a coherent political agenda. If Wright and Wiley are correct, a consistent set of economic interests may be just as difficult to formulate. The proliferation of single-issue interest groups over the past twenty-five years is the result. A citizenry that is unable to visualize, let alone to calculate, an integrated set of political positions becomes particularly receptive to the blandishments of single-interest groups.[15]

Today's interest groups and social movements are more likely not only to have narrowly based constituencies but also to be more moralistic or uncompromising. Etzioni (1968, p. 453) notes that such groups are more moralistic because they "draw from . . . unbalanced subcollectivities [that] are often . . . more intensely committed in their conduct than their positions in the stratification structure would suggest (e.g., small business is more radical than big business)." That is, when interest groups and social movements feel compelled to mobilize cross-pressured public-tier actors around a single or a narrow range of issues, both tend to use a passionate, uncompromising rhetoric. Such public-tier actors are also likely to be more knowledgeable about particular special interest issues than noncross-pressured citizens with whom they share social attributes.

Thus public-level cross pressures help explain the rise of single-interest groups as well as the zealousness exhibited by such entities and by their constituents. They also account for the apparent anomaly that increasingly cynical, complacent, and hypocritical sectors of the public are simultaneously becoming more intensely issue-oriented (see, e.g., Nie, Verba, and Petrocik 1976, pp. 319–44). The answer, it seems to me, lies in the fact that otherwise apathetic cross-pressured citizens are likely to be "turned on" by one or two single-issue groups and hence to be well informed about these special issues and cognate ones (but few others). The multiplication of single-interest pressure groups over the past three decades goes a long way to clarify the uneasy coexistence of an intense public awareness of many disparate issues side by side with increasing signs of overall public apathy.

In one sense the label "moralism" obscures the nature of the current single-issue phenomenon, however. Single-interest means *special interest*. For every monistic status-politics pressure group (e.g., pro-choice, the gun lobby, animal rights, and so forth) there exists a plethora of special-interest class-politics advocates who pursue pecuniary objectives for narrowly defined constituencies. Often these monistic self-interest organizations are labeled economic or industry "lobbies," such as the dairy lobby, the sugar lobby, the aerospace lobby, and the hospital lobby. This alone should signal that such advocates hardly represent the polity's most underprivileged constituencies; the rise of such groups has not apparently led to a substantial reduction in historic inequalities in influence. Moreover, these entities should not be equated with broader-scope class-politics lobbies, such as the AFL-CIO and the Business Roundtable. These latter agencies deal with a wide array of economic issues and speak for larger and more diverse constituencies. The common proposition that economic interest groups employ less dogmatic and more pragmatic rhetoric (as stated, for instance, by Huntington 1981, p. 105) thus requires specification.

I suspect that status-politics advocates are likelier to be social movements (core interest groups with dedicated adherents at their periphery) and that economic advocates more often are "plain" interest groups (organizations with paid staffs and lacking passionate adherents who can be turned out for special events). Moreover, status-politics advocates are probably still more likely to have a "popular" constituency, while class-politics advocates probably continue to have a more "elite" profile (labor unions, of course, being a major exception here). Nevertheless, narrow pecuniary lobbies that have spread so widely in the past two decades are increasingly using the same passionate, persistent, and uncompromising rhetoric as the typical "moralistic" status-politics group. In a word, social movement tactics and rhetoric are becoming more frequent among them. It is hard to say, for example, whether the representatives of farmers or the leaders of Operation Rescue are more ardent in putting their cases forward. In addition, single-interest advocates of various stripes have played a disproportionate role in the growth of PACs since 1974, a development that many believe distorts U.S. campaign financing and subverts the democratic process (see Drew 1983; Etzioni 1984).

The moralistic surge, therefore, is more complex than first meets the eye. Cross pressures on the public tier have indeed made life difficult for broad-based, multi-interest groups. The newer single-minded, single-interest groups are known for their fervor and dedication as well as the anger and fear they arouse in their opponents. Yet their passion is increasingly as likely to be focused on achieving economic gains for a narrow band of beneficiaries (e.g., import quotas on shoes or textiles) as on the pursuit of a "moral" agenda (e.g., the protection of human life). The intensity of the rhetoric (zealotry over pragmatism) and the heightened reliance on social movement tactics, *not* programmatic content (status politics over class politics), is what renders both pecuniary and nonpecuniary single-interest groups *moralistic*.

Further, the rise of single-interest advocates affects the *overloading* of the American system. Their monistic zeal, along with their proliferation, better accounts for the state's inability to absorb their claims than does the sheer number of advocates in today's political marketplace. Daniel Bell correctly notes that an overloaded polity is plagued by the dilemma that "the greater the number of groups, each seeking diverse or competing ends, the more the likelihood that these groups will veto one another's interests, with the consequent sense of frustration and powerlessness as such stalemates incur" (Bell 1973, p. 160). Yet the organizational glut Bell warns of is more the result of the individuation of issues and interests than of the number of groups engaged in the process. More and more pressure groups pursue isolated issues (of either an economic or moral complexion) in the name of narrow constituencies with a zeal that makes bargaining, compromise, and mutual accommodation increasingly difficult.

Conclusions

Our alternative paradigm insists that the problems of political inefficiency cannot be reduced to issues of state ineffectiveness or crises of legitimacy. This chapter has fleshed out the implications of the case. Our multidimensional analysis allows us to observe that when cross pressures are treated in multilevel, macrosociological terms, a clearer picture of contemporary inefficiencies emerges. In particular, a revised cross-pressures approach provides a more theoretically open and empirically comprehensive way to look at the turbulent environment that the American political party system faces at the moment. It has permitted me to hypothesize that macroscopic cross pressures on the public level and between the public and organization tiers have contributed to today's lowered confidence in authorities, declining party loyalties, and ebbing voter turnouts as well as to a self-deluding "new patriotism" and the rise of moralistic single-interest advocates. The proliferation of such monistic groups over the past quarter-century does not seem to have reduced the clout of powerful corporate elites, but it has accelerated the tendency for intensified organization-level moralism to coexist alongside cynicism, complacency, and hypocrisy on the public tier. These forces are probably playing a more powerful role than the commonly more acclaimed adverse consequences of the mass media. In such an environment the prospects for strong, proactive parties, let alone a new majority party, are bleak.

We have considered how our paradigm illuminates the contemporary problems of state effectiveness and political inefficiency. Viability has one final ingredient: political legitimacy. How does the approach developed throughout this book advance our understanding of this pivotal component in a way that the legitimation-crisis paradigm has failed to accomplish?

4 A Crisis of Political Legitimacy?

One of the few propositions on which Marxist and neoconservative sociologists agree is that the United States has been facing a crisis of legitimacy.
—Alan Wolfe, review of Lipset and Schneider's
The Confidence Gap

"The crisis of political legitimacy" . . . is a formulation compatible with the long-standing concern of political sociologists with the vulnerabilities of democratic institutions in mass society. . . .

However, the crisis of political legitimacy also is an ideological slogan which distorts and oversimplifies sociological investigation of modern political institutions.
—Morris Janowitz, The Last Half-Century

Those who explicitly or implicitly rely on the legitimation-crisis paradigm are set off from other political sociologists by their single-minded bonding of the questions of state effectiveness and political legitimacy. While both dimensions are essential features of this broad approach, a focus on the loss of legitimacy as the ultimate "crisis" of modern democracies is unquestionably the defining feature of the paradigm. Indeed, we have seen that the view that the United States and other capitalist democracies face the prospect of such a crisis is held across the ideological spectrum; at the extremes, neo-Marxists confidently predict its inevitability, while neoconservatives wring their hands and bewail its possibility.

While no precise accord exists about what this malaise entails, a rough consensus holds that it has something to do with diminished trust in the agents of political power. Diagnoses that avoid confounding legitimation crisis with problems of confidence, social entitlements, or economic growth (see Chapter 2) take two possible turns—sometimes both at the same time. They treat the crisis of political legitimacy as either a shift in the *doctrines* of legitimation (toward more rational-legal or, as we have seen, sometimes even "economistic" themes) or a decline in the *degree* of legitimacy (from higher to lower), irrespective of content.

Careful examination of both approaches casts doubts about the reality of a legitimation crisis in the United States (where the threat is allegedly most acute). Yet such an examination also highlights two apparent paradoxes. First, while Americans morally approve of their system, political authorities confront a widening "confidence gap." Second, although political legitimacy remains high in our society, an erosion of the core values in our general culture has been observed. This chapter shows why each of these is less paradoxical upon closer study. Specifically, I argue that shifts in the doctrines of legitimation have helped lower political confidence but not the degree of legitimacy, and that when some commentators talk about a decline in the degree of legitimacy, they are really referring to an ambiguity in the core values of the general American culture. Such analysis requires scanning the empirical evidence as well as providing conceptual clarification.

My goal is to challenge the inner logic of claims that a legitimation crisis is at hand. To accomplish this: I divide this chapter into three sections, defining political legitimation, examining the impact of doctrines of legitimation on confidence, and separating general cultural trends from changes in degree of legitimacy.

What Is Political Legitimation?

Before we can talk about a legitimation crisis, we need a clear understanding of what this concept encompasses. In Chapter 1, I discussed Lipset's ([1960] 1981) treatment of political legitimation as prototypical of the confusion that abounds in the use of this analytical tool. He, like many others who lean on the legitimation-crisis paradigm, variously locates legitimacy in the political culture and in the political system. Of course, we can all agree that expressions of legitimacy appear in the repertoire of symbols that both authorities and potential partisans produce and reproduce in order to orient themselves to political events (political culture) as well as in the networks of relationships they produce and reproduce as they seek to shape political power (the polity). To do otherwise is to relapse into the type of one-dimensional analysis I have been cautioning about.[1] Yet the notion of legitimacy requires a *primary analytical site* if the concept to be used most effectively. If a definition were to fuse social and cultural terms, some of the vital questions of social science and political sociology could not be handled without slipping into tautology. A perennial question is how the structure of a collectivity articulates with what its members believe, value, and feel (including how and whether they render political arrangements moral, plausible, and appropriate). Such a question cannot be studied scientifically unless the realms of social system and culture are kept *analytically* distinct.

In line with its Weberian roots, Chapter 1 argued that legitimacy's primary analytical site should be in the realm of culture. Political culture includes both political values and political legitimations (Lehman 1977, pp. 21–42). Political values are the general rules embedded in recurrent political conduct—what are often called the "rules of the game."[2] In the United States (and most other Western polities), democratic rules are among the most pivotal of these values. Lipset ([1960] 1981, p. 17) notes that such rules specify (1) the actors (e.g., political parties, a free press, and so forth) who are the appropriate players in the political game, (2) the prerogatives of and limitations on officeholders, and (3) the rights of "one or more set of recognized leaders attempting to gain office."

But values do not of themselves contain the moral imperative capable of fostering willing compliance. Some rules are subscribed to because those subject to them are afraid to deviate, others because citizens calculate that it is in their material interests to do so, and still others because of a moral imperative. The rules of the game work best when a moral imperative is operative—that is, when they are associated with a set of symbols that integrate, explain, and render them plausible. Berger and Luckmann (1966, pp. 47–123) call these imperatives "legitimations." Political legitimations are handy tools for both state authorities and potential partisans. (Swidler [1986] provides a cogent discussion of how cultural items can be thought of as tools or repertoires used by social actors.) For authorities, political legitimations are useful in making their goals and their domination of others more palatable. For potential partisans, these doctrines provide a moral frame with which to judge authorities and decide whether and how to cooperate with them. As I have indicated, a crisis of political legitimacy tends to be discussed as either a shift in doctrines or a drop in moral approval, although many analysts slide back and forth between the two. In particular, those who focus more on a shift in doctrines tend to assume that such an alternation leads to a lowering in the degree of legitimacy. Neither of these orientations has accurately forecast a crisis, however. Doctrinal shifts have helped foster the "confidence gap" but not a decline or crisis of legitimacy. Discussions that seem to focus on a slippage in degree of legitimacy often are really jeremiads against contemporary core American values—notably a purported shift away from the "work ethic" or achievement values toward hedonistic ones.

Doctrines of Legitimation and the "Confidence Gap"

Max Weber's ([1924] 1968, pp. 941–1372) classification still provides the most useful starting point for a discussion of doctrines of legitimation. Rules of the game are routinely legitimated in one of two ideal-typical ways: by a body of sacred symbols viewed as the product of immemorial lore—traditional doctrines, or by a set of abstract criteria perceived as rational, from which lower-level commands are assumed to be logically derived—rational-legal doctrines. Weber's third type, charismatic legitimations, is the antithesis of the other two because it arises in revolutionary interludes during which routine doctrines have lost their moral clout. Charisma rests its claim to obedience on the extraordinary qualities of a unique person, not on the virtues of an established system.

One defining feature of modern polities is their employment of at least some rational-legal appeals, although they vary in the degree of reliance on such appeals. Moreover, rational-legal doctrines are associated with a variety of rules of the game. In the United States, for example, such doctrines have been invoked to justify democratic procedures, while in the People's Republic of China they have been used to legitimate nondemocratic ones. We shall see that the interaction between rational-legal doctrines and democratic rules has a distinctive impact on how Americans give their trust to political authorities.

Neo-Marxist advocates of the legitimation-crisis paradigm (Habermas 1975; O'Connor 1973; Offe 1974; Wolfe 1977) have been particularly sensitive to the shifts in the doctrinal grounds for legitimation. They believe that the crisis of political legitimacy stems from a need of the state to jettison remaining traditional themes and justify itself more and more explicitly on rational-legal grounds. They often prefer terms such as "technocratic" rather than rational-legal to emphasize the doctrines' immersion in formal as opposed to substantive rationality.[3] These analysts say that the organizing principle of capitalist society continues to be the pursuit of profit by the capitalist class. The state's quest for economic growth is fundamentally a device to abet this class in fostering capital accumulation. However, the state must assuage the masses with entitlements to ensure continued popular support. In the process of doing both, the state seeks to convince citizens that its decisions derive from an "instrumental consciousness" (see Chapter 2) and are apolitical. In this view, the mounting inability of the state to purchase economic growth and trust from civil society simultaneously (the "fiscal crisis of the state") has brought about the crisis of political legitimacy because, inevitably, the capitalist state must give primacy to capital accumulation over legitimacy.

Without a doubt these neo-Marxist analyses illuminate the conundrums of modern states. But their key theoretical and empirical deficiencies undermine their insights. For present purposes, I see their pivotal deficiency as arising from a tendency to equate legitimation with all types of political support, including both confidence in incumbents and overall moral approval for the system. The conflation of legitimation with confidence is unwarranted (see, e.g., Citrin 1974; Easton 1965; Lehman 1987; Miller 1979; Sniderman 1981). *Theoretically*, the two processes are analytically distinct. *Historically*, the two have become progressively more empirically separated as we have moved to a world increasingly legitimated by rational-legal standards. *Politically*, the modern separation of legitimation and confidence contributes to the contemporary "confidence gap." Let us look at each of these points more closely.

THEORETICAL DIFFERENCES

The previous chapter discussed how confidence and demands form the principal channels through which civil society exerts influence on a state. Confidence points to the credibility of officeholders; when offered abundantly it confers a "zone of indifference" on them; and it tends to be highest early in an administration. Legitimation refers to the moral approval of the existing political order rather than of particular incumbents; it confers a "zone of indifference" on offices and agencies (irrespective of particular incumbents); and it is far less susceptible to short-term fluctuations than is trust in particular persons. Both confidence and legitimation can be studied with survey data (that is, public opinion polls). Studies of electoral data are more commonly used to tap confidence when they examine whether a particular candidate's percentage of the vote has increased or decreased since the previous election. Voting behavior can also be used as an indicator of legitimacy, however. Lipset's ([1960] 1981, pp. 27–63) use of the proportion of the electorate supporting extremist, antisystem parties as a gauge of degree of legitimacy is a striking example (see below). Global and qualitative ("historical") data have more often been employed as indicators of degree of legitimacy, as in the use of popular accounts about mass participation in national political rituals to measure how much citizens accept political institutions.

In modern polities, the interaction between legitimation and confidence is complex. For one thing, while legitimation provides a ground for confidence, it cannot deliver confidence automatically to officeholders. Moreover, declines in confidence do not register directly as lowered commitment to the system. For example, the shift reflected in the confidence withheld from Jimmy Carter and bestowed on Ronald Reagan is neither the result of how much Americans revere their polity nor a cause of changes in this reverence. It is likely that only a series of administrations that lack citizens' trust can erode legitimacy. As I noted in Chapter 2, the years from Lyndon Johnson to Jimmy Carter barely dampened faith in the system. Yet, as Arthur H. Miller (1979, p. 3) warns, "if the process of elections does not succeed in producing popular incumbents, the discontent generated by a series of distrusted authorities may accumulate and eventually be directed at the institutions of government."

HISTORICAL SEPARATION

The tendency to conflate legitimation and confidence probably arises from the fact that moral approval of the system and trust in sitting authorities were more fused in the past than they are today. Theoretical distinctions, after all, do not always point to real divisions in the empirical terrain. Yet whenever rational-legal doctrines become ascendant in the political culture, the differences between legitimation and confidence tend to become more real. This hypothesis rests on Weber's observation that the rationalization of modern life is expressed in bureaucratization and that this entails the uncoupling of individual and office. In the bureaucratic world, officeholders are subject to authority solely in terms of their specifically defined spheres of impersonal obligations; personal and bureaucratic assets are strictly segregated; and individuals are routinely promoted, demoted, moved laterally, or fired and replaced by others. In short, the pervasiveness of rational-legal doctrines makes persons and positions separable phenomena capable of being judged by different standards (see Weber [1924] 1968, pp. 956–1003).

In charismatic and traditional settings the subjects would regard any attempt to separate confidence from moral evaluation as absurd. Charisma represents the limiting case of the empirical fusion of confidence and legitimation. The institutional order is in disrepute, and the moral responsibilities that usually burden institutions fall on the shoulders of a revolutionary figure who possesses extraordinary personal traits. Charisma is inherently volatile. If the would-be prophet falters in the eyes of followers, the movement enters into crisis and may ultimately die because its moral grounding (which centers on the leader) has evaporated (see Weber [1924] 1968, pp. 1111–56).

While the fusion of confidence and legitimation is a destabilizing element for the charismatic order, it serves as a source of strength for traditional domination. The charismatic leader carries the burdens of legitimation alone; but in the traditional domain the institutional order carries the load for particular leaders. The sanctity of institutions covers authorities who occupy their positions on ascribed (versus achieved) grounds. Discontent, if expressed, is ordinarily directed against advisors or ministers, not the leaders themselves. When, at rare moments, the leaders are challenged, only they, and not the system, are regarded as "illegitimate." "Unjust" monarchs and "tyrants" are categories developed by jurists, moralists, and ecclesiastical authorities under traditional legitimations to sanction the removal of such leaders (Weber [1924] 1968, pp. 1114–15). The sanctity of the institution remains intact, and a more "just" and legitimate figure replaces the one who has strayed from the path of traditional virtue. The gods abandon the failed charismatic; but it is the impious traditional leader who is seen as abandoning the gods—and the system. The traditional order goes on and during tranquil interludes appears indistinguishable—and indeed draws sustenance—from the "faithful" leaders who rule under its aegis (Weber [1924] 1968, pp. 1104–09, 1114–15).

I contend that a systematic differentiation between legitimation and confidence becomes possible only in a polity that emphasizes rational-legal standards. It follows that people in such settings should more regularly be able to separate trust in incumbents from support of the system. Since the United States is seen as a highly rationalized polity, one might predict that our fellow citizens make crystal-clear distinctions here. Inevitably, however, the real world is always a little more complicated than theoretical distinctions imply. In the American polity a third element stands between the rating of individual officeholders and moral commitment to prevailing institutions: the public's degree of satisfaction with the performance of the larger system. Americans recognize a difference between incumbents and the system; yet their ratings of the actual accomplishments of the two in practice tend to be similar. Public opinion surveys, for instance, have found a high correspondence between respondents' judgments of how well *particular people* are running the branches of government (e.g., the executive, Congress, the military) and their satisfaction with how well these *branches* deliver on their goals. The ratings of both are far below what they were in the early 1960s, leading some to invoke the notion of "confidence gap."[4]

Dissatisfactions with incumbents and the performances of particular branches of the state are not synonymous with loss of faith in the American polity, however. In the United States, citizens continue to believe that "since failures of the system are the fault of incompetent power-holders, the situation can be greatly improved by changing the incumbent authorities. The cure for a government and an economy that are performing poorly is a change of leadership—brought about by the democratic process" (Lipset and Schneider 1983, p. 390). Faith in the beneficial effects of turnover based on the democratic rules of the game is an indirect yet unequivocal indicator of persistence of high moral commitment to American political institutions. Legitimacy, in other words, continues even in the midst of a "confidence gap." Paradoxically, then, while Americans tend to fuse evaluations of actions of individuals and of the larger system, they still believe that incumbent turnover will save an essentially moral system.

POLITICAL IMPLICATIONS

The separation of legitimation and confidence has not been an un-mixed blessing for the United States or other democratic polities. It has helped to widen the "confidence gap," which in political life over the past three decades translates into increasing dissatisfaction with the achievements of both incumbents and state branches as well as a decline in citizen loyalty to the two major parties (Braungart 1978; Janowitz 1978, pp. 101–13; Lipset and Schneider 1983, particularly pp. 292–99; Milbrath and Goel 1977, pp. 43–85; Nie, Verba, and Petrocik 1976; Piven and Cloward 1988, pp. 149–59). While the American public's continued enthusiasm for the salutary effects of "throwing the rascals out" is not identical with the "confidence gap," it has historically been a precondition for this phenomenon.

In modern democracies, rational-legal doctrines encourage higher demands, particularly from civil society's more organized sectors. Such doctrines cast social problems as historical products susceptible to political mediation rather than as the result of fate or the will of God. State authority is bureaucratized, and officials come to see themselves and their agencies as delivery systems. The public also adopts this frame of reference, and interest groups that profess to speak in its name (or the name of some special constituency) regularly press claims upon the state. Spiraling demands, particularly from the polity's more organized sectors, commonly result. The state finds it difficult to respond to the volume and breadth of petitions it receives, even when demands have been initiated by its own activities. The balance between confidence and demands is delicate at best (see Chapter 3). Incumbents cannot use the protective mantle of rational-legal justifications for very long, as they are then subject to grueling, short-term citizen evaluations based heavily on these very rational-legal criteria. Public and interest group confidence quickly begins to slip.[5]

In short, I argue that demands tend to expand more rapidly than confidence when polities rely heavily on rational-legal doctrines.[6] The specter of discontent with how well claims are being considered haunts not just long-standing capitalist democracies but other polities as well. But discontent takes different forms and is likely to have different outcomes depending on the degree of legitimacy. For example, discontent is bound to remain much more acute in the new polities of Central and Eastern Europe and the former Soviet republics and in the one that survives in China because they have recently gone through (or continue to experience) authentic legitimation crises. Low legitimacy stimulates rampant discontent.

Yet, ironically, high legitimacy does not mean a free ride. Indeed, pervasive moral support for democratic values carries special problems. All ongoing modern democracies are backed by a relative consensus over doctrines that contain major rational strands. The justification of democratic rules of the game with rational-legal themes leads to exaggerated expectations that electoral turnover of leaders is an efficacious cure for incumbents' "failures."

Huntington (1981, pp. 31–60) goes too far in arguing that political consensus creates instability only in the United States. But he is probably correct that the specific content of the American Creed intensifies the inevitable clash between political ideals and institutional realities. The Creed's moral imperative, he says, "constitutes an external standard for judging institutions, and often judging them harshly" (Huntington 1981, p. 32). Thus our current "confidence gap" springs partially from the high standards set by the doctrines that legitimate American political institutions—not from a rejection of these doctrines or standards.

Of course, our doctrines, notably the Creed, are hardly free of "sacred" elements. The impact of our this-worldly ascetic Protestant heritage on American life has been particularly singled out by many, from Weber ([1904–05] 1958) to Lipset (1990). This heritage reinforces the tendency of rational-legal themes to foster high demands and to subject incumbents to grueling scrutiny and the frequent risk of democratic turnover. The Protestant moralism embedded in the American Creed has also had a countervailing impact, however. Skillful leaders from time to time have been able to evade the Creed's suspicion of officeholders. Indeed, they have been able to isolate and mobilize the remaining "sacred" (and hence more traditional) themes in U.S. legitimation doctrines and thus attenuate the most adverse effects of the separation of legitimation and confidence. The manipulation of such symbols, I believe, provides *part* of the explanation for Reagan's "Teflon presidency" in particular and the greater sustained popularity of post–World War II Republican presidents generally.

Ronald Reagan's eight years in office stand as a challenge to those who see the "confidence gap" as an inevitable feature of rationally legitimated democratic life. No American president in nearly half a century, not even Eisenhower, managed to sustain such high levels of public trust. Indeed, Reagan was the first president since Eisenhower to finish eight full years in office and the first one since Andrew Jackson to leave office safe in the knowledge that his vice president had been elected to succeed him. How does the Reagan phenomenon jibe with the reality of the "confidence gap"? Most analysts have searched for an answer among either idiosyncratic factors (Reagan's personal charm or his "good luck") or macroinstitutional ones (e.g., growing presidential access to television or the possibility of party realignment toward a new Republican majority). Although it is beyond the scope of this chapter to render a full account of the "Teflon presidency," I want to suggest that *some* of the answer lies in Reagan's ability to embody traditional aspects of the American political culture and thus to evade the corrosive effects of rational-legal legitimation on confidence.

Our two most beloved postwar presidents have been Republicans who draped themselves in the classic American pieties of patriotism, family, and God. Is it too farfetched to argue that both Eisenhower and Reagan tapped some of the remaining sacred, more traditional reservoirs in our now heavily rational-legal doctrines of political legitimation? If this is so, it is possible that they reduced the usual separation of legitimation and confidence. That is, since their claims to moral worth, more than those of other presidents, drew on more traditional themes, citizens' judgments of presidential performances were more trusting and less exacting. One corollary of this hypothesis is that adept conservative presidents may have a potential political advantage if they succeed in enveloping their administrations in some of the popular nonrational themes from our ascetic Protestant heritage. Liberal Democrats, on the other hand, seem more susceptible to pitfalls stemming from the separation of legitimation and confidence, because they are less successful in manipulating such symbols. In this regard, note that three elected Republican presidents since World War II (Eisenhower, Nixon, and Reagan) have won reelection (by landslides, incidentally), while not a single Democratic president (Truman, Kennedy, Johnson, and Carter) has. A number of factors have had an impact here (an assassination and a war being the most obvious), but I suggest that the ability to exploit traditional themes is part of the story of presidential politics since 1948.

Of course, the interaction between doctrines of legitimation and confidence does not account for all the variance in presidential and state effectiveness or in the inefficiencies of contemporary political participation. Strains in the American social, political, and economic structure and the vagaries of history have no doubt also had a great impact. Yet we saw in Chapter 2 that doctrines of legitimation have an impact on states' self-conceptions as goal-delivery systems and perhaps on their ultimate effectiveness. Moreover, I have argued that, since citizens also use doctrines of legitimation as a moral frame with which to judge political events, when these events are couched mainly in rational-legal rhetoric, the public and interest groups are likely to put forward many demands and subject officeholders to grueling scrutiny, linked to a relatively short "grace period." Democratic rules of the game only heighten this tendency. On the other hand, traditional doctrines yield more generous and stable assessments of authorities. Judgments are most volatile in charismatic settings that alternate between awed submission and intense demands for effective performance. The sustained compliance of followers depends on regular demonstrations of extraordinary gifts by the charismatic leader, which puts enormous burdens on such a person.

Degree of Legitimacy and the General Culture

Shifts in doctrines of legitimation have not yielded the crisis foreseen in some neo-Marxist variants of the legitimation-crisis paradigm. Other diagnosticians have defined the crisis as a straightforward decline in the degree of legitimacy, regardless of doctrinal content. A decade ago most of the proponents of this approach were labeled as neoconservative, although in retrospect they are hardly a homogeneous group. Analysts as diverse as Daniel Bell, Irving Kristol, Michael Novak, and Aron Wildavsky wrote that a crisis of legitimacy had overtaken the United States and Western polities generally. Political authority was being sapped of its moral justifications, they believed. Yet they saw the crisis of authority as only part of a larger spiritual or "cultural" crisis. Diagnoses of this legitimation crisis are interwoven with such other issues as "adversary culture," "moral decline," and "failure of nerve." (For an overview of these approaches, see Steinfels 1979, pp. 53–63.) Indeed, just as neo-Marxists frequently conflate crises of legitimation and confidence, so-called neoconservatives have tended to confuse inconsistencies in the general culture with a decline in political legitimacy.

Moreover, contrary to neoconservative (indeed all legitimation-crisis) diagnoses, Lipset and Schneider (1983) have shown that opinion surveys report continuing high moral approval for the American system. While some might argue that the survey method is not a sufficiently sensitive instrument for plumbing such subtle but strategic shifts in mood, I find that no compelling demonstration of this point has ever been made. Certainly such a position is not widespread among so-called neoconservatives nor anywhere else within the legitimation-crisis paradigm. Nevertheless, before moving to the core of the neoconservative diagnosis, one more look for a sign—for a "structural manifestation"—of declining legitimacy is appropriate in order not to close the door on the "crisis of political legitimacy" with unseemly haste.

STRUCTURAL MANIFESTATIONS AND DEGREE OF LEGITIMACY

Political culture—and not the political system—is legitimacy's primary analytical site. Yet legitimacy is reflected in how authorities and potential partisans produce and reproduce relationships as they seek to shape political power and *not* just in the repertoire of symbols that they produce and reproduce in order to orient themselves to political events. That is, degree of legitimacy has manifestations in the structure of relations within the polity, although its analytical anchor is in political culture. If pivotal interactions did not reflect the level of moral approval for political institutions, the concept of legitimacy would be an empty shell. Certain political practices are peculiarly sensitive to the degree of legitimacy. Indeed, these structural manifestations can be used as a litmus test of the moral worth attributed to the system.

In Chapter 2, I alluded to participation in shared national rituals as one such manifestation. The bicentennial and Statue of Liberty centennial celebrations as well as the Gulf War victory parades were offered as examples. In a similar vein, Lipset notes:

> A major test of legitimacy is the extent to which given nations have developed a common "secular political culture," mainly national rituals and holidays. The United States has developed a homogeneous culture in the veneration accorded the Founding Fathers, Abraham Lincoln, Theodore Roosevelt, and their principles. These common elements, to which all American politicians appeal, are not present in all democratic societies. In some European countries, the left and the right have a different set of symbols and different historical heroes. France offers the clearest example of such a nation. ([1960] 1981, p. 68)[7]

Since our focus is now on degree of legitimacy (high versus low), structural manifestations reflective of a willingness (or unwillingness) to allow crucial political activities to proceed loom as particularly important. Three structural manifestations closely mirror our polity's degree of legitimacy in this way: the absence of major political movements opposed to the democratic rules of the game, the smoothness of political succession, and the availability of "third-party backing" for authorities and "political minorities."

Lipset ([1960] 1981, pp. 30–31) uses the absence of antidemocratic movements as his prime indicator of legitimacy in European and English-speaking nations in his celebrated chapter on economic development and democratic "stability." He focuses on the failure of all totalitarian movements, either Communist or Fascist, to receive 20 percent of the total vote over a twenty-five year period in these nations. That is, Lipset interprets voting for parties that abide by the democratic rules as a sign of moral approval for the existing institutions. Certainly, nothing in the last quarter-century of U.S. electoral politics indicates anything but massive support for present political values.

Predictable turnover in leadership provides another structural manifestation of the extent of moral compliance with democratic procedures. Legitimacy and predictable turnover are intricately bound together. For Weber ([1924] 1968, pp. 1121–48), the succession crisis is the decisive event in the routinization of a charismatic movement. The method chosen to replace a departed charismatic leader (e.g., consulting oracles, drawing lots, the introduction of hereditary rights, or bureaucratization) goes a long way in helping to decide whether the new order will be rendered moral and, if so, by traditional or rational-legal doctrines. Conversely, how unquestioned the subsequent turnover of leaders is reflects the degree to which such doctrines have taken hold. The successful implementation of rules of succession is an important structural manifestation that the routinized order has begun sinking moral roots. However, when key actors refuse to accept the rules regarding the circulation of leaders, factions, or parties, we have a reliable sign of low or declining legitimacy.

Americans' overwhelming acceptance of election results is itself an unambiguous indicator of high political legitimacy. But less routine turnover is also unchallenged. The two most recent atypical structural manifestations are the transitions from Kennedy to Johnson and from Nixon to Ford. Lyndon Johnson's assumption of the presidency after John F. Kennedy's assassination in November 1963 was treated as nonproblematic by most Americans. In fact, the transfer of power was neither natural nor self-evident. Vice President Johnson had been relegated to the periphery of executive power. Robert F. Kennedy, the president's brother and the attorney general, had been the administration's real second-in-command. Johnson's constitutionally mandated accession presaged a political decline for the younger Kennedy and his allies. Yet the succession was never challenged, indeed was never in doubt, and hence reflects the presence of high legitimacy.

Richard Nixon's replacement by Gerald Ford in August 1974 is perhaps an even more striking atypical structural manifestation. The political climate was radically different from that of 1963. More than a decade of mounting controversy over the Vietnam War had followed Kennedy's assassination. There was no revered martyred president to be replaced. Instead, Nixon resigned rather than face impeachment by the House and a trial by the Senate because of his involvement with the Watergate scandals. Ford, moreover, was not an elected vice president. He had been chosen by Nixon and confirmed by the Senate less than a year earlier to replace the convicted Spiro Agnew. Yet again, the legitimacy of the system guaranteed the uncontested accession of America's only "unelected president."

Stinchcombe (1968, pp. 158–62) argues that the third key structural manifestation, the availability of third-party support, is virtually coextensive with legitimacy. He states: "*A power is legitimate to the degree that . . . the power-holder can call upon sufficient other centers of power, as reserves in case of need, to make his power effective*" (Stinchcombe 1968, p. 162 [italics in original]). Here, he shifts the primary analytical site of legitimacy from culture to social system. Stinchcombe is less concerned with legitimacy as an "estimation of the state of public opinion or . . . ideological enthusiasm" than with its manifestation in social interaction. He also focuses concern away from the subjects of commands to the contingency of third-party support: from the acceptance of subordinates to the responses of other power centers. In effect, Stinchcombe tells us that a key structural manifestation of legitimacy is the backing given to official orders by other mobilized groups.

All branches of the American state have substantial third-party backing. Large segments of the public and other societal institutions stand behind the appropriateness of a range of commands from the national executive, Congress, the federal bureaucracy, the judiciary, military and police agencies, and state and local governments. Even when the Supreme Court has issued controversial rulings on abortion, flag burning, religious displays on public property, desegregation, and affirmative action, its *right* to do so has never been challenged; nor has the obligation of citizens to treat current decisions as the law of the land been questioned widely. (Further, reversals of "unpopular" rulings are usually pursued through constitutional means.) State actors cannot count only on citizens and outside institutions to back up their rights; they can also be certain that support will be forthcoming from other state branches. This has not always been the case. The American Civil War, after all, occurred precisely when the national executive lost the third-party backing of the sub-central governments in the South.

Third-party support is also available for potential partisans. Extensive backing exists for the right of "minorities" (such as blacks, Hispanics, women, the disabled, the elderly, and gays and lesbians) to mobilize to push new claims upon the state. The support of powerful actors (within and outside the American state) for the right of such partisans to participate regularly in the channels of political influence has, if anything, grown during the past half-century.

Perhaps the most pivotal legitimacy issue for democratic polities is the right of opposition and defeated factions to compete for office. The perspective of third-party support is especially instructive here. If we focus on legitimacy as simply a symbolic expression, we come away with the impression that once democratic values are pervasive, the right to oppose and compete is a *fait accompli*. Nothing is further from the truth. Democracy is an "unnatural" state of affairs. The adversary nature of competitive politics inevitably raises the temptation that a victorious faction will look for ways to restrict the prerogatives of the losers, regardless of the lofty sentiments everyone may subscribe to officially. After all, the opposition is the "enemy," they are advocating "error," and, more important, they are after my job (or the job I want). Therefore, a highly legitimate democratic polity still needs periodic structural manifestations that third parties are willing to protect the advocates of "error." In the United States, these safeguards, it seems to me, are as strong now as they have ever been.

Is there then a crisis of political legitimacy? We have seen that a "confidence gap," however large and persistent, does not necessarily indicate such a crisis. Indeed, the American public's enduring optimism that "throwing the rascals out" makes a difference points to a long-term coexistence of low trust in officials and deep faith in the system. Yet the very fact that the United States' heavily rational-legal doctrines (reinforced by ascetic Protestant moralism) retain wide support guarantees that incumbents will be judged severely. Grueling criteria enhance the prospect of frequent turnover. On the other hand, the near-universal rejection of antidemocratic movements and acceptance of democratic turnover and succession reflect broad reservoirs of moral approval for the rules of the political game. The same may be said for the prevalence of third-party backing for "outs" and "losers" to compete again in the struggle.

"VALUE CRISIS" IN THE GENERAL CULTURE

The question of a crisis of political legitimacy and potential problems in the general culture are not the same. The absence of the former does not mean the United States lacks "moral" or "spiritual" problems. Even some of the neoconservatives' severest critics (e.g., Steinfels 1979, p. 58; Harrington 1984) accept the possibility that a "spiritual" malaise haunts the West in general and the United States in particular. These diagnoses warrant closer scrutiny. When this is performed, we see that the heart of the neoconservatives' crisis—even when they invoke "legitimacy"—has little to do with political culture but is lodged in our society's general culture.

A society's *general culture* is the pattern of beliefs, values, and sentiments produced and reproduced by its members as they attempt to achieve shared orientations in directing their lives. It is not the same as its *social system*, which refers to the totality of relationships that are produced and reproduced by its members. Like the notion of social system, however, the concept of culture is more fruitful when it is treated as a multitiered category. Culture is multileveled in the sense that the general culture forms a symbolic supraunit that contains a number of subunits. While the former is the pattern formed by all the symbols used by members of society, the subunits have been conceptualized in several ways. At different times, these "parts" of the cultural "whole" have been treated, for example, as class culture (e.g., working-class versus bourgeois culture), regional culture (e.g., East Coast versus Sunbelt culture), racial or ethnic culture (e.g., white versus black versus Hispanic culture), and religious culture (e.g., Protestant versus Catholic versus Jewish culture). In light of this book's focus, the subunits are treated here primarily in terms of *institutional realms*. We talk about the general culture as a "whole" of which the "parts" are the political culture, the economic culture, the family and kinship culture, the educational culture, the religious culture, and so forth.

The general culture forms a higher-order symbol system; it is more than the sum of the parts. Neoconservative laments about "cultural crisis," "adversary culture," "moral decline," "failure of nerve," and (even) "legitimation crisis" are really about how the "whole" and the "parts" are articulated. This can be a problem especially because the relationship between an overarching culture and its subcultures is not one-directional. Sociologists probably have more frequently spoken about how the general culture shapes the individual subcultures. We are fond of citing Tocqueville ([1835–1840] 1954), for example, who noted the influence of America's general cultural values of equality on our democratic political culture. But we must also recognize that the "part" sometimes plays a role in transforming the general culture. How often, for instance, have we told our students that the culture of medieval Europe was shaped heavily by religious values but that modern culture reflects the impact of economic values more?

Indeed, economic values—especially achievement values or the work ethic linked to the rise of capitalism—have generally been seen as the *primus inter pares* among the institutional subcultures that have shaped the general cultures of modern Western societies. In recent times, it has become commonplace to assert that capitalist achievement values have lost much of their relevance. Yankelovich (1981), for example, argues that the "ethic of self-denial" is being replaced in America by the "ethic of self-fulfillment." Perhaps the most celebrated label used in this diagnosis is that of the "cultural contradictions of capitalism" (Bell 1970, 1976). For Bell,

American capitalism . . . has lost its traditional legitimacy which was based on a moral system of rewards, rooted in a Protestant sanctification of work. It has substituted . . . a hedonism which promises a material ease and luxury, yet shies away from all historical implications which a "voluptuary system"—and all its social permissiveness and libertinism—implies. (1970, p. 43)

Here, the ascendancy of hedonism (Yankelovich's "ethic of self-fulfillment") in advanced capitalist societies is seen as a key feature of our cultural malaise. Hedonism offers no firm moral anchor nor does it represent a final liberation. The removal of obligation, as Hobbes and Durkheim (among others) showed us long ago, does not yield transcendence but the "war of all against all," anomie, and moral disorientation. The earlier, Reformation-rooted values of achievement, discipline, deferral of gratification, hard work, rationality, and objectivity sustained the capitalist industrial order and resonated with a polity legitimated by rational-legal doctrines.[8] The work ethic and the polity as a "government of law" seemed to reinforce each other.

The so-called neoconservative diagnoses have failed to recognize that we face, at the moment, the apparent paradox of a polity whose legitimacy remains high, encased in a society whose core values have come to be suspect in some circles. This pattern of consensus-amid-erosion would seem to pose unique challenges for the political sector. Is it possible that democratic societies only need political consensus but can live with cultural flux? And, *if* we require new core values that the economic subculture is now unable to provide, are political values a plausible alternative? After all, one aspect of the struggles of the late 1960s and early 1970s was an effort by "progressive" movements to push the public agenda permanently to center stage at the expense of the privatism that marks the capitalist ethos in all its guises. (On the alternation between public and private emphases in American political history, see Hirschman 1982; Huntington 1981.) The current eclipse of these "progressive" forces suggests the (at least temporary) failure of this effort to promote the primacy of public or political values. The Reagan era provided traditionalist interests with a "bully pulpit" from which to reassert the centrality of the older work ethic pieties (sometimes clothed in neoclassical economic jargon) against the claims of both hedonism and public responsibility.

Moreover, the tenacity of those values that extol achievement and hard work should not be underestimated. No compelling argument has been put forward as to why the last decades of the twentieth century will be their last hurrah. Indeed, while production values (which stress achievement or the work ethic) and consumption values (which prize hedonism) are *logically* contradictory, they have managed to coexist in the *real* world. Cherishing both simultaneously does not appear to be as perverse as it did a couple of decades ago. This constellation of values looks to be particularly pronounced among younger, urban professionals—the so-called yuppies discussed in Chapter 3. The "yuppie ethic" says you must work hard *and* play hard. (Or in the words of the beer commercial of a few years ago: "Who says you can't have it all?") Production and consumption are both seen as matters demanding serious pursuit. In fact, the yuppie ethic holds that hard work is the only sure guarantee of satisfactory play.

Achievement and hedonism, therefore, can coexist comfortably over a significant period of time. And, of course, they have been aspects of American culture from the very beginning of our society. When Weber ([1904–05] 1958, p. 182) almost a century ago berated "specialists without vision, sensualists without heart," he had hedonistic American capitalists in mind. It is also possible that the primacy of achievement and hedonism may alternate in the American mood at any moment. Lipset's (1963b, pp. 99–104) analysis of the interaction between achievement values and egalitarian ones is an instructive model here. He argues that one permanent aspect of American culture is the fluctuation between these values that coincides with conservative and liberal periods in U.S. political history. Lipset believes that values that stress rewarding people for their accomplishments (particularly in the marketplace) both conflict with and reinforce those that proclaim that all persons must be respected as human beings and that distinctions among them should be reduced.

Of course, equality and hedonism are not the same thing. Achievement versus equality and achievement versus hedonism are two distinct dimensions on a complex American cultural landscape. Yet both equality and hedonism—and their ambiguous relationships with achievement—constitute a permanent feature of our culture. Thus it may be that achievement and hedonism alternate in preeminence in a manner analogous to the cycle of preeminence between achievement and equality. What seems to be erosion in the short run may actually turn out to be alternation over the longer haul. No evidence exists, however, to link such alternation with a crisis of political legitimacy.

Conclusions

In sum, the legitimation-crisis paradigm is both theoretically deficient and empirically incorrect. No acute crisis of legitimacy plagues the American polity nor probably any other advanced capitalist democracy. A deep reservoir of moral approval for political institutions remains. Rational-legal doctrines do subject incumbents to rigorous judgments under which they have only a very short time to prove their mettle. Yet people continue to have great faith that changing leaders according to democratic rules will make a difference. Thus, we are not faced with a legitimation crisis so much as an endemic "confidence gap." A few leaders, like Ronald Reagan, have even been able to dodge the full brunt of this "confidence gap" through skillful use of the remaining traditional themes in our political culture. If an air of crisis hovers about our political culture, it has more to do with the uncertainty over whether political values can become the dominant themes in our general culture, replacing the work ethic. The immediate prospects are bleak, but future dominance is possible *if* the decline of achievement values is real and irreversible. Hedonism has replaced the work ethic, some have argued, and hedonism is an unsatisfactory theme with which to inspire a society. Still others worry about the possibility of a firmly anchored set of values in the absence of a plausible transcendental justification, what Harrington (1984) called the "God question."

The imminent collapse of capitalist achievement values as the leitmotif of our culture is unlikely, however. Indeed, of late these have been embraced with an enthusiasm in East Asia and Eastern Europe that is nothing short of startling; rather than disappearing these values may be becoming universal. In our own country, the Reagan years saw a revival of old-time achievement values. Moreover, achievement and hedonism, despite logical contradictions, seem peacefully to coexist over the long haul in the real world and as they currently do in the yuppie ethic. Indeed, achievement values have been in eclipse before, and there is likely a periodicity in their rise and fall. At best, then, our general culture can be accused of fostering a chronic, but "subclinical," spiritual malaise, but hardly an acute moral fever—let alone a crisis of political legitimacy.

We, therefore, will have to look elsewhere for the sources of misery and discontent in modern societal and political life. Endlessly dwelling on "cultural crises" while neglecting the social systems that contain them does not get us very far. I hope the previous two chapters have shown that enough questions abound about how Americans organize the effective pursuit of collective goals and the efficient mobilization of political participation to occupy the most ardent seeker for a more viable polity and society. It is the treatment of these factors that should be the principal focus of our attention.

5 The End of History—The End of the State?

> *What we may be witnessing is not just the end of the Cold War, or the passing of a particular period of postwar history, but the end of history as such: that is, the end point of mankind's ideological evolution and the universalization of Western liberal democracy as the final form of human government.*
> —*Francis Fukuyama, "The End of History?"*

> *At the very time when the state appears to be making sure of its own ascendancy, we seem, paradoxically enough, to be witnessing its decline and fall also.*
> —*Pierre Birnbaum,* States and Collective Action

The closer we get to the end of our era's second millennium the more widespread the itch for grandiose prognostications. While social scientists' final chapters have been chronically prey to these temptations, I try to resist such impulses here. But since I have argued that this book's alternative paradigm is not only more "theoretically comprehensive" but also more "empirically open" than the legitimation-crisis paradigm, it behooves me to say something about what is going on around us. Indeed, I have made a considerable number of empirical statements about what is happening within modern polities while advancing my case for a more satisfactory set of "first principles." The aim of this concluding chapter is to reflect on these hypotheses (admittedly, often informally phrased) within the framework inspired by our presuppositions and models. I also hope to demonstrate that our paradigm may have implications for changing the world and not just for better understanding it.

In a summation of this book's core empirical statements, a scenario of merely "business as usual" or "more of the same (maybe a *little* better or worse)" should strike a discordant, indeed surreal, note. On the other hand, heralding the final triumph of Western liberal democracy, particularly its American variant, seems at best a bit odd just now. In fact, the U.S. polity's creaking ability to respond "viably" to the dramatic challenges here and throughout the world is perhaps the central domestic feature of the political moment. In the fall of 1989, *Time* magazine noted:

> Abroad and at home, challenges are going unmet. Under the shadow of a massive federal deficit that neither political party is willing to confront, a kind of neurosis of accepted limits has taken hold from one end of Pennsylvania Avenue to the other. Whatever the situation—the unprecedented opportunity to promote democracy in Eastern Europe, the spreading plague of drugs, the plight of the underclass, the urgent need for educational reform—the typical response from Washington consists of encouraging words and token funds. Yet voters, especially the party organized ones, continue to demand—and often receive—more benefits and services while rejecting higher taxes. (Goodgame and Hornik 1989, p. 29)

Hardly the foreshadowing of the triumph of liberal democracy and the "end of history," is it? By the time this book appears in print, a few of these questions may have been addressed—but, most likely, incrementally and grudgingly. Yet I doubt that the "neurosis of accepted limits" will have been met head on. The preceding multidimensional analyses help us see why it is not going to disappear quickly—or, in the language I prefer, why the deeper forces undercutting the viability of the American polity have become a matter of greater popular as well as scholarly concern. These analyses have been neither constricted by the narrow binary formula at the heart of the legitimation-crisis paradigm nor centered on the concrete political problems of the moment per se (e.g., on the problems of the Middle East, budget and trade deficits, the drug problem, the plight of the underclass, and lowered voter turnout). Rather, they have dealt primarily with the *symbolic and structural barriers* to grappling with whatever problems inevitably arise, especially in the United

States (but in other advanced democracies too). Those pages isolated a number of "master trends" that have reinforced these barriers, eroded viability, and contributed to the distorting rhetoric of "crisis" (or "neurosis," to use *Time*'s even more reductionist but more graphic metaphor). These "master trends" remind us of the premise with which this book opened: Greater viability entails more than facing up to a congeries of unrelated challenges. Through this analysis a more comprehensive and complex picture of the barriers to enhanced political success has emerged.

Ironically, we have seen that the most trumpeted challenge to established democracies—legitimation crisis—is in fact the most illusory. The actual obstacles are to be found mainly in the operations of political systems—although symbolic factors play an indirect role too. Yet the deeper problems being experienced by advanced democratic polities are not brand new nor are they likely to disappear quickly. Thus to see some or all of these as avatars of the "end of the state" (as, for example, Birnbaum [1988] does) is a bit farfetched. Challenges to viability are permanent parts of political life and do not necessarily foreshadow the state's "decline and fall" (any more than our capacity to get along despite them signals the "end of history").

Paradigmatic Grounding

This analysis has been built on the assumption that putting one's "first principles" on the table advances sociological discourse. A more theoretically comprehensive and empirically open consideration of the barriers to success in political life begins with fundamental assumptions that are robust enough to generate the key questions in a reasoned manner and sufficiently restrained not to answer them peremptorily.

As we saw in Chapter 1, three fundamental issues stand out as especially pivotal for the analysis of success and failure in modern democracies. They hinge on three pairs of differences between inter-member and political power, the state and the political system, and state effectiveness and political viability.

Politics, broadly conceived, focuses on the chances for getting others to do what we want when they might otherwise not do so. That is why the notion of power looms so large in the conceptual arsenals of most political sociologists. But in modern societies, power takes two distinct tracks according to the ends being pursued: as systems of either intermember or political power. Intermember power, with its focus on particular ends, has traditionally been the subject matter of the specialty of social stratification, because it leads one to ask: Who are the relevant societal actors in the prevailing structures of inequality, and what key resources are they struggling over (see Lehman 1977, pp. 93–121)? Superficially, one might be tempted to argue that political sociology should deal exclusively with the study of political power, insofar as the latter concept considers the capacity to set, pursue, and implement society's collective goals, and because the state has become the agency that specializes in political power. Yet, in the final analysis, political sociology remains incomplete unless it studies *both* systems of power and concentrates especially on their *interaction*. Therefore, a truly multidimensional paradigm for political sociology is neither "state centered" nor "society centered"; rather, it is open to the possibility that both sets (or either set) of forces may be definitive at any given moment.

Any spotlight on political power compels us to examine more than the state. A society's entire system of political power—its polity—contains other actors as well. Recognition that the state is but one (albeit decisive) part of a political system allows us to reject an unduly formalistic view of politics. Political life is more than the conduct of state authorities. Moreover, "outside," prospective challengers for power are just as much members of their polity as the institutionalized contenders are (Tilly 1974, 1978, to the contrary). All modern political systems contain unruly elements who do not share the institutionalized contenders' willingness to play by official rules. The political system also has several levels, which is why it may be characterized simultaneously by conflicting tendencies such as intense participation by interest groups and social movements yet apathy within the general public.

Finally, since a political system encompasses more than the state, its success or failure involves more than what government officials do or fail to do, that is, more than state effectiveness. We have seen that the growth of state capacities is increasingly treated as the prime ingredient of political viability, but it can never be the only one. The binary effectiveness-legitimacy formula of the legitimation-crisis paradigm has also been shown to be inadequate. The notion of viability makes one question not only a state's ability to deliver on its goals but also how efficiently the rest of the polity participates in the exercise of political power as well as how and to what degree the prevailing rules of the political game are rendered moral.

Political viability, therefore, has a minimum of three dimensions, none of which is endowed with ultimate causal priority by theoretical fiat; all must be examined when barriers to political success are at issue. This final chapter considers the major factors that previous discussions have suggested impinge on such viability in the U.S. polity. These factors divide themselves readily into two broad classes: barriers to greater viability that are (more or less) exceptional to the American case, and those that are also common to advanced liberal democracies. This distinction shapes the bulk of subsequent discussion.

"Only in America!"

In the course of the analysis I identified three peculiarly American patterns that have had a dampening impact on political viability in the cultural, state, and stratification systems. Of course, fragments of all these barriers are present in other advanced democratic societies, but most observers agree that their most florid political implications are probably found here. The first two (in the cultural and state sectors) have encroached on the functioning of our polity since the founding of the Republic. Each, in its own way, reflects persistent contradictory threads of American life that have affected the course of political history. The third pattern—in the stratification system—is a more recent phenomenon just now becoming fully apparent.

CULTURAL FACTORS

The impact of cultural values on viability has often been overstated. For instance, a mythic, national past of hard-working Americans was constructed by critics of the Reagan era to reproach our supposedly profligate, consumption-oriented present. In fact, the constant tension between achievement and hedonistic values is a distinctively American cultural pattern. And Americans' moral ambivalence about these, I argued in the last chapter, is not new. Nor is it, despite its possible political costs, a crisis of political legitimacy. Our fellow citizens have coped for a long time with contradictory values that extol both production and consumption—not by rejecting one or the other entirely but by alternating over time which of the two they celebrate more.

The tension between achievement and hedonism has frequently been related to another currently "hot" cultural item with more overt political overtones: the conflict between communitarian and individualistic values. Some analysts who yearn for less hedonism also pine for an earlier time when Americans allegedly were more partial to collective ("republican") actions and solutions. The rise of hedonism, in their eyes, has undercut our sense of civic duty. Other commentators argue that individualism has always been a distinctively American strength. (Compare, for example, Bellah et al. 1985 and Gans 1988 on this issue.) I do not intend to delve into the complexities of cultural history here, but the proponents of an idealized *Gemeinschaft* America of yore need to be reminded of the special role of individualistic values in our society that Tocqueville recognized almost a century and a half ago. As Lipset (1989, p. 906) notes: "Some of the behaviors the critics disdain—business corruption, huckstering, commodification—have long been with us, and are endemic in a competitive mobile society." In reality, achievement and hedonism are each rooted in American individualism and are but two faces of that more fundamental ethic.

Indeed, values that encourage personal economic success and ones that extol self-gratification probably reinforce the exceptional position of individualism on our cultural landscape. Although the political implications of a permanent tension between achievement and hedonistic values have undoubtedly been exaggerated, the interaction of these two values certainly has not been conducive to political viability. Specifically, a preference for either achievement or hedonism is congenial with the dominance of personal (or microsocial) over collective (or macrosocial) interests (although, as I argue below, hedonism's impact is more thoroughgoing). People labor for material success and they consume, not for some greater good, but for the intrinsic satisfactions that these actions bring.

Why should this matter for political viability? The answer lies mainly in the fact that individualistic values dampen moral investment in state capacities. This limitation is not necessarily a matter of restrictions on the array of state goals. We have seen in Chapter 2 that the American polity's assortment of goals is no less extensive than that of other advanced systems. Rather, individualism often constrains political means more than general political ends; that is, it restricts the range of acceptable options even when problems are acknowledged. According to the authors of *Habits of the Heart*:

> The extent to which many Americans can understand the workings of our economic and social organization is limited by the capacity of their chief moral language. . . . The limit set by individualism is clear: events that escape the control of individual choice and will cannot be encompassed in a moral calculation. . . . [Thus] many individuals tend not to deal with embedded inequalities of power, privilege, and esteem in a culture of self-proclaimed moral equality." (Bellah et al. 1985, p. 204)

America's grudging acceptance of the welfare state, I suggested in Chapter 2, springs in part from what Farer (1982) calls our distinctive "ideology of individualistic capitalism."

But this is hardly the only instance when such values have a negative effect on state capacity. Their affinity with other American values intensifies this negative impact. For instance, our individualistic preferences resonate with the *antistatist* strands in our culture; together they generally sustain our hesitance to seek collective and public solutions for social problems, even when these have been treated as appropriate in most other advanced polities. Examples range all the way from how we deal with homelessness to the mechanisms we are inclined to favor for the protection of the environment and the allocation of health care.

Achievement and hedonism discourage the scope of public actions over and above the nurturing of individualistic values. Their influence is felt because of both their protracted *coexistence* and their tendency to *alternate* in primacy.

The long-standing coexistence of these values in American culture saps our capacity for sustained public actions in at least two ways. For one thing, the simultaneous presence of values that extol productive success and personal gratification (often in the same individual or group—as in the yuppie ethic) helps to legitimate *mixed motivation* as a normal feature of purposive social action. It is perfectly right and proper, in other words, to find fulfillment in both disciplined work and self-indulgence. Indeed, the same act may be justified in both rhetorics without embarrassment. Yet mixed motives are not equally acceptable in the private and public domains. Business people can more easily admit to working hard for the sake of living well than can public figures. The latter's rhetoric must still be saturated in the discourse of the older work ethic pieties. Mixed motives are "impure" and the sign of the hypocrite. Consequently, as Hirschman (1982, p. 129) notes, "once public man reels under the accusation of hypocrisy—the charge, that is, that public action is essentially self-serving—the turn to the private can be viewed as a move toward reality, sincerity, and even humility."

The coexistence of the two values also likely exacerbates the inefficiencies spawned by macro–cross pressures. Chapter 3 examined why U.S. political participation is plagued by both *apathy* (particularly disappointing voter turnouts, erosion of party identification, and a loss of confidence in incumbents) and *overload* (especially the rise of moralistic, single-issue pressure groups and social movements). Macroscopic cross pressures within a multitiered polity, I argued, account for a great deal of the apparently contradictory inefficiencies that afflict the same overall system. The public level is characterized by cynicism, complacency, and hypocrisy, while the organization tier is buffeted by a surge of moralism.

While hedonism does not create public apathy, it condones self-gratificatory behaviors once they are in place. Thus, for many, it is not until

> their private sanctuaries [are] threatened, [that] such people often feel the need to get involved in politics . . . They often call themselves "concerned citizens." Implicit in this designation is the idea that one can be a good citizen simply by being passively law abiding, and that one need become actively involved in public issues only when one becomes concerned about threats to the interests of one's self and one's community. (Bellah et al. 1985, p. 181)

Conversely, achievement values in our society inspire organized rational goal–oriented conduct. While achievement values have an individualistic tilt, they also foster an instrumentalist sense that mobilization can sometimes make a difference. Achievement-oriented persons, in turn, are more likely to embrace the notion that the formation of movements and pressure groups is useful in advancing one's interests. This "can do" outlook is *one* of the reasons that Americans seem to be so accepting of single-issue pressure groups (and why we have so many of them).

The American tendency to *alternate* in giving greater weight to hedonism or achievement also adversely affects political viability. Alternation intensifies the uncertainty about the proper scope of state actions, which is already more precarious here because of our system of divided federalism (see below). While achievement values often have a strong personal or microsocial focus, this is not inevitable. As just noted, the active instrumentalism inherent in such values has an affinity with the American inclination to pursue organizational responses to problems. In other words, those who value achievement are more likely to favor banding with others to seek collective and maybe even political solutions. On the other hand, state officials and citizens in advanced capitalist democracies (not just in the United States) have increasingly made "expressive" interests matters of private concern rather than public morality. Hence, a greater emphasis on hedonism deepens individualistic preferences and diminishes the room for public concerns. Insofar as both sets of values persist, ambiguity over the suitable range of the public sector is a permanent feature of American political life. In the absence of a strong, centralized state, shifts back and forth between the two values further cloud what should be the appropriate responsibility of government. In order to appreciate this point, one need only compare what liberals and conservatives alike saw as the state's proper scope during the late 1960s and early 1970s with both groups' more restricted views today.

STATE FACTORS

Culture never works in a sociological vacuum. Most often it impacts on viability by mediating among the more direct effects of structural forces, such as those linked to the state and social stratification. In

Chapter 2 we saw that the American state's capacity for effective goal attainment has historically been "awkward and incomplete" (Skowronek 1982, p. 287). Our system of divided federalism—a federal state with the separation of powers on the national level as well as below—has been invoked as the prime structural ingredient of this impaired state power. This does not mean that state effectiveness is a less important matter here. Instead, it forces us to ask directly "whether the much vaunted American Constitution, deep-frozen in the late-eighteenth century when 'checks and balances' were a more important consideration than national [effectiveness], does not hinder—or nowadays even paralyze—the taking of unpopular but necessary reforms" (Kennedy 1990, p. 40). In short, when the Founders built safeguards against tyranny into the American polity, they placed a light burden on the shoulders of the minimalist state of the time. But has fate decreed that this light burden should become an iron cage for state builders during the twentieth century? And, as I have just noted, divided federalism does not mean that the American state has fewer goals than other advanced states. Rather, our "awkward and incomplete" Constitution has produced a goal-attainment capacity that is more prone to be incremental, dispersed, and localized. It is incremental insofar as policymaking remains the science of "muddling through"; it is dispersed since the objectives of one government agency are at best loosely coordinated with those of others; and it is localized because so many collective goals are pursued below the national level, and even by private actors (e.g., employer-sponsored health insurance).

Difficulty in trading off between economic growth and other goals is a universal conundrum of advanced polities (see below). However, these symptoms of fragmentation are sharpened in our system. Incremental, dispersed, and localized decision formation makes the effective adjudication among the exigencies of economic growth, the welfare state, internal order, national security, and quality of life far more complex than in more centralized state systems.

The United States' fragmented state capacities have also probably helped weaken its citizens' faculty for calculating consistent, broad-based interests—even class-based interests. In Chapter 3, I attributed this tendency primarily to the separation of home and work and the "contradictory locations in class relations" (see also below).

Yet the American state's highly incremental, dispersed, and localized style aggravates this penchant (see, e.g., Skocpol 1985a, pp. 23–24). One crucial consequence is that both workers and capitalists are less able here than in other democracies to operate as unified forces on the national level.

Weir, Orloff, and Skocpol note:

> Within a state structure that so discourages unified, persistent class politics as does U.S. federal democracy, it is perhaps not surprising that social policy breakthroughs have clustered in widely separated "big bangs" of reform: during the Progressive Era from about 1906 to 1920; during the New Deal of the mid-1930s; and between the mid-1960s and the mid-1970s, during and right after the Great Society period. (1988, p. 22)

They offer slightly different scenarios for why this should be so for both workers and capitalists. In the case of the former, they focus on the separation of home and work, emphasizing the roles of universal suffrage and our patronage-oriented parties in our relatively weak state. "Because in the United States manhood suffrage and competing patronage parties were in place at the very start of capitalist industrialization," they argue, "American workers learned to separate their political participation as citizens living in ethnically defined localities from the workplace struggles for better wages and employment conditions" (Weir, Orloff, and Skocpol 1988, p. 21; see also Katznelson 1981, 1985; Shefter 1986). They see intracapitalist conflicts over state policies implicitly more as the result of contradictory locations within class relations and as reflecting:

> the frustration that American capitalists recurrently experience in their dealings with this or that part of the decentralized and fragmented U.S. state structure. For not only does U.S. federal democracy impede unified working-class politics; it also gives full play to divisions within business along industrial and geographic lines. (Weir, Orloff, and Skocpol 1988, pp. 21–22)

STRATIFICATION FACTORS

The nature of inequality in the United States has also impeded viability. Stratificational obstacles have sprung up despite the relative absence of a feudal past that burdened European polities with inherited but anachronistic conflicts. (It has been argued that racism, insofar as it has its roots in our southern agrarian past, is a major exception in this regard.) Overall, the comparatively easy triumph of industrial capitalism in the United States—along with its attendant cleavages—has a good deal to do with the absence of a landed ("feudal") aristocracy north of the Mason-Dixon line. Moreover, the Civil War can be seen as the vehicle for rapidly spreading the blessings of this "bourgeois revolution" to the South (see, e.g., Moore 1967, pp. 111–16).

The failure of feudal-based cleavages to prosper on American soil does not mean, however, that inequality has moved relentlessly in a one-dimensional economic direction or that it has been politically cost-free. Far from it. The assimilation of the waves of poor immigrants who entered this country during the nineteenth and early twentieth centuries did not result in a simple stratification system based exclusively on divisions between employers and employees. Cleavages, if anything, continue to be multidimensional, beyond even the degree implied in the classical Weberian division between classes and status groups. Economic life itself has become much more variegated. Chapter 3 suggested that Wright's notion of "contradictory locations within class relations" catches the essence of this complexity, although Wiley's Weberian conception of multiple and potentially cross-cutting marketplaces (labor, credit, and commodity) makes many of the same points more parsimoniously and ties them more directly to political developments.

"Contradictory locations within class relations" does not exhaust the politically relevant dimensions of American inequalities. Janowitz's (1978) emphasis on the political impact of the growing rift between work and community spheres has given renewed plausibility to the Weberian class–status group distinction. In other words, while some Americans today find it difficult to calculate a consistent set of economic interests (because of contradictory marketplace locations), others (including women, to a growing extent) are discerning that it is increasingly arduous to reconcile economic interests with community and family concerns. Cross-cutting, multiple cleavages such as these have not produced the efficient processing of political participation envisioned by Berelson, Lazarsfeld, and McPhee (1954). Instead, multidimensional conflicts weaken citizens' capacities to reckon a comprehensive set of priorities across sectors and time. Gans notes:

> People play many roles, which increases the number of interests they must juggle and reconcile. For example, . . . the routine division of labor places people in conflicting roles. As parents they want good schools for their children; as taxpaying homeowners they prefer inexpensive ones . . . [W]hen people are under cross-pressures . . . ,they may refrain from voting. The temptation to become bystanders increases. (1988, pp. 69–70)

Moreover, multidimensional conflicts make the efforts to build broad-based interest groups especially exasperating because those affected by cross-cutting cleavages have difficulty calculating consistent interests over several sectors. The result is the appearance of seemingly antithetical inefficiencies on different tiers of the polity: apathy in the forms of cynicism, complacency, and hypocrisy on the public level and an ascendancy of single-issue moralistic social movements among interest groups. Both tendencies, as noted, are also exacerbated by America's fragmented state capacity.

Our political party system has been the principal casualty of these developments. The divisions, apathy, and moralism that stem from "contradictory locations within class relations" and the fissuring of work and home have contributed significantly to *dealignment*, that is, to the long-term absence of a durable majority party. In the late nineteenth century, dealignment was manifested in the regular turnover between the two parties in control of the White House and the two Houses of Congress. During the past generation it has been reflected in the near-permanent division of national leadership between a Republican presidency and a Congress controlled by Democrats. As I note in previous chapters, party dealignment has had two key concomitants: (1) an individuation of issues such that parties are unable to mold diverse claims into comprehensive, consistent platforms capable of mobilizing more than a momentary majority; and (2) a particularization of elections in the sense of an increased randomness in electoral choices, as the votes within or across elections reflect little or no continuity.

To be sure, much of this discussion could be placed in the next section with little intellectual shoehorning, since cleavages in European societies have also become more cross-cutting in recent times, although they likely lag somewhat behind the United States because of residual tugs from their feudal heritage. Panebianco (1988, pp. 262–74) cites the advent of such divisions as one reason that Western European party systems more and more resemble the American model, in which he feels (somewhat exaggeratedly) that "parties completely lose their organizational identity and appear only as convenient tags for independent political entrepreneurs" (Panebianco 1988, p. 274). Thus the principal danger to a democratic party system is no longer strongly institutionalized oligarchies. Panebianco believes that "multidimensional cleavages" (as well as the changing roles of interest groups and the media) have been as decisive in fostering "deinstitutionalization." This development encourages a shift *from* "mass bureaucratic parties" (marked by central bureaucracies, pursuit of committed, dues-paying members, an internal, collegial leadership, financing from members and collateral associations, and a stress on ideology) *to* "electoral-professional parties" (characterized by the ascendancy of professionals, an "opinion electorate," the preeminence of elected officials, financing from interest groups and public funding, and a stress on opportunism over ideology) (Panebianco 1988, p. 264).

Nevertheless, the impact of macro–cross pressures on the party system is probably still greater here; and it reverberates more strongly in other parts of the American polity as well. The organization level has felt the blows with special intensity. The rise of moralistic single-issue movements, coupled with party dealignment (and probably fragmented state capacities), has strengthened the role of PACs since 1974. Some see this uniquely American subversion of reform as the principal factor undermining democratic efficiency here. Whether or not this is an exaggeration should not deflect attention from the fact that PACs are the direct effect of macro–cross pressures as well as their indirect result via party dealignment. This roundabout effect develops because of the parties' growing inability to manage and finance election campaigns in either a politically or an economically efficient manner.[1]

In sum, exceptional American cultural, state, and stratification formations have hampered our ability to fashion a more viable polity. Each factor in its own way inhibits state effectiveness and contributes to a growing inefficiency of political participation—although the legitimacy of the system itself remains remarkably intact. Our failure to enhance state effectiveness may be the more discussed sign of faltering viability over the past generation; our inherited system of divided federalism has had the strongest direct effect here. American values and our multiple and cross-cutting macroinequalities also contribute to ineffectiveness, albeit more circuitously. American values undermine state building by magnifying the impact of structural forces. In particular, they strengthen the adverse consequences of divided federalism and inefficient political participation. The indirect effects of macroscopic cross pressures on state capacities also stimulate inefficiency.

Yet inefficient participation is probably the most distinctive barrier to viability spawned by our multidimensional system of inequality. Our multiple, cross-cutting stratification system is plausibly the most pivotal factor in accounting for America's problems in balancing confidence and demands. Nevertheless, as we have seen, divided federalism and the permanence of achievement and hedonistic values also inhibit our ability to mobilize influence efficiently.

Barriers in Advanced Democratic Polities

American exceptionalism should not be overemphasized, however. Our polity has many features in common with other advanced democratic systems; some of these have critical repercussions for viability as well. Foremost among these barriers is the direction that modern state building has taken. The impact of contemporary political participation has also played a role, as has the effect of rational-legal doctrines of legitimation on the "confidence gap."

STATE CAPACITIES

Viability, we now know, has at least three vital ingredients. I have stressed repeatedly that the success of all modern political systems entails more than a state's ability to pursue goals effectively. Yet the modern state's bureaucratic format, its considerable dependence on contributions from nonstate actors (especially, although not exclusively, the producers of goods and services), and the moral frames provided to authorities and partisans by rational-legal doctrines all serve to guarantee that the effectiveness of state capacities becomes the paramount component. Analysis of modern states as complex organizations subject to a "contradiction model" of effectiveness, however, ensures that we will not equate success in this regard with the satisfactory pursuit of any single goal. Although delivering the economic goods is today's dominant state goal, it can never be pursued in isolation without incurring serious backlash. Internal divisions, heterogeneous internal and external constituents, and access to diverse resources mean that every modern state also strives after additional goals, among which national security, the "welfare state," "quality of life," and internal order have been cited as pivotal. The relationship of the first three to economic growth is especially important.

In the recent past, pursuit of national security through massive military expenditures has perhaps been the paramount challenge to the primacy of economic growth in the United States and the now-defunct Soviet Union. But as Paul Kennedy (1987) has shown, this conflict has had a long life, extending for at least five hundred years, especially among the "great powers." History demonstrates that when powerful states have had to choose between national prosperity and heavy military costs, they have been inclined to pick the latter and thereby to initiate their own decline. One of the major dramas on the end-of-the-century international front is whether this is merely an empirical generalization or an iron law of history. While elementary sociological sense suggests that no deterministic law is operative here, it is far from clear to what degree the last of the late twentieth century's two great powers will be able to avoid the fate of its principal rival. The prospect for the United States, despite its far greater economic abundance, remains clouded.

In Chapter 2, we saw that a zest for economic growth conflicts with state goals other than national defense. In the post–Cold War era, the search for such growth clashes particularly with the welfare state and environmental (quality of life) agendas. As all are permanent competitors for limited state resources, the choices to be made here are prime bases for political cleavages. The battle over the relative merits of economic growth versus social services is more historically embedded in democratic politics. It has provided grounds for classic right-left divisions or so-called class politics issues. Much has been made of the "new politics" located in the clash between the quality of life movements and the proponents of economic growth. Many see these newer debates as cross-cutting the older right-left divisions; others see a natural coalition between the "class politics" left and environmentalists and other quality of life advocates. In this scenario, "new politics" debates are merely superimposed on and reinforce older cleavages. The outcome is not at all certain. Whether "new politics" and classic right-left divisions cross-cut or reinforce each other depends heavily on the trends in civil society. *If* cross pressures continue to grow in all democratic societies, *if* interest groups and movements proceed in monogoaled and moralistic directions, and *if* party-system dealignment persists, *then* prospects for the sustained success of broad-based, multi-issue coalitions are likely to remain bleak in America and decline elsewhere.

An overemphasis on economic growth affects political involvement even more directly. In particular, it fosters inefficient participation in two ways. First, as we saw in Chapter 2, a stress on material progress promotes a rhetoric of instrumental consciousness that frames problems as technical rather than political or ideological. Such a rhetoric helps to weaken the leverage of elected officials and strengthen the hand of bureaucrats in the sifting of demands and confidence; to separate parties from broad, stable bases of support in civil society; and to individuate issues for interest groups, voluntary associations, and the public. Second, state authorities' overemphasis on economic growth kindles the political business cycle, a process that merges the rhythms of two distinct societal sectors to the detriment of both. The cycle's tendency to orchestrate economic rhythms to conform to electoral cadences affects the public, organization, and party tiers in ways that resemble the workings of instrumental consciousness. On the state level, these two forces work in opposite directions, however, because the political business cycle strengthens elected officials (whose life's blood is trading policies for votes) while challenging the state bureaucracy's central role in processing political influence.

Yet together instrumental consciousness and the political business cycle do not balance out. The contradictory strains faced by elected officials and bureaucrats as they attempt to respond to lower tiers reinforces the tensions between the two government sectors. State capacity is a probable victim. All states feel pressure to make less integrated and comprehensive decisions and to give greater leeway to local authorities and the private sector (although, as we have seen, other forces also accelerate the tendency toward dispersed, incremental, and local policy formation in the United States). Moreover, the fact that the two processes join to undermine the efficient processing of demands and confidence from party, organization, and public rungs will ultimately affect state capacities adversely.

POLITICAL PARTICIPATION

The preceding chapters have implied that participation and viability do not always fit together. Indeed, closer reflection makes clear that the nature of political participation in advanced democracies may erect barriers to viability. Certainly, the *inefficient* balancing of confidence and demands dilutes viability. We have noted, for example, that Western Europe seems now to be experiencing some of the same adverse ramifications we have previously found in the American pattern of an apathetic public coupled with moralistic interest groups and a dealigned party system. But democratic participation per se also raises challenges for viability.

Democracy's most universal justification has been that it restrains arbitrary state power. The rights of legitimate opposition, due process, and the rule of law are our surest safeguards against the rise of another Hitler or Stalin. Hence, "healthy" democratic institutions must always have the ability to challenge the growth of state capacities or else lose their efficacy and credibility. Theorists as diverse as Tocqueville, Weber, Michels, and Lipset feared that the growth of the state would eventually threaten democratic rights and obligations. (For an overview, see Lipset [1960] 1981, pp. 9–12.) Yet one does not have to be an admirer of totalitarianism to turn this concern on its head and speculate about the relative costs of vibrant democracy (see, e.g., Birnbaum 1988, pp. 183–84). Must eternal vigilance against tyranny to some degree be sacrificed to achieve enhanced state capacities? If the answer is yes, we understand more fully the imprudent willingness in some circles to jettison democratic safeguards (usually disparaged as "niceties") during moments of national "crisis."

More specific features of modern democracy are also a matter of concern. For some, the apparent inevitability of a multitiered democratic process is a source of consternation. They frequently use the label of "elite pluralism" to describe and disparage the fact that confidence and demands are filtered through several progressively more "elite" layers of the polity. As I noted in Chapter 3, minority decision making guarantees chronic dangers of distortion, since interest groups always restrict, edit, and remold potential influence from lower, more populous and dispersed tiers. Moreover, these distortions are not likely to be random but, instead, have a "conservative" tilt. By "conservative" I mean that the confidence and demands most articulated by interest groups support the prevailing distribution of power and privilege. A society's more privileged individuals and groups (i.e., the more highly educated, the better paid, and members of the business sector) tend to be overrepresented in voluntary associations and interest groups.[2] Less privileged persons and the collectivities that claim to speak for them are underrepresented on, and sometimes totally absent from, the organization level. Little wonder, then, that the most successful advocates on this tier are not likely to be on the cutting edge of radical change.

Yet, "direct democracy," the alternative sometimes recommended to elite pluralism, does not seem a better prospect for enhancing viability. Often, the term has been used to mask postrevolutionary terror by both neighborhood vigilante groups and new national leaders. "Participatory democracy," a more benign variant of direct democracy, certainly mitigates the risks of totalitarianism via emphasis on local self-management. Yet it too has costs for viability to the degree that it fails to deal satisfactorily with the exigencies of comprehensive planning over a wider territory; participatory democracy is a mechanism for more responsible mobilization of influence but not a substitute for political power (see Moore 1972, pp. 65–69). Moreover, participatory democracy advocates tend to blur distinctions between public and private spheres of life. Insofar as democratic viability depends on the acceptance of such a separation, participatory democracy may have unanticipated adverse results for such systems (see, e.g., Birnbaum 1988, p. 184).

The role of the mass media in democratic participation is also a matter of concern. Democratic viability obviously requires a press and a broadcast system that can function beyond direct state control. Yet while the destabilizing impact of the contemporary mass media has been exaggerated by some, they (particularly television) do create problems for all advanced democratic polities. The media's impact cannot be neglected in any democratic polity simply because their most severe critics assume that the institutions that stand between the public and the state and parties have been pulverized. This charge remains unsubstantiated. Yet, even if the "two-step flow" of communication remains a valid picture of what happens in democratic systems, this does *not* suggest that the kind of information processed (for example, more thirty-second "sound bites" on television news and fewer in-depth analyses) is not undermining democratic viability (albeit more subtly than some believe).

DOCTRINES OF LEGITIMATION

This brings us once again to the question of legitimacy. I have repeatedly observed that those adherents of the legitimation-crisis paradigm who anticipate an imminent collapse of advanced capitalist democracies are formally and substantively incorrect. In fact, the crisis of political legitimacy that this paradigm says hangs over liberal democracies has come down instead upon heads of regimes that justified themselves as Marx's apostolic successors. The collapse of state socialist systems in Central and Eastern Europe and the Soviet Union as well as continued stresses in China and Cuba indicate that the prime sources of loss of political faith in our times are not in fact the conflicts and contradictions within capitalist democracies.[3] Liberal democracies, as we have seen, face lots of problems, but the crisis of legitimacy is not among those looming.

Yet the way in which contemporary democratic systems maintain legitimacy is not without costs. Perplexingly, the more deeply democratic institutions dig their moral roots, the greater citizens' dissatisfaction with authorities becomes. The "confidence gap," although most discussed in the United States, is an increasing barrier to viability in all advanced democratic polities. Citizens and interest groups in these systems employ moral frames that are heavily imbued with rational-legal doctrines in order to evaluate the political events they experience. Such doctrines, I have argued, eventually increase interest group demands and ensure that public trust in specific leaders will be volatile. Justification of democratic rules of the game with this type of rhetoric heightens enthusiasm for the salutatory effects of "throwing the rascals out" and is probably more acute in this country because of the pervasive commitment to the American Creed. Yet the "confidence gap" is endemic to modern democratic life everywhere.

A crisis of legitimacy down the road in democratic polities is not impossible, however. All political systems are potentially vulnerable to erosions of faith. In modern times, ineffective goal attainment has been pinpointed as the most likely source of this predicament. A state's inability to ensure growing national prosperity has been recognized as especially troublesome in this regard. Yet, as Weil (1989) has shown in his analysis of survey data from France, Great Britain, Italy, Spain, West Germany, and the United States, economic effectiveness has a direct effect on confidence (trust in incumbents) but not on legitimacy (approval of the democratic rules of the game). He finds that economic effectiveness has an impact on legitimacy indirectly, via its influence on confidence. Thus, modern democratic states' special responsibility for economic growth merely runs the risk of undercutting legitimacy over the long run after a deep and sustained growth in the "confidence gap." This scenario is remote at the moment but not totally out of the question.

Looking for Policy Levers: A Postscript

Is there then no hope for more viable liberal democracies? My intent has not been to spread needless gloom. Unfortunately, the nature of "pure" academic work—that is, theoretical and empirical exercises that aim more to describe and explain things as they are and less as they ought to be—can foster distorted impressions about the prospects for deliberate political change. Such exaggerations can take several directions, intended and unintended; but they invariably create an aura of dashed hopes or a sense of futility. At different times, these formulations have been too utopian or too pessimistic and occasionally too "Olympian." The first two, more common possibilities overstate the ease or difficulty in bringing about significant political transformation. Sociological writings in the late 1960s tended more in the first direction; works in the 1980s were more inclined to go in the opposite track. I use the term "Olympian" for the third class of hyperbole to call attention to those highly abstract prognostications that are so obscure as to defy ready labeling as either too utopian or pessimistic. Recent proclamations of the "end of history" and the "end of the state" are prototypical here. All major developments (for good or ill), "Olympian" theorists tell us, are the result of impersonal (indeed, "mindless") forces and not the conscious interventions of human agents.

Whatever its specific manifestation, distortion springs to some degree from the nature of "pure" social science. Sociological theory by itself is not an ideal guide for policy formation. Our discipline's major schools of thought (such as the interpretative, rational-choice, functionalist, and conflict approaches) may help gauge the broad constraints faced by policy initiatives and point to which classes of factors are most or least susceptible to human interventions (e.g., to show that a group's structure is more easily modified than its culture).[4] But theory per se does not lend itself directly to the solution of concrete problems precisely because of its abstract formulations. For instance, the application of either structural-functional or labeling approaches to deviance hardly provides a detailed guide to effective national policy on crime, drug abuse, or high mortality rates in the inner cities. Such conceptual schemes must be "translated" before they can have any reliable practical impact. Two preliminary steps are essential. First, the key dimensions of each concept must be specified. This specification should always be in the direction of lower levels of abstraction than the original category. Second, one or more valid empirical indicators for each dimension must be found and used in the testing of explanatory statements (see Lehman 1978).

Yet, although the use of valid measurements is a step toward making social science more compatible with effective policymaking than theory alone is, a distorted picture of the prospects for planned change is still likely. "Pure" academic researchers are mandated to search out those factors that have contributed the most strongly to what has happened or failed to happen. In other words, they assign weights or ranks to likely explanatory variables in proportion to how much of the variance in a dependent variable they actually produce. Etzioni (1971) reminds us that this should not be the main objective of those seeking the most suitable levers for social change. In contrast to "pure" researchers, these latter specialists are called policy researchers. Their mission is to seek out the most "movable" variables, those that point us to the factors that are most readily molded by deliberate human interventions. In other words, a variable's "movability" is "the degree to which the phenomenon it characterizes is malleable" (Etzioni 1971, p. 11).[5]

Since this not the best of all possible worlds, the most movable variables do not always explain the most variance. At first glance, this might seem a formidable impediment to the pursuit of conscious social change. Yet, simply because the prime explanatory variables and the most movable ones do not coincide does not mean that we must abandon a scientifically grounded search for transformation. Unfortunately, both advocates of change and their critics often foster utopianism or undue pessimism because they conflate the two types of variables and thus fail to grasp this point. Reformers, in an attempt to justify their policy recommendations, are prone to equate the remediation of a problem with its initial causes. Even someone as sophisticated as Wilson (1978, 1987) does not always clearly disentangle his recommended treatment for urban minority poverty from the long-term cultural and social factors that helped bring it about in the first place. It makes perfectly good sense to put forward an urban jobs program as the best way to ameliorate inner-city poverty. But one does not have to intimate that employment patterns are the pivotal explanatory variables in accounting for the rise of the urban minority poor to validate such a recommendation.

Conservative critics of reform, on the other hand, feel that, by arguing or demonstrating that the suggested movable variables are not the ones that explain most of the variance, they have exposed a fundamental inadequacy of a proposed policy. In the area of urban poverty, they are particularly fond of invoking the "culture of poverty" as their key explanatory variable. Thus, for example, Mead (1986) contends that Great Society programs were doomed because they failed to consider the maladaptive values, behaviors, and life-styles of the poor. Needless to say, such an explanation is open to considerable dispute. Yet the question is not simply whether critics such as Mead are correct about the alleged role of cultural factors in explaining the origins of minority poverty. Even *if* these factors were decisive in accounting for beginnings, the policy recommendations that conservatives abhor would not be vitiated. Since cultural variables are very difficult to change over the short run (Lehman 1977, pp. 31–34; see also note 4), equating movable with explanatory variables unduly restricts the range of policy options. It prevents us from asking, "What can be fixed?"

Let me sum up: Academic social science can make a contribution to building a more viable polity and more decent society once its limitations as well as its strengths are made explicit. Theoretical formulations about political life are, by their nature, sufficiently complex to warrant explicit definition in multidimensional terms. Normally, use of more than one empirical indicator for each of the dimensions not only enhances valid measurement but brings us closer to being "policy relevant." However, we must always appreciate the fundamental differences between "pure" social research and policy research. The fact that accounting for variance is the central aim of the former and movable variables are the target of the latter is probably most vital here. (For other differences, see note 5 and Etzioni 1971.)

This book has not concentrated on the quest for movable variables for the sake of solving concrete problems. Its primary concern has been the development of a more adequate paradigm for the analysis of the constraints liberal democracies face in dealing with whatever problems arise rather than an examination of a particular set of problems ; but this should not cloak my conviction that broad-ranging policy innovations on a variety of fronts are essential for enhanced viability. From the perspective of a policy analyst, my focus has been more on the conditions of political action and not on the formulation of explicit means or ends. In a sense, this final chapter has pulled together the strands from the earlier discussions regarding which constraints on political initiatives are specific to the U.S. situation and which ones are common to most advanced capitalist democracies. Understanding the exigencies that surround effectiveness, efficiency, and legitimacy advances our political discernment. It also shapes our capacity to transform society, although this effect is inevitably more nebulous. An enhanced ability to study the barriers that we encounter while struggling to achieve greater viability as a liberal democracy with a special history is a contribution in itself. Successful planning is also advanced by the unequivocal recognition that we must look elsewhere for the *tangible levers* to overcome our specific problems.

Yet the kind of constraints we have been looking at are not cast as equally intractable. In fact, there is a range: Some of the factors we discussed have intrinsically low malleability; some are probably malleable but "cost" too much to manipulate; and others seem to be fruitful candidates for lowering existing barriers to successful policy initiatives. Patterns of culture are the clearest instances of low malleability. Generally, symbol systems crystalize, diffuse, and gain acceptance quite slowly. This low short-term variability makes culture a poor vehicle for planned social change. Beliefs, values, and sentiments cannot be easily molded for the sake of transformation. For instance, we have seen that American individualistic values and the modern world's preference for rational-legal legitimations both affect political life. But how seriously should we take recommendations to alter either or both of these—by, for instance, fostering "communitarian" values—for the sake of democratic viability? New values or doctrines might be helpful, but the struggle for more effective, efficient, or even legitimate polities can hardly wait for several generations for cultural metamorphosis to occur.

Although structural factors, as a rule, are more malleable than cultural items, not all of them offer the same prospects. Divided federalism, it has been repeatedly noted, raises barriers to more effective state capacities. In the abstract, it is easier to change the "awkward and incomplete" U.S. Constitution than to modify American values. Yet, in the final analysis, those who are worried about our problems with productivity, education, health, crime, etc., would do well to avoid constitutional battles as well as culture tampering. The political costs of constitutional reforms would be so high that a focus on this area might actually delay dealing with the more pressing, specific predicaments. Much the same may said about recommendations to reduce cross pressures built into modern inequality. Of course, macro–cross pressures promote inefficient processing of confidence and demands. But even if the reduction of inequities is a specific policy objective, the contraction of cross pressures per se is so innately costly that any victories on this front would be Pyrrhic.

However, there are structural factors whose deliberate manipulation can enhance a polity's guidance capacity without raising insuperable costs. Outside of specific programs to relieve individual problems (e.g., reform of campaign financing or restructuring of the federal budget process), one other general area looks particularly promising. In Chapter 2, I argued that economic growth, despite its acknowledged primacy, can never be pursued in a political vacuum. Modern states must also deliver social entitlements, internal order, national security, and quality of life. We saw that entitlements and quality of life often fall victim to a single-goal enthusiasm for economic growth, while the pursuit of national prosperity is sometimes a casualty of the exaggeration of the importance of national security and internal order. Thus, state capacities become more effective when policymaking is more coordinated, comprehensive, and centralized—that is, when the pursuit of any goal (economic growth, for example) occurs in the context of concern for the practical implications for all the others. Mishra's (1984) Integrated Welfare State (IWS) presents at best a partial model here, because it provides only a guide for reconciling economic growth with social entitlements goals. Such a binary view of state agendas is too one-dimensional.

A more ambitious neocorporatism is very much in the political air and cuts across party lines in the post-Reagan era. By neocorporatism I simply mean policymaking that is antithetical to the current pattern of dispersed, incremental, and localized decisions, and hence more coordinated, comprehensive, and centralized, while also formally incorporating relevant constituencies into the process. The more successful such strategies are, the more the overall effectiveness of state capacities will be. By definition, a neocorporatist approach to decision making will check the tendencies for state actions to be fragmented. Neocorporatism with a democratic face will also enhance efficient participation in a number of ways. In particular, I anticipate that it will lead to a greater uncoupling of the political business cycle because policy will be more long-term and comprehensive and not merely manipulated for short-term electoral advantage. Also, neocorporatist approaches will mitigate the individuation of issues and hence possibly arrest party dealignment.

Neocorporatism will not come to the United States overnight. We noted in Chapter 2 that certain European democracies (notably Austria, Sweden, Germany, and the Netherlands) have already made significant progress on this front. Yet we also saw that structural impediments to neocorporatism persist here (and in Great Britain to some degree). However, the political climate is right at the moment to begin neocorporatist ventures on selected fronts in the United States. The need to shore up vital American industries in the face of Japanese and other foreign competitors that have strong state support seems a relatively noncontroversial entry point into our own neocorporatism. From these beachheads, gradual expansion to more and more policy sectors is plausible.

Neocorporatism is not without risks. In the early part of this century advocates of a corporatist state were uniformly antidemocratic, awareness of which should promote permanent vigilance. Even today, neocorporatism clearly does little in the short term to revitalize the electoral process and may well contribute to its further erosion. I am especially concerned about the possibility that the advocates of neocorporatism may further promote instrumental consciousness. In Chapter 2 I discussed this policy style's deleterious effects on democratic political participation. Yet if neocorporatism is to embody something like an expanded version of Mishra's IWS, then perhaps even the type of rhetoric that political practitioners are going to employ will move beyond a narrow instrumentalism. For example, when economic growth and the welfare state are reconciled not only with each other but with quality of life goals, a broader, more elevating political discourse may emerge among policymakers.

Yet lofty objectives and compelling rhetorics cannot be custommade. Thus I offer none here, just as I have eschewed specific policy recommendations. Both activities are vital but fall beyond the scope of this book. On the other hand, although I have not focused on what and how things should be changed, I hope I have shown why change is important—and also why it is possible. Since history is not over, and since the state will not disappear, the quest for political transformation is more than a passing stage in the human experience. The twentieth century has taught us that there are no ultimate political answers. The shattered hopes of those who believed themselves to be on the cutting edge of history lie all around us. But this record must not deter us. The rational understanding and pursuit of political viability are worthy goals. The need to avoid hubris is not a call for passivity. It is instead a call to avoid barren ideologies and "static utopias" (Moore 1972) while pursuing a more effective, efficient, and legitimate political order—and passing on this enterprise to the next generation.

Notes

Introduction

1. Kuhn (1970) believes that the social sciences are "pre-paradigmatic." Others question the applicability of the concept of paradigm to sociology in particular and the social sciences in general (see, e.g., Eckberg and Hill 1979; Turner 1991, p. 29).

Clearly, no single paradigm exists in sociology. Nevertheless, we can speak of our specialty as divided into a number of schools of thought or general theoretical orientations set off from one another by distinctive metaphysical, epistemological, ideological, and aesthetic views of reality and advancing competing theoretical and empirical strategies. The term "paradigm" may safely be applied to these varying approaches without doing undue damage to Kuhn's original intent—and indeed consequently profiting from appropriating some of his insights (see, e.g., Alexander 1982; Ritzer 1990).

2. The source is a private communication from Goodwin (October 11, 1991).

3. Indeed, a "paradigm" in this sense may influence scholars without their being aware of its existence.

4. See Chapter 4 for a more complete analysis of Weber's contributions to our understanding of legitimacy.

5. Chapter 1 examines the strengths and weaknesses inherent in Lipset's definition of "democratic political stability." Chapters 2 and 4 ponder, among other things, the special interaction between effectiveness and legitimacy that he hypothesizes for modern states.

6. I return to this issue in Chapter 4.

Lipset's former student Juan Linz (1988) has tried to break out of binary formulations in another way, by adding the dimension of the growth of international capitalism. He believes that with the rise of this new factor the capitalist state is now more protected from legitimation crisis because citizens no longer blame it for economic ineffectiveness. I find this argument provocative, but Linz's theoretical framework for analyzing state success and failure remains too closely wedded to the binary mode.

7. Of course, there are important variations within the neo-Marxist approach. Different emphases on which dimension is the primary site of the crisis are probably the most significant cleavages. Most works give centrality to the loss of public trust, which they equate with the evaporation of legitimacy. This is the "purer" version of legitimation-crisis analysis (see Offe 1974; Habermas 1975; Wolfe 1977). Another version gives greater consideration to the strains that appear in state capacities. The decisive predicaments are then sometimes given different names such as the "fiscal crisis of the state" (O'Connor 1973) or the "crisis of crisis management" of the capitalist welfare state (Offe 1984).

For a detailed critique of Marxist and neo-Marxist analyses of the state, see van den Berg (1988).

8. Dennis Wrong in a personal communication (October 25, 1991) reminds me that neither Riesman nor Kornhauser, the earliest users of the term "veto group," necessarily deplored the pluralism such groups generated. The opposite is true in Riesman's case; he was concerned with contrasting the reality of broadly based veto power in our society with claims that Wall Street or monopoly capitalism actually ran the show. Kornhauser was simply comparing pluralist and elitist theories, not bewailing existing conditions.

The pessimistic view of pluralism that one finds in the writings of authors such as Bell and Janowitz only becomes prominent a decade later in the 1970s.

9. In Chapter 3 I attempt to specify this insight in order to show that the American polity is simultaneously apathetic and "hyperactive."

Chapter 1

1. For an understanding of how this approach to metatheory fits in with other uses of the term, see Ritzer (1990).

2. Of course, Alexander's (1982) continuum of scientific work—which is intended as a rebuke to monistic interpretations of science—is itself one-dimensional. All the elements of scientific paradigm are arrayed along a single plane. The scientific enterprise is probably better seen as inevitably even more complex. A more complete rendering of the components of a paradigm would require respecifying in detail all the items on Alexander's continuum and forming them into a multidimensional matrix. However, given the overall purpose of this book, such an effort would take us too far

afield. Alexander's scheme—for all its closet monism—is more than adequate for the points I wish to make about paradigm building in general and fundamental assumptions in particular.

3. Nor is this predilection currently confined to the legitimation-crisis paradigm. Much of the research on political culture, for example, tends to have a unidimensional bias insofar as it relies exclusively on a symbolic framework and ignores the role of structural and environmental factors in explaining political processes (see Lehman 1977, pp. 21–42).

4. Some might argue that Giddens is less multidimensional than Alexander because he remains more ambiguous about the emergent, *sui generis* aspects of social structure. Yet, for my purposes here, this issue is beside the point. In the present circumstance I regard Giddens as robustly multidimensional because he casts the problem of order in terms of a duality of agency and structure rather than opting for one or the other of these two dimensions.

5. The realm of presuppositions contains other elements, of course. Ideology is perhaps the most important of these (Alexander 1982, pp. 39–44). Ideological presuppositions penetrate concrete activities in all sciences. The penetration is most explicit in analyses of social, economic, and political life, however. I do not deny the importance and possible inevitability of ideological intrusions in the conduct of political sociology. Yet, in the final analysis, my "ideology" is that the objective of all social scientists should be to restrict the impact of nonrational ideology as much as possible and to optimize the range of the cognitive, nonevaluative aspects of science. This position, coupled with the realization that we will never attain an ideological consensus comparable to the ones *possible* about power and viability, leads me to forgo detailed discussion of prospective ideological presuppositions.

6. Wrong (1980, p. 86) notes that Weber's definition "is often interpreted, whether critically or approvingly, as insisting on the primacy of force in politics, echoing Thrasymachus, Hobbes and Machiavelli, the last of whom Weber praised as an ancestor." Wrong, however, goes on to suggest that there is more ambiguity here than first meets the eye (see Wrong 1980, pp. 86–87).

7. In a private communication (June 10, 1989), James B. Rule has reminded me that one cannot use this aphorism to infer a simplistic, one-dimensional reading of Mao's views of power or the state. Rule himself believes that these views are not so different from those of Weber, Pareto, and a number of other classical theorists who never minimized the role of symbols and ideas.

8. Yet, as Etzioni (1968, p. 106) notes: "As in all organizations, the

state's pyramidal pattern does not preclude the possibility of the partial autonomy of sub-units, though—in a fashion typical of other organizations—sub-unit autonomy tends to exist within limits set by the overriding unit."

9. Most of the pivotal projects of modern life are accomplished through complex organizations. This close association of complex organizations with the activist potential in politics has wider implications as well. For the most part, my discussion has focused on the organizational capacities of the state. Yet complex organizations (i.e., deliberately created agencies for the pursuit of specific goals) appear on at least three of the four intrasocietal levels of the polity and probably on all conceivable transnational tiers too. Thus interest groups, political parties, and other states, as well as transstate actors (e.g., the United Nations, the EEC) are all organizations with some transformative potential. In short, autonomy and agency are critical potentials on the state level, and our concern with political viability makes these topics especially important. On the other hand, our analysis becomes unduly restricted if as a matter of definition we confine these potentials to the state alone. We also lapse back into a one-dimensional mode of thinking when this happens.

10. They also disagree, of course, because neo-Marxists say economic growth is being overemphasized, while neoconservatives argue that too much weight has been given to entitlement. See Chapter 2 for a more comprehensive discussion of this issue and the general question of state effectiveness in modern politics.

Chapter 2

1. This potential strain between confidence and demands has proven a handy vehicle for delving into the nature of political efficiency and inefficiency. Chapter 3 presents an image of efficient participation as fundamentally entailing the ability to balance these two inputs (see also Berelson, Lazarsfeld, and McPhee 1954, pp. 305–23). That chapter also examines in depth the implications of a multilevel polity for the processing of confidence and demands (in general) and political efficiency (in particular).

2. It could be argued that the impact of rational-legal doctrines in emphasizing effectiveness is fully conveyed under the rubric of the bureaucratization of state capacities. I disagree, because to accept this possibility is to conflate the realms of culture and social system generally and the realms of political culture and political system particularly (see Lehman 1977, pp. 21–42). Moreover, as we saw in Chapter 1, theoretical and empirical confusions ensue when one slips back and forth between making legitimacy part of political culture and making it part of the political system.

Sociological analysis prospers when we separate the shared symbols that members of any collectivity produce and reproduce in order to orient themselves (their culture) from the network of relationships they produce and reproduce among themselves (their social system). If the two systems are conflated, many of the vital questions of social science become tautologies. Perhaps the classic question in this regard has been termed the *sociology of knowledge* and concerns the relationship between how people are organized and what they believe, value, and feel. In political analysis this means that the primary analytical site for legitimacy ought to be in the realm of political culture. As a result, the study of the interaction between doctrines of legitimation and political-system phenomena such as bureaucratization and the stress on effectiveness can proceed in a more empirically open manner.

3. As Flora Lewis (1987, p. A19) noted at the time, these states "all know that most of Iran's arms supplies are delivered clandestinely, . . . but through channels they cannot admit. Iran and Iraq have become the world's greatest consumers of munitions and there are thousands of jobs that depend directly on these secret exports, national arms industries that could not maintain competitive unit costs for their countries' defense needs without lucrative Iran and Iraq markets. Over 30 countries engage in the trade, most with both sides in the war."

4. Goal succession is intricately intertwined with goal multiplication. For one thing, extensively available assets encourage not only an increase in the number of goals but also the continued search for new ones. Sills's (1957) study of how the March of Dimes replaced the conquest of polio with a new goal of overcoming arthritis and birth defects is perhaps the classic inquiry into goal succession. But succession and multiplication are also intertwined because the unambiguous supplanting of one goal by another is rare, mainly because few goals are ever definitively attained (particularly in political life). The military, for example, shifts resources from a "warfare" goal to a "preparedness" one when armed hostilities end. Yet victory in any given war does not mean that the warfare goal has been permanently replaced. In most political circumstances, therefore, resources are rarely shifted permanently from one goal to another. Rather, goal succession is typically a subspecies of goal multiplication, and resource primacy is alternated to emphasize one goal and then another without diminishing—and probably increasing—the absolute number of goals.

5. Planning was more comprehensive in Sweden, Heclo (1974) believes, because its history of autonomous bureaucratic conduct predates modern democratic politics while Great Britain's is much more recent.

6. This is a point on "which virtually all scholars agree," according to

Skocpol (1985a, p. 12). She sees the fact that the United States did not in-
herit a bureaucratic order from a feudal past as particularly important in this
regard (Skocpol 1985a, p. 12).

7. Little wonder that the pool of professionals in the public service
sector has also formed an advocacy base for the welfare state that sometimes
has been more vocal than social service beneficiaries and their representatives. They have been among the most persistent actors on the organization
level (viz., via interest groups) in the drive against cutbacks.

8. Kennedy introduces a third state goal in the late stages of his analysis, one that resembles what has been termed here as social entitlements or
the welfare state. Thus, in his concluding chapter, he departs from the binary formula employed throughout the rest of the book when he declares
that in heading toward the twenty-first century, advanced states have a
threefold objective: "simultaneously to provide military security (or some
viable alternative security) for its national interests, *and* to satisfy the socio-
economic needs of its citizenry, *and* to ensure sustained growth, this last
being essential both for the positive purposes of affording the required guns
and butter at the present, and for the negative purpose of avoiding a relative economic decline which would hurt the people's military and economic
security in the future" (Kennedy 1987, p. 446). Nevertheless, a social entitlements goal does not constitute a pivotal element in Kennedy's overall analysis. In fact, he subsequently equates socioeconomic needs with "consumption" (Kennedy 1987, p. 446).

9. National security also has a crucial historical link to internal order.
Both flow from the state's capacity to monopolize the means of violence
effectively. The heightened order inside the modern state's borders has permitted "a concentration on military power 'pointing outwards' towards
other states in the nation-state system" (Giddens 1985, p. 192). While states
vary by the degree of separation between internal policing and external military prowess, the overall pattern is a distinguishing feature of contemporary
political life, especially in democracies.

10. This is understandable in the present context, since the boundaries of
the modern state were shaped primarily by the physical limits of its military
capacities (see, e.g., Poggi 1978). Even today a state's official borders reflect
this capacity more than the scope of its economic, cultural, and linguistic
reach. Indeed, military prowess remains the ultimate resource in the relations
among states, although nuclear arsenals have produced an unprecedented
threshold of violence and, thus, have raised questions about what shape military force will have to take in the future to pursue national security effectively.

11. Further, the anti-Communist internationalism consensus provided a
rationale for an array of domestic actions that had implications for economic

growth and public welfare. Government support for research and development, the space program, area studies and foreign language training, and science education depended on anti-Communist internationalism to get off the ground in the 1950s and early 1960s. With the decline of this consensus, then the end of the Cold War, and the persistence of the incrementalist DWS, no compelling domestic rationale to sustain such programs emerged immediately. Little wonder that the backing for these programs then eroded to the point where their renewed effectiveness has become a matter of broad national concern.

12. Certainly, no one doubts the conflict between military spending and other key goals, particularly social entitlements. The Reagan era, after all, was marked by massive increases in the former and efforts to cut back on the latter. Still, we might recall that in the preceding two decades federal welfare expenditures rose more sharply than the proportion of the budget devoted to defense.

13. Certainly, the neoisolationist visions from both the right and the left provide no effective guidance here. The former calls for a turning inward now that communism has been "defeated"; the latter continues to be haunted by specters of new Vietnams around every corner.

14. Some proponents of more entitlements have also come to believe that environmental programs may siphon off funds from social programs and, thus, benefit the affluent and the suburban (the members of the Sierra Club, for instance) more than the poor and the urban.

15. While I feel comfortable about including both under the general rubric of instrumental consciousness, distinguishing between the two permits Jasper (1990) to analyze why France, the United States, and Sweden developed divergent approaches to developing and regulating nuclear power as well as managing opposition. In France, the technological enthusiasts prevailed, resulting in the continued development of nuclear power and the muting of debate below the state level. In Sweden and the United States, on the other hand, the cost-benefiters won. The result was increased debate and policy stalemate.

16. Nor is the United States alone here. Other polities continue to depend on traditional (or at least nonrational) themes too. The monarchist symbolism in Great Britain—and to lesser degrees in Belgium, Denmark, the Netherlands, Norway, and Sweden—continues to inspire some authorities and citizens. Other, albeit less graphic, examples come readily to mind. Party leaders in Cuba and China still try to invoke the rhetoric of revolution (granted with decreasing success) in order to give their efforts to retain dominance a moral anchorage. Nationalism's vitality in new and in long-established polities (as well as in the former Soviet Union and the formerly

Communist systems of Eastern Europe) is probably the most universal demonstration that economic themes have not achieved a singular preeminence and that other strands—including nonrational ones—remain important in the process of legitimation.

Chapter 3

1. While voting serves as a gateway to more intensive and extensive forms of participation, it may also be an impediment to higher levels of involvement. Albert O. Hirschman (1982, pp. 111, 117), for instance, notes that elections are "a method of aggregating preferences that places a ceiling on citizen involvement . . . and . . . *delegitimizes* more direct, intense, and 'expressive' forms of political action that are more effective and more satisfying."

2. What Olsen means by "partisan" differs from my usage. I follow Gamson's (1968) distinction between "authorities" (those who set goals and issue commands) and "potential partisans" (those who are affected by the goals and commands). In effect, I employ the terminology to distinguish between the polity's state and nonstate members and between "potential" and "actual" partisans. I also use the terminology to spotlight my disagreement with Tilly (1974, 1978) over what constitutes a polity member. Actual "partisans," to my way of thinking, may be either "contenders" or "challengers." In short, polity members (or participants) are divided into "potential partisans" (those who are subject to state controls but are otherwise inactive) and "actual partisans" (who include both "contenders" and "challengers").

3. The term "zone of indifference" was introduced by Barnard (1938, pp. 167–71, 185–89) to account for the range of commands for which an organization's leaders can assume automatic acceptance, that is, do not need to back up with sanctions. Herbert Simon (1957) calls the same phenomenon the "zone of acceptability."

4. Thus the cross-pressured voter is simultaneously someone who currently copes with incompatible affiliations by withdrawing more from the political process and someone who in the longer run helps reduce polarization and provide a basis for future political formations. The coping mechanisms are not the basis of the political formations, however. Rather, both are the products of how relations are structured within a society.

5. Not the least important of these is that it makes us look to the organization of society for the principal sources of political formations and conflicts and not to the subjective dispositions of citizens individually or in the aggregate.

6. Of course, the structure of the state and the general character of political institutions also mold the forms that political participation is likely to take. Amenta and Zylan (1991), for example, have found that state struc-

ture and policies (along with differences in political party system) are decisive in accounting for both why the Townsend movement, which sought pensions for the elderly during the Depression, was larger in some states than in others and why its size fluctuated throughout the 1930s.

7. Although I use both "interest group" and "social movement" in this chapter, I do not regard them as distinct species. Rather, as I observe in Chapter 1, social movements are a highly visible and potent type of interest group. Although they share a bureaucratized core with interest groups generally, social movements also include a periphery of fervent adherents who are not technically organizational participants but who are capable of mobilization for limited but intense events.

8. Exceptions occur when officials believe compliance to the demands of an organized group is personally rewarding. Bribery is the crudest instance here. The "revolving door" between regulatory agencies and the industries they purport to regulate has only recently become subject to legal sanctions, for example.

Exceptions may also occur when the organized group claims *expertise* and not special interest as its justification for exerting influence. Brint (1990) argues that lawyers, economists, physicians, and educators have been especially adept in making claims on the state with little or no need to vindicate their demands in the name of some public-based constituency.

9. Hamilton and Wright (1986, p. 376) conclude: "This theory, we think more than any other, is destined for a *retour éternal* in intellectual affairs." For a concise critique of mass society theory and the "irrationalist" tradition of which it is a part, see Rule (1988, pp. 91–118).

10. The antithesis of parties of representation are "parties of integration." The latter have homogeneous constituencies, aim at high intrusion into their followers' private lives, and are predisposed toward high political moralism. They are more likely to be interested in representing only one or a few groups. Because they are concerned with "great ideals," they see their responsibility as extending beyond politics as it is conventionally conceived. Their goal is also to encapsulate and shape the lives of their adherents by fostering associations that restrict contacts with outsiders and by imposing values for appropriate behavior in the private sector (regarding such matters as family life, sex, religion, recreation, and aesthetics, for example). European Catholic and socialist parties during the interwar period came close to being the "ideal type" examples of parties of integration.

For a comprehensive view of party systems on the world scene, see Sartori (1976). For a distinction between parties similar to the representation-integration classification, see Panebianco (1988) on the difference between mass bureaucratic and electoral-professional parties.

11. This was the year in which Ronald Reagan defeated an incumbent

Democratic president (Jimmy Carter) in a "landslide" election and the Republican party regained control of the United States Senate for the first time since 1954.

12. I employ this somewhat awkward usage deliberately. It still would be excessive under our "party of representation" system to cast Democrats (especially in the House and Senate) as consistently liberal and Republicans as consistently conservative. More accurately, each party has lost most of its "outliers," that is, ultra-conservative Democrats and ultra-liberal Republicans.

13. Hirschman's treatment of privatism (1982, pp. 92–134) is also worth looking at regarding this issue, despite his predilection for rational-choice theory.

14. The fact that other forms of political participation have not decreased even while voting has slid downward somewhat is worth noting here in support of the idea that overall involvement has not eroded. In particular, levels of involvement in interest groups and political organizations remain higher in the United States than in any other advanced democratic nation (Ladd 1987, pp. 458–60). Nevertheless, this phenomenon points to interactions between the organization tier and the public and is more appropriately discussed when we analyze moralism.

15. Of course, the shape of American interest groups is probably influenced by factors other than those tied to "upward" participation processes. The nature of state capacities may also play a key role. Skocpol (1985a, pp. 23–24), for example, observes: "Such basic (and interrelated) features of the U.S. state structure as federalism, the importance of geographic units of representation, nonprogrammatic political parties, fragmented realms of administrative bureaucracy, and the importance of Congress and its specialized committees within the national government's system of divided sovereignty all encourage a proliferation of competing, narrowly specialized, and weakly disciplined interest groups."

My analysis here is not a rejection of Skocpol's contention. Rather, I merely add that this "proliferation" has rapidly accelerated in recent times because of macro- and multitiered cross pressures. Moreover, such interest groups have now adopted more passionate, "moralistic" rhetorics (see below).

Chapter 4

1. I discuss below the key political-systemic ("structural") manifestations of legitimation and how examining them casts further doubt on the plausibility of a legitimation crisis.

2. The term "rules" is often equated with "norms," the specific standards of conduct produced and embedded in social interaction. Yet I believe that those who write about the "political rules of the game" are speaking about broader statements of preference—about what is generally desirable and appropriate and what is not. These kinds of rules are part of patterns of values set in a collectivity's culture.

3. Chapter 2 considered the fact that such diagnoses often went further; they suggested that appeals to economic effectiveness have usurped the place of classic rational-legal doctrines. For present purposes I restrict my analysis to the implications of the shift Weber pointed out to us—the movement from traditional to rational-legal legitimations. See Chapter 2 for a discussion of why the more extreme claims for an economic turn remain at best conjectural. Let me just note that such diagnoses are not confined to neo-Marxists, however; see, for example, Poggi (1978).

4. For a review of the data and the formulation of the notion of "confidence gap," see Lipset and Schneider 1983, especially pp. 93–96. For a similar finding—but without the same conceptual distinctions—see Hamilton and Wright 1986, pp. 361–73.

5. Conversely, in settings where rational-legal doctrines are negligible or nonexistent, a "confidence gap," as we know it, is less likely to develop. Charismatic legitimation provides a leader with virtually unbounded confidence; followers are expected to suppress their own agendas in favor of unconditional submission to their leader's will. Charisma's "viability" depends on how successfully this suppression is maintained. A rise in followers' independent demands is part and parcel of a growing doubt about a leader's claim to extraordinary qualities. It translates almost immediately into the unraveling of charisma in its pure form. Under traditional doctrines, authorities have fewer goals, and subjects generally voice fewer demands. The goals and demands that are put forward are more likely to be standardized and predictable, indeed often ritualistic. Spiraling demands in such contexts are a threat to the "normal" fusion of legitimation and confidence. If undampened for some time, such claims may lead to charges that sitting authorities are illegitimate usurpers or, less commonly, to an authentic legitimation crisis of the traditional order.

6. That is not to say that the moralistic response (more demands than confidence) is the only possible one in such systems. In Chapter 3 we noted Huntington's (1981) thesis that the American polity goes through recurrent cycles of moralism, cynicism, complacency, and hypocrisy. Moreover, I suggested that all four factors are present today as contemporaneous reflections of inefficient political participation. The existence of high levels of demands in our polity does not contradict the presence of significant pockets of apa-

thy. The former mode of involvement, as we saw in the previous chapter, is more common on the organization level, while cynical, complacent, and hypocritical manifestations of apathy are more likely to be public-tier phenomena.

7. Lipset wrote these words about France more than thirty years ago. Numerous commentators on France's own bicentennial in 1989 suggested that the cultural divisions wrought by the Revolution are now closing. Yet modern France still lacks the shared legitimating rituals that are embedded in our Fourth of July celebrations, nor they do venerate a common set of Founding Fathers (or Mothers).

8. A more recent, highly regarded variant of this approach is found in *Habits of the Heart* (Bellah et al. 1985). This work by four sociologists and one philosopher decries what they see as America's turn to an individualistic ethic that takes both "utilitarian" and "expressive" (e.g., self-help groups) forms. The authors advocate a return to older "biblical" and "republican" communal values in the American Protestant tradition. For a thoughtful critique that challenges these authors' tendency to create a mythic *Gemeinschaft* American past to hurl in the face of an allegedly lately arrived *Gesellschaft* present, see Fox (1986).

Chapter 5

1. Richard L. Berke of the *New York Times* has observed: "In Washington today, raising money takes nearly as much time as legislative work. After days in the hearing rooms or on the floor of the Congress, lawmakers make the rounds of fund-raising receptions or spend evenings 'dialing for dollars,' as many members call their telephone appeals. The average senator who was elected in 1988 spent $3.7 million on his or her campaign, a 22 percent rise from only two years before. The winning candidates for the House seats spent, on the average, $393,000, an increase of more than 10 percent over 1988" (1990, p. A1).

2. Thus, Gans notes about the American case: "People with one overriding interest have helped bring about the recent increase in single-issue politics. . . . Nevertheless, the prime participants in the political arena are the same interests that have always dominated it: the suppliers—including the manufacturers, distributors, and sellers—of goods and services. They also have a single interest, the particular goods and services they supply, and thus have a greater day-to-day stake in government than either the users of those goods and services or the supporters and opponents of particular issues" (1988, p. 70).

3. Of course, state-socialist polities' loss of viability—indeed, their disintegration in Central and Eastern Europe in 1989—entails more than a legitimation crisis. No one disputes the importance of "the identity crisis and deradicalization of the communist parties, the disintegration of the official political discourse, and the transition from legitimation claims based on Marxist-Leninist ideology to ones based on a pseudo-*realpolitik* with strong nationalist underpinnings" (Ekiert 1990, p. 2). In addition, the diminished effectiveness and efficiency of these systems were integral parts of their crises. In the realm of effectiveness, for instance, the failure of central planning to sustain economic growth is probably decisive. But inefficient mechanisms of participation were pivotal too. On the one hand, we witnessed "the disintegration of the auxiliary institutions of the party-state, such as trade-unions, professional and youth organizations" (Ekiert 1990, p. 2). On the other hand, this disintegration encouraged the emergence of new groupings (and the reemergence of old ones) in civil society that the party-state belatedly tolerated, occasionally made informal bargains with, but finally was unwilling to incorporate systematically in the political influence process. (For an overview, see Ekiert 1990.)

4. Bell provides a succinct explanation for the greater difficulty in transforming cultural factors. He notes: "Changes in moral temper and culture—the fusion of imagination and lifestyles—are not amenable to 'social engineering' or political control. They derive from the value and moral traditions of the society, and these cannot be 'designed' by precept. The ultimate sources are the religious conceptions which undergird a society; the proximate sources are the 'reward systems' and 'motivations' (and their legitimacy) which derive from the arena of work (the social structure)" (1970, p. 43).

5. The notion of malleability is perhaps the most important input from macrosociological theory to policy analysis. To inquire about malleability is to ask, "Can it be fixed in accord with conscious human intentions?" This question is but one of several important issues in macrosociology; in policy science it is the central one.

Policy science is less analytical and draws on several disciplines (Etzioni 1971). Hence it is better than macrosociology (or economics, or political science, or organizational analysis, etc.) at ranking factors by how well they can be deliberately modified. Indeed, policy *research* is indispensable for a precise delineation of the most malleable factors in any situation as well as the conditions under which less malleable ones become more open to modification.

References

Aberbach, Joel D., Robert D. Putnam, and Bert A. Rockman. 1981. *Bureaucrats and Politicians in Western Democracies.* Cambridge, Mass.: Harvard University Press.

Aldrich, Howard. 1979. *Organizations and Environments.* Englewood Cliffs, N.J.: Prentice-Hall.

Alexander, Jeffrey C. 1982. *Theoretical Logic in Sociology.* Vol. 1, *Positivism, Presuppositions, and Current Controversies.* Berkeley: University of California Press.

Alford, Robert R., and Roger Friedland. 1985. *Powers of Theory: Capitalism, the State, and Democracy.* New York: Cambridge University Press.

Amenta, Edwin, and Yvonne Zylan. 1991. "Political Opportunity, the New Institutionalism, and the Townsend Movement." *American Sociological Review* 56:250–65.

Andersen, Kurt. 1984. "America's Upbeat Mood." *Time,* September 24, 10–17.

Baker, Russell. 1976. "Between the Acts." *New York Times,* November 30, 39.

Barnard, Chester I. 1938. *The Functions of the Executive.* Cambridge, Mass.: Harvard University Press.

Bell, Daniel. 1970. "The Cultural Contradictions of Capitalism." *The Public Interest* 21:16–43.

———. 1973. *The Coming of Post-Industrial Society.* New York: Basic Books.

———. 1974. "The Public Household." *The Public Interest* 37:29–68.

———. 1976. *The Cultural Contradictions of Capitalism.* New York: Basic Books.

Bellah, Robert N. 1975. *The Broken Covenant: American Civil Religion in a Time of Trial.* New York: Seabury Press.

Bellah, Robert N., Richard Madsen, William M. Sullivan, Ann Swidler, and Steven M. Tipton. 1985. *Habits of the Heart: Individualism and Commitment in American Life.* Berkeley: University of California Press.

Bendix, Reinhard. 1974. "Inequality and Social Structure: A Comparison of Marx and Weber." *American Sociological Review* 39:149–61.

Berelson, Bernard, Paul F. Lazarsfeld, and William N. McPhee. 1954. *Voting; A Study of Opinion Formation in a Presidential Campaign*. Chicago: University of Chicago Press.

Berelson, Bernard, and Gary A. Steiner. 1964. *Human Behavior: An Inventory of Scientific Findings*. New York: Harcourt, Brace & World.

Berger, Peter, and Thomas Luckmann. 1966. *The Social Construction of Reality: A Treatise in the Sociology of Knowledge*. Garden City, N.Y.: Doubleday.

Berke, Richard L. 1990. "An Edge for Incumbents: Loopholes that Pay Off." *New York Times*, March 30, A1.

Birnbaum, Pierre. 1980. "Central Patterns: States, Ideologies and Collective Action in Western Europe." *International Social Science Journal* 32:671–86.

———. 1988. *States and Collective Action: The European Experience*. New York: Cambridge University Press.

Blau, Peter M. 1955. *The Dynamics of Bureaucracy*. Chicago: University of Chicago Press.

Block, Fred. 1977. "The Ruling Class Does Not Rule: Notes on the Marxist Theory of the State." *Socialist Revolution* 33:6–28.

———. 1987. "Rethinking the Political Economy of the Welfare State." In *The Mean Season: The Attack on the Welfare State*, edited by Fred Block, Richard Cloward, Barbara Ehrenreich, and Frances Fox Piven, 109–60. New York: Pantheon Books.

Braungart, Richard G. 1978. "Survey Essay: Changing Electoral Politics in America." *Journal of Political and Military Sociology* 6:261–69.

Brint, Steven. 1984. "'New Class' and Cumulative Trend Explanations of the Political Attitudes of Professionals." *American Journal of Sociology* 90:30–71.

———. 1990. "Rethinking the Policy Influence of Experts: From General Characterization to Analysis of Variation." *Sociological Forum* 5:361–84.

Brogan, Denis W. 1948. *American Themes*. London: Hamish Hamilton.

Bruce-Briggs, B. 1979. "A Preface on Purpose and Organization." In *The New Class?* edited by B. Bruce-Briggs, ix–xii. New Brunswick, N.J.: Transaction.

Burnham, Walter Dean. 1970. *Critical Elections and the Mainsprings of American Politics*. New York: Norton.

———. 1975. "American Politics in the 1970's: Beyond Party?" In *The Future of Political Parties*, edited by Louis Maisel and Paul M. Sacks, 238–77. Beverly Hills, Calif.: Sage.

Butcher, W. D. 1978. "The Stifling Costs of Regulation." *Business Week,* November 6, 22 *et seq.*

Cameron, David R. 1978. "The Expansion of the Public Economy: A Comparative Analysis." *American Political Science Review* 72:1243–61.

Carnoy, Martin. 1984. *The State and Political Theory.* Princeton, N.J.: Princeton University Press.

Chirot, Daniel. 1987. "Ideology and Legitimacy in Eastern Europe." *States and Social Structures Newsletter* 4:1–4.

Citrin, Jack. 1974. "Comment: The Political Relevance of Trust in Government." *American Political Science Review* 68:973–88.

Cohen, Michael D., James G. March, and Johan P. Olsen. 1972. "A Garbage Can Model of Organizational Choice." *Administrative Science Quarterly* 17:1–25.

Crozier, Michel, Samuel P. Huntington, and Joji Watanuki. 1975. *The Crisis of Democracy: Report on the Governability of Democracies to the Trilateral Commission.* New York: New York University Press.

Curtis, Richard A. 1986. "Household and Family in Theory on Equality." *American Sociological Review* 51:118–83.

Davis, Diane E. 1991. "Urban Fiscal Crises and Political Change in Mexico City: From Global Origins to Local Effects." *Journal of Urban Affairs* 13:175–99.

Drew, Elizabeth. 1983. *Politics and Money.* New York: Macmillan.

Easton, David. 1965. *A Systems Analysis of Political Life.* New York: Wiley.

Eckberg, Douglas Lee, and Lester Hill, Jr. 1979. "The Paradigm Concept and Sociology." *American Sociological Review* 44:925–37.

Ekiert, Grzegorz. 1990. "Transition from State-Socialism in East Central Europe." *States and Social Structures Newsletter* 12:1–7.

Epstein, Cynthia F. 1970. *Woman's Place.* Berkeley: University of California Press.

Etzioni, Amitai. 1968. *The Active Society: A Theory of Societal and Political Processes.* New York: Free Press.

———. 1971. "Policy Research." *American Sociologist* 6:8–12.

———. 1975. *A Comparative Analysis of Complex Organizations: On Power, Involvement, and Their Correlates.* rev. and enl. ed. New York: Free Press.

———. 1984. *Capital Corruption: The New Attack on American Democracy.* New York: Harcourt Brace Jovanovich.

Etzioni-Halevy, Eva. 1985. *Bureaucracy and Democracy.* rev. ed. London: Routledge & Kegan Paul.

Farer, Tom J. 1982. "The Making of Reaganism." *New York Review of Books,* January 21, 40–45.

Fox, Richard Wightman. 1986. Review of *Habits of the Heart: Individualism and Commitment in American Life,* by Robert N. Bellah, William M. Sullivan, Ann Swidler, and Steven Tipton. *American Journal of Sociology* 92 (July):183–86.

Freidson, Eliot. 1987. "Professionals and Amateurs in the Welfare State." In *Applied Research and Structural Change in Modern Society,* edited by L. Kjølsrød, A. Ringen, and M. Vaa, 13–31. Oslo, Norway: Norwegian Institute of Applied Social Research.

Fukiyama, Francis. 1989. "The End of History?" *The National Interest* 16:3–18.

Gamson, William A. 1968. *Power and Discontent.* Homewood, Ill.: Dorsey Press.

———. 1975. *The Strategy of Social Protest.* Homewood, Ill.: Dorsey Press.

Gans, Herbert J. 1988. *Middle American Individualism: The Future of Liberal Democracy.* New York: Free Press.

Giddens, Anthony. 1984. *The Constitution of Society: Outline of the Theory of Structuration.* Berkeley: University of California Press.

———. 1985. *The Nation-State and Violence.* Vol. 2 of *A Contemporary Critique of Historical Materialism.* Berkeley: University of California Press.

Goertzel, Ted G. 1983. "The Gender Gap: Sex, Family and Political Opinions in the Early 1980's." *Journal of Political and Military Sociology* 11:209–22.

Goodgame, Don, and Richard Hornik. 1989. "The Can't Do Government." *Time,* October 23, 28–32.

Greenhouse, Steven. 1991. "Eastern Europe's Leaders in Bind as Economic Reform Stirs Anger." *New York Times,* July 7, A1.

Habermas, Jürgen. 1975. *Legitimation Crisis.* Boston: Beacon Press.

———. 1984. *The Theory of Communicative Action,* Vol. 1. Boston: Beacon Press.

Hall, Richard. 1982. *Organizations: Structure and Process.* 3rd ed. Englewood Cliffs, N.J.: Prentice-Hall.

Hamilton, Richard F. 1972. *Class and Politics in the United States.* New York: Wiley.

Hamilton, Richard F., and James D. Wright. 1986. *The State of the Masses.* New York: Free Press.

Harrington, Michael. 1984. *The Politics at God's Funeral: The Spiritual Crisis of Western Civilization.* New York: Holt, Rinehart & Winston.

Heclo, Hugh. 1974. *Modern Social Politics in Britain and Sweden: From Relief to Income Maintenance.* New Haven, Conn.: Yale University Press.

Hirschman, Albert O. 1982. *Shifting Involvements: Private Interest and Public Action.* Princeton, N.J.: Princeton University Press.

Huntington, Samuel P. 1975. "The Democratic Distemper." *The Public Interest* 41:9–38.

————. 1981. *American Politics: The Promise of Disharmony.* Cambridge, Mass.: Harvard University Press.

Janowitz, Morris. 1978. *The Last Half-Century: Societal Change and Politics in America.* Chicago: University of Chicago Press.

Jasper, James M. 1990. *Nuclear Politics: Energy and the State in the United States, Sweden, and France.* Princeton, N.J.: Princeton University Press.

Katz, Elihu, and Paul F. Lazarsfeld. 1955. *Personal Influence: The Part Played by People in the Flow of Mass Communications.* Glencoe, Ill.: Free Press.

Katznelson, Ira. 1981. *City Trenches: Urban Politics and the Patterning of Class in the United States.* New York: Pantheon.

————. 1985. "Working-Class Formation and the State: Nineteenth-Century England in American Perspective." In *Bringing the State Back In,* edited by Peter B. Evans, Dietrich Rueschemeyer, and Theda Skocpol, 227–51. New York: Cambridge University Press.

Kennedy, Paul. 1987. *The Rise and Fall of the Great Powers: Economic Change and Military Conflict from 1500 to 2000.* New York: Random House.

————. 1990. "Fin-de-Siècle America." *New York Review of Books,* June 28, 31–40.

Klein, Ethel. 1984. *Gender Politics: From Consciousness to Mass Politics.* Cambridge, Mass.: Harvard University Press.

Kornhauser, William. [1953] 1966. "'Power Elite' or 'Veto Group?'" In *Class, Status, and Power: Social Stratification in Comparative Perspective,* edited by Reinhard Bendix and Seymour Martin Lipset, 210–18. 2nd ed. New York: Free Press.

————. 1961. *The Politics of Mass Society.* Glencoe, Ill.: Free Press.

Kuhn, Thomas S. 1970. *The Structure of Scientific Revolutions.* 2nd ed. Chicago: University of Chicago Press.

Ladd, Everett C., Jr. 1978. "What the Voters Really Want." *Fortune,* December 18, 40–48.

————. 1987. *The American Polity: The People and Their Government.* 2nd ed. New York: Norton.

Lazarsfeld, Paul F., Bernard Berelson, and Hazel Gaudet. 1944. *The People's Choice.* New York: Duell, Sloan & Pearce.

Lehman, Edward W. 1977. *Political Society: A Macrosociology of Politics.* New York: Columbia University Press.

————. 1978. "Sociological Theory and Social Policy." *International Journal of Comparative Sociology* 19:7–23.

————. 1985. "Cross Pressures Revisited: A Macrosociological Approach to Anomalies in Contemporary Political Involvement." *Journal of Political and Military Sociology* 13:1–16.

———. 1987. "The Crisis of Political Legitimacy: What Is It; Who's Got It; Who Needs It?" In *Research in Political Sociology*, Vol. 3, edited by Richard G. Braungart and Margaret M. Braungart, 203–21. Greenwich, Conn.: JAI Press.

———. 1988. "The Theory of the State versus the State of Theory." *American Sociological Review* 53:807–23.

Lewis, Flora. 1987. "Now France at Irangate." *New York Times*, July 20, A19.

Lieberson, Stanley. 1971. "An Empirical Study of Military-Industrial Linkages." *American Journal of Sociology* 76:562–84.

Lindblom, Charles E. 1959. "The Science of 'Muddling Through.'" *Public Administration Review* 19:79–99.

———. 1977. *Politics and Markets: The World's Political Economic Systems.* New York: Basic Books.

Linz, Juan J. 1988. "Legitimacy of Democracy and the Socio-Economic System of Western Democracies." In *Comparing Pluralist Democracies: Strains on Legitimacy*, edited by Mattei Dogan, 65–113. Boulder, Colo.: Westview.

Lipset, Seymour Martin. [1960] 1981. *Political Man: The Social Bases of Politics.* exp. ed. Baltimore: Johns Hopkins University Press.

———. 1963a. "The Value Patterns of Democracy: A Case Study in Comparative Analysis." *American Sociological Review* 28:515–31.

———. 1963b. *The First New Nation.* New York: Basic Books.

———. 1968. *Revolution and Counterrevolution: Change and Persistence in Social Structures.* New York: Basic Books.

———. 1985. "Feeling Better: Measuring the Nation's Confidence." *Public Opinion* 5:55–60.

———. 1989. "Exceptional Individualism." Review of *Middle American Individualism*, by Herbert J. Gans. *Contemporary Sociology* 18:905–7.

———. 1990. *Continental Divide: The Values and Institutions of the United States and Canada.* New York: Routledge.

Lipset, Seymour Martin, and William Schneider. 1983. *The Confidence Gap: Business, Labor, and Government in the Public Mind.* New York: Free Press.

Luker, Kristin. 1984. *Abortion and the Politics of Motherhood.* Berkeley: University of California Press.

McConnell, Grant. 1966. *Private Power and American Democracy.* New York: Knopf.

Mann, Michael. 1984. "The Autonomous Power of the State: Its Origins, Mechanisms, and Results." *Archives of European Sociology* 15:185–213.

———. 1986. *The Sources of Social Power*, Vol. 1: *A History of Power from the Beginning to A.D. 1760.* Cambridge: Cambridge University Press.

Marcuse, Herbert. 1964. *One Dimensional Man: Studies in the Ideology of Industrial Society.* Boston: Beacon Press.

Mead, Lawrence M. 1986. *Beyond Entitlement: The Social Obligations of Citizenship.* New York: Free Press.

Merton, Robert K. 1968. *Social Theory and Social Structure.* rev. and enl. ed. New York: Free Press.

Milbrath, Lester W., and M. L. Goel. 1977. *Political Participation: How and Why Do People Get Involved in Politics?* 2nd ed. Chicago: Rand-McNally.

Miliband, Ralph. 1969. *The State in Capitalist Society.* New York: Basic Books.

Miller, Arthur H. 1979. "The Institutional Focus of Political Distrust." Paper presented at the annual meeting of the American Political Science Association, Washington, D.C., August 31–September 3.

Mills, C. Wright. 1956. *The Power Elite.* New York: Oxford University Press.

Mishra, Ramesh. 1984. *The Welfare State in Crisis: Social Thought and Social Change.* New York: St. Martin's Press.

Mollenkopf, John. 1989. "Who (or What) Runs Cities, and How?" *Sociological Forum* 4:119–37.

Moore, Barrington. 1967. *Social Origins of Dictatorship and Democracy: Lord and Peasant in the Making of the Modern World.* London: Penguin Press.

———. 1972. *Reflections on the Causes of Human Misery and upon Certain Proposals to Eliminate Them.* Boston: Beacon Press.

Morrow, Lance. 1987. "A Change in the Weather." *Time,* March 30, 28–37.

Muraskin, William A. 1975. Review of *Regulating the Poor,* by Frances Fox Piven and Richard A. Cloward. *Contemporary Sociology* 4:607–13.

Nettl, J. P. 1968. "The State as a Conceptual Variable." *World Politics* 20:559–92.

Neumann, Sigmund. 1956. "Toward a Comparative Study of Political Parties." In *Modern Political Parties,* edited by Sigmund Neumann, 395–421. Chicago: University of Chicago Press.

Neustadtl, Alan, Denise Scott, and Dan Clawson. 1991. "Class Struggle in Campaign Finance? Political Action Committee Contributions in the 1984 Elections." *Sociological Forum* 6:219–38.

Nie, Norman H., Sidney Verba, and John R. Petrocik. 1976. *The Changing American Voter.* Cambridge, Mass.: Harvard University Press.

Nordlinger, Eric A. 1981. *On the Autonomy of the Democratic State.* Cambridge, Mass.: Harvard University Press.

Nye, Joseph S., Jr. 1990. *Bound to Lead: The Changing Nature of American Power.* New York: Basic Books.

O'Connor, James. 1973. *The Fiscal Crisis of the State.* New York: St. Martin's Press.

Offe, Claus. 1974. "Structural Problems of the Capitalist State." In *German Political Studies* Vol. 1, edited by Klaus von Beyme 31–54. Beverly Hills, Calif.: Sage.

———. 1984. *Contradictions of the Welfare State*. Cambridge, Mass.: MIT Press.

Olsen, Marvin. 1982. *Participatory Pluralism: Political Participation and Influence in the United States and Sweden*. Chicago: Nelson-Hall.

Panebianco, Angelo. 1988. *Political Parties: Organization and Power*. New York: Cambridge University Press.

Parsons, Talcott. 1937. *The Structure of Social Action: A Study in Social Theory with Special Reference to a Group of Recent European Writers*. New York: McGraw-Hill.

———. 1960. *Structure and Process in Modern Societies*. Glencoe, Ill.: Free Press.

———. 1967. *Sociological Theory and Modern Society*. New York: McGraw-Hill.

Phillips, Kevin. 1982. *Post-Conservative America: People, Politics, and Ideology in a Time of Crisis*. New York: Random House.

Piven, Frances Fox, and Richard A. Cloward. 1971. *Regulating the Poor: The Functions of Public Welfare*. New York: Vintage Books.

———. 1988. *Why Americans Don't Vote*. New York: Pantheon Books.

Poggi, Gianfranco. 1978. *The Development of the Modern State: A Sociological Introduction*. Stanford, Calif.: Stanford University Press.

———. 1990. *The State: Its Nature, Development and Prospects*. Stanford, Calif.: Stanford University Press.

Polsby, Nelson W. 1982. "The Prospects for American Pluralism: Trends in Public Sector Mediation." University of California, Berkeley, Department of Political Science, photocopy (April 30).

———. 1983. *Consequences of Party Reform*. New York: Oxford University Press.

Prewitt, Kenneth, and Alan Stone. 1973. *The Ruling Elites: Elite Theory, Power, and American Democracy*. New York: Harper and Row.

Reich, Robert B. 1987. *Tales of a New America: The Anxious Liberal's Guide to the Future*. New York: Random House.

Riesman, David, in collaboration with Reuel Denney and Nathan Glazer. 1951. *The Lonely Crowd*. New Haven, Conn.: Yale University Press.

Ritzer, George. 1990. "Metatheorizing in Sociology." *Sociological Forum* 5:3–15.

Rose, Arnold M. 1967. *The Power Structure*. New York: Oxford University Press.

Rose, Richard, and Guy Peters. 1979. *Can Government Go Bankrupt?* New York: Basic Books.

Rothschild, Emma. 1984. "The Costs of Reaganism." *New York Review of Books*, March 15, 14–17.

Rule, James B. 1988. *Theories of Civil Violence*. Berkeley: University of California Press.

Runciman, Walter G. 1969. *Social Science and Political Theory*. 2nd ed. New York: Cambridge University Press.

Sartori, Giovanni. 1966. "European Parties: The Case of Polarized Pluralism." In *Political Parties and Political Development*, edited by Joseph LaPalombara and Myron Weiner, 137–76. Princeton, N.J.: Princeton University Press.

———. 1976. *Parties and Party Systems: A Framework for Analysis*. Cambridge: Cambridge University Press.

Schumpeter, Joseph. [1950] 1975. *Capitalism, Socialism, and Democracy*. New York: Harper Colophon.

Selznick, Philip. 1960. *The Organizational Weapon*. New York: Free Press.

Shefter, Martin. 1986. "Trades Unions and Political Machines: The Organization and Disorganization of the American Working Class in the Late Nineteenth Century." In *Working-Class Formation: Nineteenth-Century Patterns in Western Europe and the United States*, edited by Ira Katznelson and Aristide Zolberg, 197–276. Princeton, N.J.: Princeton University Press.

Sills, David. 1957. *The Volunteers*. New York: Free Press.

Simon, Herbert A. 1957. *Administrative Behavior*. 2nd ed. New York: Macmillan.

Skocpol, Theda. 1979. *States and Social Revolutions*. Cambridge: Cambridge University Press.

———. 1985a. "Bringing the State Back In: Strategies of Analysis in Current Research." In *Bringing the State Back In*, edited by Peter B. Evans, Dietrich Rueschemeyer, and Theda Skocpol, 3–37. Cambridge: Cambridge University Press.

———. 1985b. "What Is Happening to Western Welfare States?" *Contemporary Sociology* 14:307–11.

———. 1987. "The Dead End of Metatheory." Review of *Powers of Theory: Capitalism, the State, and Democracy*, by Robert R. Alford and Roger Friedland. *Contemporary Sociology* 16:10–12.

Skocpol, Theda, and Kenneth Finegold. 1982. "State Capacity and Economic Intervention in the Early New Deal." *Political Science Quarterly* 97: 255–78.

Skowronek, Stephen. 1982. *Building a New American State: The Expansion of National Administrative Capacities, 1877–1920*. New York: Cambridge University Press.

Sniderman, Paul M. 1981. *A Question of Loyalty.* Berkeley: University of California Press.

Steinfels, Peter. 1979. *The Neoconservatives: The Men Who Are Changing America's Politics.* New York: Simon and Schuster.

Stinchcombe, Arthur L. 1968. *Constructing Social Theories.* New York: Harcourt, Brace & World.

Swidler, Ann. 1986. "Culture in Action: Symbols and Strategies." *American Sociological Review* 51:273–86.

Szymanski, Albert. 1973. "Military Spending and Economic Stagnation." *American Journal of Sociology* 79:1–14.

Thompson, E. P. 1978. *The Poverty of Theory and Other Essays.* London: Merlin Press.

Thurow, Lester. 1980. *The Zero-Sum Society: Distribution and the Possibilities for Economic Change.* New York: Basic Books.

Tilly, Charles. 1974. "Town and Country in Revolution." In *Peasant Rebellion and Communist Revolution in Asia,* edited by John Wilson Lewis, 271–302. Stanford, Calif.: Stanford University Press.

———. 1978. *From Mobilization to Revolution.* Reading, Mass.: Addison-Wesley.

———. 1986. *The Contentious French.* Cambridge, Mass.: Harvard University Press.

Tocqueville, Alexis de. [1835–40] 1954. *Democracy in America.* 2 vols. Edited and translated by Henry Reeve, Francis Bowen, and Philips Bradley. New York: Vintage Books.

Tuckel, Peter S., and Felipe Tejera. 1983. "Changing Patterns of American Voting Behavior." *Public Opinion Quarterly* 47:230–46.

Tucker, Robert W. 1971. *The Radical Left and American Foreign Policy.* Baltimore: Johns Hopkins University Press.

Turner, Jonathan H. 1991. *The Structure of Sociological Theory.* 5th ed. Belmont, Calif.: Wadsworth.

van den Berg, Axel. 1988. *The Immanent Utopia: From Marxism in the State to the State of Marxism.* Princeton, N.J.: Princeton University Press.

Weber, Max. [1904–05] 1958. *The Protestant Ethic and the Spirit of Capitalism.* New York: Scribner.

———. [1924] 1968. *Economy and Society: An Outline of Interpretive Sociology.* 3 vols. Edited by Guenther Roth and Claus Wittich. New York: Bedminster Press.

Weidenbaum, Murray L. 1969. *The Modern Public Sector.* New York: Basic Books.

Weil, Frederick D. 1989. "The Sources of Legitimation in Western Democracies: A Consolidated Model Tested with Time-Series Data in Six

Countries since World War II." *American Sociological Review* 54:682–706.

Weir, Margaret, Ann Shola Orloff, and Theda Skocpol. 1988. "Introduction: Understanding American Social Politics." In *The Politics of Social Policy in the United States,* edited by Margaret Weir, Ann Shola Orloff, and Theda Skocpol, 3–27. Princeton, N.J.: Princeton University Press.

Wiley, Norbert. 1967. "America's Unique Class Politics: The Interplay of Labor, Credit, and Commodity Markets." *American Sociological Review* 32:529–41.

Wilson, William Julius. 1978. *The Declining Significance of Race.* Chicago: University of Chicago Press.

———. 1987. *The Truly Disadvantaged: The Inner City, the Underclass, and Public Policy.* Chicago: University of Chicago Press.

Wolfe, Alan. 1977. *The Limits of Legitimacy: Political Contradictions of Contemporary Capitalism.* New York: Free Press.

———. 1985. Review of *The Confidence Gap: Business, Labor and Government in the Public Mind,* by Seymour Martin Lipset and William Schneider. *American Journal of Sociology* 90:947–49.

Wright, Erik Olin. 1978. *Class, Crisis, and the State.* London: New Left Books.

———. 1985. *Classes.* London: Verso.

Wrong, Dennis H. 1980. *Power: Its Forms, Bases, and Uses.* New York: Harper Colophon.

Yankelovich, Daniel. 1981. *New Rules: Searching for Self-Fulfillment in a World Turned Upside Down.* New York: Random House.

Index

Aberbach, Joel D., 88, 89, 91
Achievement values, 142, 157–60, 167–71
Action (as a presupposition), 10, 28, 29, 32–36, 40, 46, 49, 92, 109, 110, 127, 133, 136, 154, 170, 176, 186, 198. *See also* Social action
Administrative branch, 54, 68, 87, 88, 93, 94
Adversary culture, 151, 156
Agency and structure, 33, 42–44, 46–48, 193. *See also* Duality of structure
Agnew, Spiro, 154
Aldrich, Howard, 119
Alexander, Jeffrey C., 26–28, 31–33, 46, 191–93
Alford, Robert R., 1, 3, 30, 31, 57, 98
Alienation, 16, 38, 124
Allocative resources, 38
Alternative paradigm, 23–59, 61, 63, 95, 102, 137, 163
Althusser, Louis, 28
Amenta, Edwin, 198
American Civil War, 154, 174
American Creed, 128, 148, 183. *See also* American culture
American culture: alternation of achievement and equality in, 159; alternation of achievement and hedonism, 159, 160, 167–69, 171; antistatist values in, 169; coexistence of achievement and hedonism, 160, 169–71, 177; communal values in, 202; consensus-amid-erosion, 158; individualism in, 168, 169, 171, 187, 202
American exceptionalism, 64, 65, 67, 167, 168, 177
American polity, 21, 64, 151, 164, 167, 172; alternation of public and private emphases in, 158; gap between ideals and institutions, 128, 148; parties' loss

of key functions, 118; stages of inefficiency, 128, 129, 201. *See also* American state; United States (U.S.)
American state: as awkward and incomplete, 54, 64, 172, 187; burden of arms race on, 81; fragmented structure of, 68, 71, 172, 173, 175, 176, 200; internal structure of, and number of goals, 68; limits on centralized capacities of, 64; number and coordination of goals, 71, 169, 172; structure of, and interest groups, 200; third-party backing for, 154, 155. *See also* American polity; United States (U.S.)
Andersen, Kurt, 133
Apathy, 1, 10, 13, 16, 21, 47, 59, 65, 66, 91, 92, 94, 101, 104, 107, 109, 129, 131, 135, 166, 170, 175, 180, 192, 202
Arbenz, Jacobo, 83
Atomistic analysis, 109, 112, 120
Atypical minorities, 127
Australia, 30
Austria, 78, 95, 96, 189
Authoritative resources, 38
Authorities, political, 6, 10, 13, 16, 20, 22, 29, 39, 44, 45, 48, 52, 61, 62, 65–67, 71, 73, 75, 76, 78, 79, 81, 86, 87, 95, 99, 101, 103, 105–7, 110, 129–31, 137, 140, 141, 142, 144–46, 147, 150–52, 166, 178–80, 182, 197, 198, 201

Baker, Russell, 19, 66
Balancing of confidence and demands, 65, 106–8, 128, 147, 177, 179, 180, 194. *See also* Efficiency, efficient participation
Barnard, Chester I., 57, 198
Belgium, 197n16
Bell, Daniel, 5, 6, 12, 13, 16, 72, 136, 151, 157, 192, 203
Bellah, Robert N., 16, 97, 168–70, 202